COGNITIVE LITERARY STUDIES

COGNITIVE APPROACHES TO LITERATURE AND CULTURE SERIES
EDITED BY FREDERICK LUIS ALDAMA, ARTURO J. ALDAMA,
AND PATRICK COLM HOGAN

COGNITIVE LITERARY STUDIES

Current Themes and New Directions

EDITED BY ISABEL JAÉN AND JULIEN JACQUES SIMON

UNIVERSITY OF TEXAS *Austin*

Cognitive Approaches to Literature and Culture includes monographs and edited volumes that incorporate cutting-edge research in cognitive science, neuroscience, psychology, linguistics, narrative theory, and related fields, exploring how this research bears on and illuminates cultural phenomena such as, but not limited to, literature, film, drama, music, dance, visual art, digital media, and comics. The volumes published in this series represent both specialized scholarship and interdisciplinary investigations that are deeply sensitive to cultural specifics and grounded in a cross-cultural understanding of shared emotive and cognitive principles.

First edition, 2012
First paperback edition, 2013

Requests for permission to reproduce material from this work should be sent to:
    Permissions
    University of Texas Press
    P.O. Box 7819
    Austin, TX 78713-7819
    utpress.utexas.edu/about/book-permissions

♾ The paper used in this book meets the minimum requirements of ANSI/NISO Z39.48-1992 (R1997) (Permanence of Paper).

LIBRARY OF CONGRESS CATALOGING-IN-PUBLICATION DATA

    Cognitive literary studies : current themes and new directions / edited by Isabel Jaén and Julien Jacques Simon. — 1st ed.
        p.   cm. — (Cognitive approaches to literature and culture)
    Includes index.
        ISBN 978-0-292-75442-3
    1. Literature—History and criticism—Theory, etc.   2. Literature and science.
3. Cognition and culture.   I. Jaén, Isabel, 1970–   II. Simon, Julien Jacques, 1974–
PN55.C646   2012
809'.93356—dc23   2011038987

CONTENTS

FOREWORD

F. ELIZABETH HART

THIS BOOK EXPLORES the intersections of literary studies and cognitive science, contributing to a growing body of literary research emerging over the past twenty years in response to developing theories of "embodied cognition."[1] Turning gradually away from models of the mind as computer-like or as functionally autonomous, today's cognitive scientists increasingly view the mind as complexly integrated with the biological brain, and they view both the brain and the mind as organically situated within—indeed structurally enabled and constrained by—the body.[2] The implications of this paradigm shift reach far, spanning across important domains of philosophical inquiry and consequently academic disciplines.

In their 1999 study *Philosophy in the Flesh*, George Lakoff and Mark Johnson describe embodiment theory in a way that shows how it combines the priorities of phenomenology, epistemology, and ontology: "Cognitive science provides a new and important take on an age-old philosophical problem, the problem of what is real and how we can know it, if we can know it. Our sense of what is real begins with and depends crucially upon our bodies, especially our sensorimotor apparatus, which enables us to perceive, move, and manipulate, and the detailed structures of our brains, which have been shaped by both evolution and experience" (17). In such a view, perceiving, knowing, and being become intricately intertwined, collapsing category boundaries that may forever shift the terms of academic analysis. Scholars in the humanities and social sciences—literature, fine arts, history, philosophy, anthropology, and linguistics—are being drawn to embodied cognition, some influenced by the rise of connectionism (and other symptoms of nonlinear dynamic systems theory, with which embodied cognition proves highly compatible). Decades of exposure to postmodern philosophies have conditioned humanists and social scientists toward interdisciplinarity in general and toward more context-friendly models in particular. Eschewing "liberal" notions of a human essence—of a humanity that can be circumscribed and ontologically distinct from its surroundings—these scholars strive to place the human within its larger material, social, and cultural contexts. It may seem odd at first to consider how their curiosity has led them to cognitive science, a discipline so apparently distant from their interests and (usually) their formal training. But shifts in the humanities and social sciences have occurred in tandem with changes in the sciences, and the result so far has been a small-scale and tentative but also energizing recognition of mutual interests.

The Literature and Cognitive Science Conference held in the spring of 2006 at the University of Connecticut, Storrs, and for which I was privileged to serve as co-coordinator with Alan Richardson of Boston College, constituted an important step in this collaboration. The researchers who attended were, for the most part, humanists or fine arts researchers: literary critics, philosophers, and theatre and performance specialists. But the event also attracted a handful of scientists, including cognitive psychologists, neuroscientists, and empirically oriented philosophers of mind. As a group these researchers represented a degree of interdisciplinarity that is on the rise in academia and that is indicated by the founding and flourishing of various scholarly organizations dedicated to the crossing of these major divides. These include (but are not exclusive to) the Society for Literature, Science, and the Arts (SLSA), incorporated in 1985; Harvard University's "Cognitive Theory and the Arts" seminar, established in 2001; Yale University's "Literary Theory, Cognition, and the Brain" seminar, begun in 2005; and Purdue University's "(Co)Ignition" discussion group, founded in 2008 as part of Purdue's Center for Cognitive Literary Studies. Evidence of the Connecticut conference's success soon followed in the form of similar gatherings at Bucknell (2007), Purdue (2007), and Haverford College (2008) and in the inauguration of two new book series by scholars who had been among the conference's participants: the University of Texas Press's Cognitive Approaches to Literature and Culture (edited by Frederick Luis Aldama, Arturo J. Aldama, and Patrick Colm Hogan) and Palgrave MacMillan's Cognitive Studies in Literature and Performance (edited by Bruce McConachie and Blakey Vermeule).

The present volume features the work of some of the scholars who have been engaged in these interdisciplinary conversations (at the University of Connecticut and elsewhere). Through it, the editors hope to demonstrate that, just as the study of the mind is becoming an evocative new way to approach the problems of literary analysis, so too are literary studies becoming interesting and useful to scientists. Literary scholars bring training and insight to the analysis of acts of reading, writing, and interpretation—acts symptomatic of uniquely human and general-level cognitive capacities that are extremely difficult to test using empirical methods. Literary texts may serve as laboratories in which language processing, narrative comprehension, creativity, memory, emotions, and many other cognitive functions are brought intensively into focus—and are, in a sense, isolated and performed for study—thus bespeaking instances not just of extraordinary cognition (what has traditionally drawn literary critics) but also of general or "everyday" cognition (what now appeals to scientists' interests). Researchers of all kinds variously trained in the workings of brains, minds, and texts stand to gain from a conversation that brings their differing methodologies to the table.

Cognitive Literary Studies bears a resemblance to other important essay collections in cognitive literary studies that began appearing about a decade ago and are steadily proliferating even at this writing. Notable among them are Herman (2003), Gavins and Steen (2003), Richardson and Spolsky (2004), Gottschall and Wilson (2005), Turner (2006), McConachie and Hart (2006), Zunshine (2010), Aldama (2010), and Herman (2011). The Richardson and Spolsky collection has been especially influential as a primer for newcomers to the field because of Richardson's invaluable introductory essay "Studies in Literature and Cognition: A Field Map."[3] Despite its similarities to these predecessor and companion collections, however, *Cognitive Literary Studies* differs in key ways. One difference, as I just mentioned, is that it actively performs the collaboration between humanists and scientists that these other volumes have tended to hypothesize—but have not generally realized—as an ideal research scenario for the field. Richardson himself has recently articulated the terms of this ideal scenario (in the introduction to his 2010 monograph): "[A] healthy interdisciplinarity does not involve one group converting to the norms, aims, and ethos of another, but rather participants from all groups joining in a serious and mutually critical conversation in the interests of a new consensus that none could have produced singly" (Richardson 2010, xiii). Literary scholars, Richardson writes:

> bring to the interdisciplinary encounter a long and elaborate history of careful scrutiny of figurative language, representations of mind and behavior, narrative and discursive modes, and other linguistic phenomena currently of great interest to their colleagues in neuroscience and cognitive science. They can bring to the table as well their own sorts of evidence, including a huge, diverse, multilingual and multicultural text base, spanning over two millennia, that most scientific researchers can only begin to access. (Richardson 2010, xiii)

A second key difference that this book marks, and one that is just as significant as its methodological eclecticism, has to do with its very active explorations of the theory of "embodied cognition" and the unusual combinations of philosophical frameworks—phenomenological, epistemological,
and ontological—that a perspective based on mind-embodiment enables.
Because embodied cognition configures the brain/mind as a constraining
medium through which all human knowledge and experience must filter—
at the same time that it also accounts for the context-dependent nature of
the brain/mind's development and "online" processing—any theoretical approach using this science commits itself to the epistemological position of
"constrained constructivism."[4] This position, whose particular expression I
have borrowed from the literary critic N. Katherine Hayles, has been variously
described by the philosophers Maurice Merleau-Ponty and Hilary Putnam (as
"embodied consciousness" and "internal realism" respectively), by the cognitive linguist and philosopher George Lakoff and Mark Johnson ("experien-
tialism"), and more recently by the cognitive literary critic Nancy Easterlin
("weak constructivism"), among others. It represents a third position nestled
between the epistemological extremes of realism and relativism—or rather
a *set* of positions that together define a continuum of positions running between the two without ever fully committing to the extremes of either.

The resulting epistemology emphasizes not ultimate knowledge but possible knowledge, the only kind of knowledge actually available to us humans,
whose relationships both to reality and to the symbol systems we create to
accommodate reality are always mediated by our cognitive systems. Hayles'
term "constrained constructivism" refers to the mutual perceptions within
and even across animal species (including the human animal) that are not
a matter of positive associations but of negativities.[5] These negativities are
"consistent constraints," adhering at a level of philosophical analysis that refuses to rise above local interactions into abstractions.[6] The idea that consistencies might hold between one individual knower's perceptions and another
individual knower's perceptions is in itself a powerful qualification of relativism and its companion concept, social constructivism. This may appear
to be an apologetics for scientific empiricism if not for the fact that it also
recognizes the limits of observation, taking in the culturally determinant and
context-dependent nature of all representations, including scientific ones, and
erasing the fantasy of a scientific positivism. Constrained constructivism is
committed, therefore, to both limited constructivism and limited empiricism.
This orientation places cognitive theory—and the literary theories influenced
by it—at a crucial remove from others that have evolved during and through
postmodernism, first, by deconstructing the realism/relativism binary of

long-established critical practice and, second, by recasting that polarity onto a continuum of relations, offering instead a set of combinatory integrations. Neither realism nor relativism remains intact within a system that takes brain/mind-filtered knowledge or experience as its ground. Yet, at the same time, because cognition itself is grounded in both the real world and in the constraining structures of sensory, perceptual, and conceptual interiority, knowledge and experience must be based on both, although in varying degrees, and hence the shift to the non-idealizing measure of the continuum.[7]

All cognitive-based literary studies share this philosophical orientation along the epistemological continuum, oscillating between the poles of realism and relativism. And because literary experience is itself quite wide in scope, encompassing a range of experience from the relatively narrow processing of a text's form to the larger-scale analyses of a text's myriad contexts, I believe that cognitive-inflected literary studies, such as those exemplified in *Cognitive Literary Studies*, have the potential to bring much-needed coherence to the cornucopia of approaches representing today's literary studies in general. This book, through its investment in the epistemological and interpretive nuances engendered by embodied cognition, inhabits a necessary middle space of critical reading between the narrower scope of textual processing and the wider scope needed to situate texts within their historical and cultural contexts.

NOTES

1. Some early examples of cognitive literary studies include Holland 1988, Turner 1991, and Tsur 1992; those appearing in a kind of "second wave," starting from the mid-1990s, include Spolsky 1993 and 2001, Turner 1996, Crane 2001, and Richardson 2001; some more recent highlights include Herman 2002, Hogan 2003, Palmer 2004, Zunshine 2006 and 2010, and Richardson 2010.

2. The literature on embodied cognition is now too vast to cite comprehensively, but some important deep background studies include Rosch and Lloyd 1978, Lakoff and Johnson 1980, Lakoff 1987, Johnson 1987, Varela, Thompson, and Rosch 1991, Lakoff and Johnson 1999.

3. Although now somewhat dated, this survey is still indispensable as an introduction to the field because of the way Richardson categorizes the approaches that have emerged since Holland 1988.

4. See Hayles 1993.

5. Hayles describes cross-species perceptual studies showing that basic perceptions are species-specific, differing, say, between frogs, dogs, and human beings according to the differing stimulation-processing tools that each species possesses. Yet despite the perception-specific nature of different species' encounters with their environments, objects within their environments nevertheless exist; they are not figments of any single species' perceptual apparatus. Furthermore, Hayles argues, communication about the environment can, in fact, take place across the gaps between species (and presumably within species) in spite of their differ-

ences. Responding differently to the same environmental stimulus, different perceivers have responses that coalesce, or overlap, such as, to cite Hayles' example, a dog and its human owner both reacting simultaneously—in their differing and species-specific ways—to the sight of a rabbit suddenly crossing their path: "[Reality] impinges on [the dog], impinges on me. . . . We both know that we are responding to an event we hold in common, as well as to a context that includes memories of similar events we have shared" (Hayles 1993, 31). Nancy Easterlin's discussion of "weak constructivism," following Hayles' by a few years, makes a similar argument but on the basis of shared "cognitive predispositions" in humans specifically (Easterlin 1999, 139).

6. Hayles writes: "A model of representation that declines the leap into abstraction figures itself as species-specific, culturally determined, and context-dependent. Emphasizing instrumental efficacy rather than precision, it assumes local interactions rather than positive correspondences that hold universally. It engages in a rhetoric of 'good enough,' indexing its conclusions to the context in which implied judgments about adequacy are made. Yet it also recognizes that within the domains specified by these parameters, enough consistencies obtain in the processing and in [reality] to make recognition reliable and relatively stable" (Hayles 1993, 32). See also Richardson's discussion of the same analysis by Hayles (Richardson 2010, 4).

7. I previously offered some of the ideas in this analysis of Hayles' work and its implications for cognitive literary epistemology in a 2001 essay that appeared in *Philosophy and Literature*. That journal has kindly given permission to use them here. See also Richardson 2010, 3–5.

WORKS CITED

Aldama, Frederick Luis, ed. 2010. *Toward a cognitive theory of narrative acts*. Austin: University of Texas Press.

Crane, Mary Thomas. 2001. *Shakespeare's brain: Reading with cognitive theory*. Princeton, NJ: Princeton University Press.

Easterlin, Nancy. 1999. Making knowledge: Bioepistemology and the foundations of literary theory. *Mosaic* 32, no. 1: 131–47.

Gavins, Joanna, and Gerard Steen. 2003. *Cognitive poetics in practice*. London: Routledge.

Gottschall, Jonathan, and David Sloan Wilson, eds. 2005. *The literary animal: Evolution and the nature of narrative*. Evanston, IL: Northwestern University Press.

Hart, F. Elizabeth. 2001. The epistemology of cognitive literary studies. *Philosophy and Literature* 25, no. 2: 314–34.

Hayles, N. Katherine. 1993. Constrained constructivism: Locating scientific inquiry in the theater of representation. In *Realism and representation: Essays on the problem of realism in relation to science, literature, and culture*. Edited by George Levine. Madison: University of Wisconsin Press.

Herman, David. 2002. *Story logic: Problems and possibilities of narrative*. Lincoln: University of Nebraska Press.

———, ed. 2003. *Narrative theory and the cognitive sciences*. Stanford, CA: Center for the Study of Language and Information.

———, ed. 2011. *The emergence of mind: Representations of consciousness in narrative discourse in English*. Lincoln: University of Nebraska Press.

Hogan, Patrick Colm. 2003. *Cognitive science, literature, and the arts: A guide for humanists*. London: Routledge.

Holland, Norman N. 1988. *The brain of Robert Frost: A cognitive approach to literature*. London: Routledge.

Johnson, Mark. 1987. *The body in the mind: The bodily basis of meaning, imagination, and reason*. Chicago: University of Chicago Press.

Lakoff, George. 1987. *Women, fire, and dangerous things: What categories reveal about the mind*. Chicago: University of Chicago Press.

Lakoff, George, and Mark Johnson. 1980. *Metaphors we live by*. Chicago: University of Chicago Press.

———. 1999. *Philosophy in the flesh: The embodied mind and its challenge to western thought*. New York: Basic Books.

McConachie, Bruce, and F. Elizabeth Hart, eds. 2006. *Performance and cognition: Theatre studies and the cognitive turn*. London: Routledge.

Palmer, Alan. 2004. *Fictional minds*. Lincoln: University of Nebraska Press.

Richardson, Alan. 2001. *British Romanticism and the science of mind*. Cambridge: Cambridge University Press.

———. 2010. *The neural sublime: Cognitive theories and Romantic texts*. Baltimore: Johns Hopkins University Press.

Richardson, Alan, and Ellen Spolsky, eds. 2004. *The work of fiction: Cognition, culture, and complexity*. Aldershot, UK: Ashgate.

Rosch, Eleanor, and Barbara B. Lloyd, eds. 1978. *Cognition and categorization*. Hillsdale, NJ: Lawrence Erlbaum Associates.

Spolsky, Ellen. 1993. *Gaps in nature: Literary interpretation and the modular mind*. Albany: State University of New York Press.

———. 2001. *Satisfying skepticism: Embodied knowledge in the early modern world*. Aldershot: Ashgate Publishing.

Tsur, Reuven. 1992. *Toward a theory of cognitive poetics*. Amsterdam: North-Holland.

Turner, Mark. 1991. *Reading minds: The study of English in the age of cognitive science*. Princeton, NJ: Princeton University Press.

———. 1996. *The literary mind*. Oxford: Oxford University Press.

———, ed. 2006. *The artful mind: Cognitive science and the riddle of human creativity*. Oxford: Oxford University Press.

Varela, Francisco J., Evan Thompson, and Eleanor Rosch. 1991. *The embodied mind: Cognitive science and human experience*. Cambridge, MA: MIT Press.

Zunshine, Lisa. 2006. *Why we read fiction: Theory of mind and the novel*. Columbus: Ohio State University Press.

———, ed. 2010. *Introduction to cognitive cultural studies*. Baltimore: Johns Hopkins University Press.

ACKNOWLEDGMENTS

Cognitive Literary Studies would not have been possible without the interdisciplinary minds that have helped us make it tangible. We are truly grateful to those who have so generously shared their expertise, enthusiasm, and friendship, encouraging us to pursue and complete this project.

We thank particularly Jim Burr, our editor, and Frederick L. Aldama, Arturo J. Aldama, and Patrick Colm Hogan, our series editors, for believing in the book from the start. We also thank Leslie Tingle, Molly R. Frisinger, Chris Dodge, Nancy Bryan, and everyone who assisted us with the editing process at the University of Texas Press.

Our deepest gratitude to our contributors, for their work, energy, and patience, to our reviewers, and to the many scholars who helped us with the initial steps of the project or read this manuscript, in whole or in part, at different stages in its development: Andrew Gordon, David Herman, Nancy Easterlin, Liz Hart, Howard Mancing, Charles Ganelin, Keith Oatley, Mary Thomas Crane, Matthew Belmonte, Alan Palmer, Richard Schweickert, Raymond Mar, David Miall, Marie-Laure Ryan, Maja Djikic, Amy Cook, Barbara Dancygier, John Frow, Elena Semino, Peter Stockwell, Joanna Gavins, Teenie Matlock, Alan Richardson, Joseph Bizup, Anne Varty, Eric Olofson, Eric Freeze, Marjorie Taylor, Bruce McConachie, Rhonda Blair, Arnold Heidsieck, and Don Kuiken. We are also grateful to Cynthia Sloan, Simon Taylor, Eva Núñez, George Karnezis, Roger Market, Julia Rosenberg, and Josidalgo Martínez for their insightful comments.

For their valuable help, advice, and warm support we would also like to thank Jonathan Brent, Lisa Zunshine, Attilio Favorini, Frank Hakemulder, Paula Leverage, and Floyd Merrell.

Finally, Julien Simon would like to thank Indiana University East for granting him a fellowship to work on this book.

COGNITIVE LITERARY STUDIES

INTRODUCTION

ISABEL JAÉN AND JULIEN J. SIMON

I. THE STUDY OF MIND AND LITERATURE: AN INTERDISCIPLINARY ENDEAVOR

For years we have been adding tiles to the vast mosaic of research on the cognition of literature. Patterns have been created and have diversified. As we step back now to observe the current shape of cognitive literary studies, we begin to discern a clearer picture. There is still much to compose; the renewed energy that scholars have brought to the assemblage guarantees the health and permanence of a field whose diversity and far-reaching nature forces it to take the slow steps of a giant. Cognitive literary studies may indeed look like an impressive and intimidating Colossus of Rhodes, or perhaps like a Hercules attempting to create a smooth passage between the humanities and the sciences.

The study of literature in relation to the human mind and its natural and social context enjoys a long tradition. Commonly cited examples of early philosophical interest in the creation and reception of verbal art are Plato's *Republic* and Aristotle's *Poetics*. There are many medieval accounts of the socioritual and didactic function of tales, such as Boccaccio's *Decameron*, Chaucer's *The Canterbury Tales*, and Don Juan Manuel's *The Book of Count Lucanor and Patronio*. The power of acted narratives to provoke a psychological reaction in audiences was well known to the participants in classical tragedies, and artists would consistently exploit the allure of rhythm and pitch to create verses as well as musical and dance accompaniments for other artistic forms.

Medieval and early modern thought inherits Platonic warnings as much as Aristotelian recipes to deal with the transformative power of literature. Humans can recognize the impact that fictional narratives have on the mind and the community, as evidenced by Lope de Vega's manual on writing successful plays, *The New Art of Making Comedies*, and Juan Luis Vives' *Works of*

Education, where he distinguishes between personal experience and the stories and fables that are imagined for the instruction and warning of mankind. One of the most widely read novels, Cervantes' *Don Quixote*, is perhaps the perfect example of the impact that fiction can have on the mind and on culture.

The European Enlightenment revives this interest in the reception of literature and its didactic function, a line of investigation that the Romantics will continue to pursue. Questions such as how to educate by poetry (see Sullivan in this volume) are part of the cognitive project of Romanticism, a period in which literary criticism emphasizes the agency of both author and reader. As Alan Richardson has noted, this is the period in which the brain is finally established as the material site of thought (2001, 1), when literature and the mind sciences interact in ways that lead to a new understanding of human subjectivity and its relation to the environment.

At the dawn of the twentieth century, literary critics' interest in the mind continues and is revitalized by post-Freudian psychoanalysis and reader response theories. In the face of neuroscientific evidence, the psychoanalytic road that had been taken by some poststructuralists will eventually demand a revision (see Holland 2009). The reader response tradition, for its part, finds continuity in empirical studies of literature, which are carried out today from a variety of disciplines, including psychology, literary criticism, anthropology, and philosophy. These studies are rapidly becoming one of the most fruitful realms for collaboration between humanists and scientists and show promise of an auspicious future.

During the second half of the twentieth century, "cognitivism"—based on computational models of the mind, the view of the "mind as machine" (see Boden 2006)—and the development of generative grammar paradigms allowed for further investigation into the role of language and pattern in human cognition. This linguocentrism was paralleled in literary theory, which in the 1950s and 1960s radicalized its program of closely examining texts, often pushing context to the background, or even disregarding it completely. The critical method of isolating the text as the object of study quickly became problematic, mainly because of its assumption of stability and objectivity of meaning. However, the embodied and enactive approach to cognition that flourishes during the 1990s (see Varela, Thompson, and Rosch 1991) moves us away from the "mind as computer" metaphor and reconnects the human mind with its biology and environment, while grounded theories of cognition emphasize multimodal representation along with the role of simulation, situated action, and bodily states (see Barsalou 2008). In the humanities, post-structuralist theory stressed relativism, hoping to be the antidote to the positivist reductionism of earlier studies of discourse. More recent critical approaches such as gender or postcolonial studies recover the cultural and social context of human cognition and art. Nonetheless, some fundamental questions remain unanswered: How do we build a literary theory that integrates all those aspects of verbal art—author, text, reader, context—that previous criticism only considered fragmentarily? How do we account at the same level for agency, artifact, and context in human literary manifestations? And, more importantly, how do we reconcile the binaries biology and culture, science and the humanities?

Seeking to answer these questions, in the late 1980s some literary scholars began to further explore disciplines such as cognitive science, psychology, and linguistics. Thanks to the contributions of Norman Holland and Reuven Tsur, among other pioneers, the new field of cognitive literary studies gestated for more than a decade, feeding on the research of colleagues from diverse fields outside literary criticism. A turning point was the foundation of the Modern Language Association discussion group Cognitive Approaches to Literature in 1998. By the end of the twentieth century, cognitive literary studies began to establish itself firmly as a new and exciting field aiming to understand literature in the context of the embodied mind and its dynamic interaction with the environment. Over the last decade the field has grown exponentially. It is now experiencing a boom characterized by the proliferation of books, articles, conferences, and discussion groups. Today cognitive scholars may reach a much deeper understanding of the relation between brain and culture, as a result of major technological breakthroughs such as functional magnetic brain imaging and recent discoveries like the mirror neuron system. Moreover, not only are literary critics turning to the mind sciences to make sense of literature but also scientists, in their quest to understand human cognition, are beginning to approach literary critics and recognize the value of their contributions, making cognitive literary studies a truly multidirectional endeavor.

Indeed, cognitive literary studies are now in dialogue with a wide spectrum of disciplines, such as developmental and evolutionary psychology, neuroscience, psychiatry, cognitive linguistics, anthropology, and philosophy. Critics like Marcus Nordlund (2002) stress the importance of being guided by the light of consilience—unity among the different realms of knowledge—when engaging in literary studies. The consilient approach to literature is both a call for pluralism and for the consideration of human biology, along with human culture, in the study of literature (see Gottschall 2008). Consilience, as envisioned by E. O. Wilson (1998), implies cooperation among disciplines. Rather than conceiving our particular fields as isolated tiles that constitute a local pattern, we must consider their role in the whole epistemological mosaic. Reaching out is the key to ensuring that we continue to advance our knowledge of cultural phenomena, particularly as we see the need to retool our fields and adjust our methodologies in order to coherently adapt our perspectives to our evolving realities.

Although it seems legitimate that we should turn to other disciplines in search of new points of view and methodologies, Patrick Colm Hogan and other cognitive scholars warn us against the dangers of using cognitive literary studies as a novelty approach (2003, 2). It is not a question of abandoning previous beliefs in favor of the exciting cognitive credo. In fact, almost as important as reflecting on what cognitive literary studies are, is considering what they are not. They are not a new theory or a new school or a way of producing new readings of literature directed at critics, but rather a call for inclusiveness and cooperation, an interdisciplinary approach to knowledge, a stance if you will. There is no such thing as a cognitive literary method (Mancing n.d.), but there is a willingness to leave our comfort zone, our discipline's shell, for the sake of contributing to the construction of a more complete and coherent image of the human mind and its manifestations.

Such a desire and effort to travel to foreign lands for new insights pertains equally to the sciences and the humanities, to all representatives of the myriad disciplines that constitute human epistemology beyond this traditional science-humanities dichotomy. It is perhaps time to realize that the increasingly close collaboration among scholars in cognitive literary studies may erase "that erstwhile line drawn in the sand" (Aldama 2010, 1) that keeps scientists and humanists apart. If methods, points of view, and, more importantly, minds are constantly crossing the boundaries of this traditional separation, we might be able to continue blurring lines, turning our perspective into that of a Velázquez or a Goya, where the strength of our view resides in the subject's natural integration within the wider context.

The consideration of other views and strategies for the valuable insights that they could provide us is not only worth the effort, but necessary to exercise a genuine and responsible investigation of the human and natural world in which we are immersed. In this regard, Bruce McConachie's question, "can we continue to rely on our business-as-usual theories and orientations for responsible epistemologies?" (2006, xii), becomes quite relevant. Investigating the human mind and its cultural products beyond our disciplinary boundaries is not simply a matter of enriching and complementing our own methods and perspectives but, more importantly, of refocusing on the ethical commitment the intellectual has to society. The more we know about our neighbors' intellectual endeavors and engage in interdisciplinary conversations and collaborations, the more complete and coherent our studies and conclusions, and therefore, the more ethically responsible we become.

The present volume contains the contributions of scholars in a variety of fields both in the humanities and the sciences. We believe that it will encourage further exploration of the literary phenomenon from a pluralistic and inclusive perspective, as well as collaboration among scholars who see themselves as institutionally separated from those with whom they would like to work. We are certainly not advocating a feel-good, idealistic approach to knowledge. Everyday realities often place obstacles to our well-intentioned efforts to explore other fields. Indeed, the volume of yearly publications on just one idea renders it difficult to maintain currency within our own particular disciplines, let alone in other distant fields that we would like to explore in order to strengthen our research. This is why collaborations become especially important and why the creation of interfaces such as cognitive literary studies, which channels interdisciplinary efforts to delve into human narratives, proves an inspiring and practical avenue. Cognitive literary studies can help us not only through the organization of the numerous interests that an inclusive approach to literature and cognition encompasses but may also facilitate dialogue and provide opportunities for fruitful exchange. The scholar who engages in cognitive literary studies does it by bringing a rich background to share. It is precisely in the diversity and heterogeneity of all these contributions that the strength of the field resides.

II. VOLUME OVERVIEW

The essays included in this volume have been arranged by the area of inquiry that they address. We have chosen to employ section titles that are, in our view, consistent with the current state of the field. Although we certainly haven't been able to represent each of the many paths that cognitive literary studies present today, we aim to provide readers with a sample of some of the themes that scholars have been exploring in their study of literature and cognition during the last few years.

The book begins with an overview of recent developments in cognitive literary studies (Section I) and continues with an inquiry into the bidirectionality of the field from both a scientific and a literary point of view (Section II). It then moves to more specific explorations of the neurological underpinnings of the literary experience and the role of emotion in literature (Section III). A discussion follows on language, literature, and mind processes, with an emphasis on pattern and embodiment (Section IV). From a cultural-historicist perspective, the next set of articles addresses questions about the role of literature in the development of self (Section V). Finally, the return to our original point of departure on the symbiosis of literature and the cognitive sciences is completed by a discussion of present and future directions in the psychology of fiction (Postscript).

Following our overview on the current state of cognitive literary studies, the two essays included in Section II, "The Cognitive Sciences and Literary Theory in Dialogue," discuss the relationship between science and narrative, as well as the extent to which literary critics and scientists can benefit from each other's work. In "Why Literature Is Necessary, and Not Just Nice," Richard Gerrig outlines how literary analysis can and should inform the cognitive sciences. He provides us with case studies of phenomena, such as the paradox of suspense, which have been examined from a literary and aesthetic standpoint and have important implications for the study of memory representations and other cognitive processes. In "Theory of Mind in Reconciling the Split Object of Narrative Comprehension," Joseph Murphy proposes a model of narrative as a midlevel cognitive phenomenon, correlated to acquisition of theory of mind, in which the imagination of characters moving through time introduces subjects to the abstract environment of trajectories through space, preparing the way for social being and suggesting the adaptive function of narrative. In doing so, he considers the possibility of designing an interdisciplinary experimental program that includes neuroscientific and developmental insights and methods and in which literary critics play an indispensable role.

Murphy's piece leads readers to Section III, "Neurological Approaches to Literature," in which Norman Holland, Patrick Colm Hogan, and Aaron Mishara explore the physiological underpinnings of the literary experience. In "*Don Quixote* and the Neuroscience of Metafiction," Holland offers a neuropsychoanalytic view on the disconcerting effect of metafictional games as they appear in novels, plays, and films. He pays particular attention to Cervantes' masterpiece, the first and greatest of metafictions, where Don Quixote and his squire Sancho are aware of their existence both as real beings and literary characters. Holland concludes his essay with a reflection on the brain and the arts, particularly on the role that the prefrontal cortex plays when we experience fictional events, and also deals with the emotional effect of dissolving the borders between the physically real and the imaginary. Hogan's "The Mourning Brain: Attachment, Anticipation, and Hamlet's Unmanly Grief" draws on appraisal and subcortical arousal theories of emotion and the work of Antonio Damasio and other neuroscientists in order to account for complex human emotions such as grief in literature and life. The puzzle with Hamlet isn't why he fails to act, but why he does act in some instances. Hogan analyzes the connection between the prince's behavior, grief, and anger. His proposed account of emotions considers not only cultural influence, but also gender and other forms of ideology, and focuses on the role of anticipation in emotional experience. Aaron Mishara's "The Literary Neuroscience of Kafka's Hypnagogic Hallucinations: How Literature Informs the Neuroscientific Study of Self and Its Disorders" explores neural mechanisms in the processing of self during hypnagogic (between waking and sleep) states. Mishara also discusses the neurobiological underpinnings of autoscopy (the projection of an imaginary double) to illustrate how Kafka's writings help to elucidate the underlying cognitive and neural mechanisms of hypnagogic hallucinations. He concludes that the literary experience is rooted in the embodied subjectivity of self/other and shows us how literature may inform clinical neuroscience research.

Section IV, "Language, Literature, and Mind Processes," explores language and mind processes in relation to poetry and narrative. The first two essays, by Margaret Freeman and Michael Sinding, address the central question of how new meaning is created in literature, and significantly broaden the scope of this area's investigations. Freeman explores the ways in which blending theory can better account for the creative imagination, while Sinding brings Mikhail Bakhtin's insights to his analysis of the emergence and complexity of the novel. In her article, "Blending and Beyond: Form and Feeling in Poetic Iconicity," Freeman deals with the artistic process of blending form with feeling, or felt life (the conscious realization of internal emotions and external sensations), in order to create poetic meaning. She demonstrates how poetic iconicity works in Emily Dickinson's poetry, whose metaphoric blend creates identity among self, poem, and nature. Freeman advocates a reassessment of conceptual blending, stressing that the role of feeling needs not only to be recognized, but also modeled. Sinding's essay, "'A sermon in the midst of a smutty tale': Blending in Genres of Speech, Writing, and Literature," discusses the importance of genre mixture for both literary and discourse studies. He reminds us that genres are cognitive schemata involving multiple subschemas for aspects of form and content. He examines how different conceptual networks produce different categorizations, meanings, and responses by showing us how Laurence Sterne framed his famous sermon "The Abuses of Conscience Considered" in *Tristram Shandy* and three other rhetorical situations, thus modifying its genre in four ways. This section continues with two different perspectives on verbal art and pattern. Nigel Fabb and Morris Halle explore the cognitive processes behind counting in metrical poetry. Within a generative framework, they describe the rules that govern syllable grouping in poetic forms such as the French alexandrine meter. Pointing at what metrical verse, word-stress rules, and metrical music have in common, they suggest that metrical counting depends on a specific mechanism that is shared across literary, linguistic, and musical cognition. Claiborne Rice's "Fictive Motion and Perspectival Construal in the Lyric" explores how our somatosensory responses to motion verbs in poetry help create the sense of a virtual self that is acting and observing in an imaginary world. Looking at poems by Billy Collins and Lyn Hejinian, Rice argues that the dynamic construal demanded by fictive motion helps guide shifts in construal perspective consonant with an observer in motion, which in turn can trigger minor somatic effects associated with bodily movements. Rice's somatic view of the poetic experience reminds us that language and consciousness are fundamentally embodied.

In Section V, "Literature and Human Development," Brad Sullivan's essay "Education by Poetry: Hartley's Theory of Mind as a Context for Understanding Early Romantic Poetic Strategies," introduces us to Romantic theories of imagination. He explores David Hartley's 1749 work *Observations on Man*, which stresses the importance of sensory experience in the shaping of human thinking and feeling. Sullivan follows the poetic strategies of William Wordsworth and Anna Barbauld to show us how these poets investigated the ways in which the mind forms associations, focusing on personal experience and affective states. He also explains how they created poetic strategies seeking to encourage readers to form positive associations in order to develop good habits of mind. In "Leafy Houses and Acorn Kisses: J. M. Barrie's Neverland Playground," Glenda Sacks explores literature, child development, and gender construction, focusing on J. M. Barrie's design of Neverland as an environment where children can simulate, experiment, empathize, and experience adult life. Neverland provides a flexible imaginary space and an alternative world in which the children's pseudo-adult play not only assists them in their cognitive development, but simultaneously challenges societal norms by subverting vestiges of strict Victorian child-rearing ideas prevalent in Edwardian society.

The volume ends with a postscript by Keith Oatley, Raymond A. Mar, and Maja Djikic, "The Psychology of Fiction: Present and Future," a discussion of fiction as a topic of interdisciplinary research by literary scholars, psychologists, and cognitive scientists. They review some of the work that has been done in areas such as empirical testing of literary theory, the use of literature in psychological investigations, and the effects of fiction on selfhood and social ability, along with their educational and therapeutic implications. Oatley, Mar, and Djikic provide us with evidence of the strong current interest of researchers in these areas of inquiry while pointing at future exciting directions in the study of psychology and fiction. By emphasizing the need for interdisciplinary dialogue and collaboration, they take us back to the original theme of this volume, perfectly closing our inquiry into the cognitive study of literature.

WORKS CITED

Aldama, Frederick Luis. 2010. Introduction. In *Toward a cognitive theory of narrative acts*, 1–9. Edited by Frederick Luis Aldama. Austin: University of Texas Press.

Barsalou, Lawrence W. 2008. Grounded cognition. *Annual Review of Psychology* 59: 617–45.

Boden, Margaret A. 2006. *Mind as machine: A history of cognitive science*. 2 vols. Oxford: Clarendon Press.

Gottschall, Jonathan. 2008. *Literature, science, and a new humanities*. Cognitive studies in literature and performance 1, ed. Bruce McConachie and Blakey Vermeule. New York: Palgrave Macmillan.

Hogan, Patrick Colm. 2003. *Cognitive science, literature, and the arts: A guide for humanists*. New York: Routledge.

Holland, Norman N. 2009. *Literature and the brain*. Gainesville, FL: PsyArt Foundation.

Mancing, Howard. n.d. *The context of literary theory: Linguistics, biology, psychology*. Unpublished manuscript.

McConachie, Bruce. 2006. Preface. In *Performance and cognition: Theatre studies and the cognitive turn*, ix–xv. Edited by Bruce McConachie and F. Elizabeth Hart. London: Routledge.

Nordlund, Marcus. 2002. Consilient literary interpretation. *Philosophy and Literature* 26: 312–33.

Richardson, Alan. 2001. *British Romanticism and the science of the mind*. New York: Cambridge University Press.

Varela, Francisco J., Evan Thompson, and Eleanor Rosch. 1991. *The embodied mind: Cognitive science and human experience*. Cambridge, MA: MIT Press.

Wilson, Edward O. 1998. *Consilience: The unity of knowledge*. New York: Random House.

COGNITIVE LITERARY STUDIES TODAY

The purpose of this section is to present the reader with an informative, concise overview of some of the main directions that cognitive literary studies have taken during the last few years. The featured essay is organized around two relevant themes in the cognitive study of literature: 1) literary discourse in relation to the embodied mind, and 2) the interplay in human narratives between biological universals (features that we all share as humans) and historical-cultural specifics (pertaining to the particular cultures and historical circumstances in which humans are immersed). Within these two main lines of inquiry, the authors discuss mind processes in relation to literary discourse, the search for the neurological underpinnings of the literary experience, evolutionary approaches to literature, and the role of fiction in human development and human societies. They also address the relation of cognitive literary studies to post-structuralist critical theory, particularly to cultural studies.

CHAPTER 1

AN OVERVIEW OF RECENT DEVELOPMENTS
IN COGNITIVE LITERARY STUDIES

ISABEL JAÉN AND JULIEN J. SIMON

COGNITIVE LITERARY STUDIES emerged in the 1980s from the investigation of literature in relation to the embodied mind. Today we may define the field as an interdisciplinary initiative that integrates humanistic and scientific approaches and methodologies into a powerful tool to explore the complex dynamics between cognition and literature.[1] In this chapter we provide readers with a sense of how some of the most significant lines of inquiry in cognitive literary studies have evolved during the last few years. We will highlight a few representative themes and studies, focusing on recent developments and what we see as new directions. Our objective is to emphasize both the continuity and the vitality of a field that is based on a dialogue among a variety of disciplines.[2]

I. FURTHER EXPLORING DISCOURSE
AND THE EMBODIED MIND

Several cognitive literary approaches have placed language and mental processing at the core of their inquiry, with humanists and scientists exploring literature both as a cognitive act but also as a key to understanding how the mind works. Over the last few years, researchers have stressed the need to consider cognitive processes and literary artifacts in relation to phenomenological and contextual factors, such as feeling or medium (the format in which stories come to us), in order to obtain a more coherent picture of literature as a discursive phenomenon.

1. LANGUAGE, LITERATURE, AND MIND PROCESSES

By turning to the mind processes behind language structure, cognitive linguistics in the 1980s offered a new theoretical framework that favored the advent of cognitive poetics. Foundational texts that opened a path for this field included Lakoff and Johnson's *Metaphors We Live By* (1980), Langacker's *Foundations of Cognitive Grammar* (1987, 1991), and the work of Leonard Talmy (see 2000a, 2000b).

In cognitive linguistics, "the formal structures of language are studied not as if they were autonomous, but as reflections of general conceptual organization, categorization principles, processing mechanisms, and experiential and environmental influences" (Geeraerts and Cuyckens 2007, 3). The ideas of situatedness (the position of our organism in relation to the physical and social environment) and embodiment (the mind/brain is shaped by the body in its interaction with the world), along with the realization that metaphor, projection, and parable—traditionally considered specific to the literary domain—are in fact fundamental components of our everyday cognition and that our mind is therefore "literary" (Turner 1996), brought about a new way to think about literature beyond previous aesthetic, structuralist, and cultural considerations. In this context, literary discourse also became a vehicle to study the workings of the human mind.

Cognitive poetics scholars have drawn from a variety of fields in the cognitive sciences, such as cognitive psychology and artificial intelligence, in addition to the research in cognitive linguistics. While this inclusive posture was already part of the project of cognitive poetics pioneer Reuven Tsur (1992), Gavins and Steen further emphasized the need to go beyond a linguistics-based analysis by including the work of psychologists Keith Oatley and Raymond Gibbs in their *Cognitive Poetics in Practice* (2003).

The last decade has represented a consolidation phase for cognitive poetics, characterized by the proliferation of books that are introductory in nature or meant to be used as textbooks (Semino and Culpeper 2002; Gavins and Steen 2003; Stockwell 2002) and by an effort to reflect on the position and role of cognitive poetics as well as the accomplishments and shortcomings of the field (Brône and Vandaele 2009). Additionally, during the last few years, cognitive poeticians have, among other undertakings, a) continued to explore the connection between poetic discourse and embodied cognition by considering aspects such as perspectival construal, fictive motion, and somatic feedback (see Rice this volume); b) emphasized the need to consider emotion (Burke 2011) and phenomenological aspects of the literary experience, such as feeling, vis-à-vis literary form (Freeman 2009, this volume); c) further explored literary discourse and intertextuality in relation to text world theory (Gavins 2007; Semino 2009); and d) stressed the inclusive and interdisciplinary nature of the cognitive poetics approach (Gavins and Steen 2003; Stockwell 2002, 2009), while attempting to bridge the gap that anomalously separates literary criticism from linguistic inquiry (Freeman 2007; Stockwell 2009).

Conceptual integration (the integration of mental patterns to create new meaning that is at the core of human thinking), also known as blending (see Fauconnier 1997; Fauconnier and Turner 2002, 2008), has also received much attention from both cognitive linguists and literary scholars. Conceptual blending is part of both Freeman's cognitive poetics project (see Freeman 2005, 2006, this volume) and Michael Sinding's cognitive approach to genre, in which he integrates the work of Fauconnier and Turner to account for an important aspect of genre theory: genre mixture and hybridization (Sinding 2005, this volume). Recent studies on blending and literature also include the work of Vera Tobin (2006), Amy Cook (2007, 2010), Sarah Copland (2008), and Cristóbal Pagán Cánovas (2010).

Literary discourse and mental processes have also been explored from the perspective of a generative linguistics tradition by English scholar Nigel Fabb and linguist Morris Halle (2008). Focusing on metrical pattern, these authors seek to underscore the connections among the mental abilities involved in the cognition of literature, music, and aspects of language, by suggesting that the specific cognitive mechanism behind counting in verbal art is shared across those domains (this volume).

2. NARRATIVE AND COGNITION

During the 1980s and 1990s, traditional narratology, in contact with the cognitive sciences, entered a post-classical phase (see Herman 1999, 8) in which it benefited from "concepts and methods that were unavailable to story analysts such as Barthes, Genette, Greimas, and Todorov during the heyday of structuralism" (Herman 2009a, 26). In this context, cognitive narratology was born. At the outset, the field was greatly influenced by Ray Jackendoff's "preference rules" of the reading process (1987), and artificial intelligence's concepts of frames, scripts, and schemas (Minsky 1975; Schank and Abelson 1977).[3] Research in psychology also had an important impact on cognitive narratology, particularly the work of Jerome Bruner (1986) and Theodore Sarbin (1986) in the nascent field of narrative psychology. Their proposal, as Richard Gerrig reminds us, was that "human thought is fundamentally structured around stories" (Gerrig 2005, 473). In that sense, as an intrinsic aspect of how we make sense of the world, narrative—and the accumulation of findings of narrative theorists—can be, for some cognitive narratologists, a way to engage in a fruitful conversation with the cognitive sciences to arrive at a fuller picture of human cognition (see Herman 2003).

In addition to enriching the study of narratives through a dialogue with the cognitive sciences, cognitive narratologists have expanded their scope of research to consider factors such as a) the media in which stories come to us

(Ryan 2004, 2006a), b) genre specificity, often focusing on drama, which had been excluded from traditional narratology discussions (Jahn 2001; Fludernik 2008), c) narratives in face-to-face interaction (Herman 2007), d) the role of intentionality in narrative understanding (Herman 2008), e) narrative world-making (Herman 2009b), f) virtual reality and possible worlds (Ryan 2001, 2006b), and g) the representation of consciousness in narratives across time (Herman 2011).

Richard Gerrig has investigated narratives and discourse processing from a cognitive psychological standpoint, contributing to research in cognitive narratology (see Gerrig and Egidi 2003). In his oft-cited *Experiencing Narrative Worlds* (1993), he stated that "all a reader must do to be transported to a narrative world is to have in place the repertory of cognitive processes that is otherwise required for everyday experience" (239). This assertion that our engagement with fictional worlds employs the same cognitive processes that we need in real life has had a remarkable resonance among cognitive and empirical literary studies scholars alike. Gerrig's research on narrative comprehension, memory, and readers' experiencing of fiction, as well as his defense of interdisciplinary collaboration in the study of mind and narrative (see this volume), make him one of the scholars exploring furthest down cognitive studies' new paths.

The empirical exploration of human narratives has also been carried out by a group of scholars known as the International Society for the Empirical Study of Literature and Media, or, in German, IGEL (Internationale Gesellschaft für Empirische Literaturwissenschaft), which employs methodologies borrowed from the social and natural sciences to delve into the engagement of readers (novices or experts) with literature. Their studies involve the use, among other techniques, of questionnaires, computerized text analysis, and, more recently, brain imaging (see "Neurological Approaches to Literature" section below).[4] By proposing theories of the act of reading and submitting them to empirical testing, they turn their project into "a continual two-way interweaving of theoretical proposal and empirical investigation" (Miall 2006, 2).

We can identify three main lines of research that scholars involved in the empirical study of literature have been following: a) a search for the cognitive underpinnings of literariness (the distinctive features of literary discourse) through the study of the effects on readers and film viewers of stylistic features such as foregrounding (Van Peer, Hakemulder, and Zyngier 2007a; Hakemulder 2007; Miall 2008), b) the study of the affective aspects of readers' responses to literature by looking into phenomena such as self-modifying feelings and self-implication (Kuiken et al. 2004; Kuiken 2008), and c) a socio-psychological orientation that traces the effects of literary reading on self and society (Hakemulder 2000, 2001, 2008; Mar et al. 2006; Mar, Djikic, and Oatley 2008; see "Literature and Human Development" section below). The research produced by IGEL since its creation by Siegfried Schmidt in 1987 inspired cognitive literary scholars who sought to open up to empirical methodologies and collaboration with researchers from scientific disciplines (see Bortolussi and Dixon 2003; Van Peer, Hakemulder, and Zyngier 2007b; Zyngier et al. 2008).

3. NEUROLOGICAL APPROACHES TO LITERATURE

Over the past decade there has been a slow but steady attempt at investigating narrative and the literary experience in relation to neural processes, with a clear interest coming from a variety of areas such as neurology, neuropsychiatry, psychology of fiction, literary studies, studies of text comprehension using fMRI (functional magnetic resonance imaging), and theory of mind.

Kay Young and Jeffrey Saver's article "The Neurology of Narrative" (2001) is one of the first inquiries into the neurological structures underlying the act of reading or writing literature. Using Jerome Bruner's theory of the narrative construction of reality and delving into the cognitive neuroscience research of the time, they tried to answer the following question: "How and why does the brain cause us to experience life and our individual lives as narratives at all?" (75). Alice Flaherty, in her book *The Midnight Disease* (2004), centers more specifically on the neurology of literary creation, bringing together her personal experience as a fiction writer with that of her career as a neurologist. She examines the neural substrates of the absence or presence of a writer's muses: writer's block and the drive to write. Aaron Mishara, a neuropsychologist, follows a similar path by looking at how the writing process and literary texts can help to elucidate cognitive and neural mechanisms (this volume), while Irving Massey in *The Neural Imagination* (2009) focuses on the contributions of neuroscience to aesthetics by offering a comparison between neuroscientific and humanistic approaches to the study of the arts.

Furthermore, neuroimaging research is helping us understand the neural underpinnings of reading stories (see Ferstl and von Cramon 2007; Ferstl, Rinck, and von Cramon 2005; Xu et al. 2005; Yarkoni, Speer, and Zacks 2008; Speer et al. 2009)[5] and viewing films (see Hasson et al. 2004, 2008; Kauppi et al. 2010; Zacks et al. 2010). Additionally, the fMRI research on theory of mind (see Mar and Oatley 2011), an important line of inquiry in the field of social cognitive neuroscience, often makes use of stories and cartoons as part of their experimental design (Fletcher et al. 1995; Gallagher et al. 2000; Völlm et al. 2006; Jenkins and Mitchell 2010) and may have an impact on the emerging research at the confluence of the neurosciences and literary studies.

Another instance of the value of neurological research for literary scholarship is the discovery of the neural correlates of imitation, mirror neurons (see Gallese and Goldman 1998; Iacoboni et al. 2005; Rizzolatti 2005; Iacoboni 2008; Rizzolatti and Sinigaglia 2008). This research opens exciting prospects for the study of literature with respect to theory of mind and simulation (see McConachie and Hart 2006, 5; Zunshine 2008, 60–61; and "Literature and Human Development" section below).

One of the latest contributions to this area of study, from a literary criticism standpoint, is Norman Holland's *Literature and the Brain* (2009), which crowns almost three decades of research at the crossroads of psychology and literature. Holland's investigation into the literary response explores the neurobiology of "being transported" when we read literature, "poetic faith," why we enjoy engaging in fictional worlds, and how we make meaning of and evaluate literature. Drawing on neuroscience, Holland invites us to reconsider the following questions: "Why do we lose ourselves in books and dramas?" "Why do we feel real emotions at things we know are fictional?" "How do we 'set' our brains for literary effects?" "What is the difference between creating a work of literature and the work of creating an ordinary life?" "Does literature confer an evolutionary advantage?" The wide scope of Holland's research program, which has included approaches and disciplines as diverse as reader response criticism, psychoanalysis, cognitive psychology, and, more recently, neuroscience, illustrates the difficulty of setting definite boundaries in a field that is based on integrating disciplines and reaching out in order to expand our possibilities of investigation.

II. CONSIDERING HUMAN BIOLOGICAL UNIVERSALS IN HISTORICAL-CULTURAL CONTEXTS

One of our recurrent themes throughout this chapter is the need to adopt an inclusive perspective and methodology when undertaking the study of human cognition and literary phenomena. The previous section focused on approaches that emphasize the materiality of the mind as the site of linguistic and literary activity. In this section we will outline three approaches that consider the role of literature in human communities by focusing on biological, environmental, evolutionary, developmental, social, historical, and cultural variables, while reflecting on how we can best theorize about the connection between mind and culture.

1. BIOLOGY AND CULTURE REUNITED

In 1995, Joseph Carroll published his *Evolution and Literary Theory*, in which he claimed that "literary works reflect and articulate the vital motives and interests of human beings as living organisms" (3). Almost fifteen years later, in the preamble to a special issue of *Style* dedicated to his work and to the field of evolutionary literary study (2008), Carroll revisited evolutionary critical approaches, emphasizing, a) their epistemological position: "like Wilson, they [literary Darwinists] regard evolutionary biology as the pivotal discipline uniting the hard sciences with the social sciences and the humanities," (105) and b) the "biocultural" nature of their ideas: "they argue that the genetically mediated dispositions of human nature interact with specific environmental conditions, including particular cultural traditions" (105).

The anthology *Biopoetics*, edited in 1999 by Brett Cooke and Frederick Turner, offered a good sample of interdisciplinary work on evolutionary approaches to the arts by scholars in anthropology, psychology, literature, and art, among other fields. *Practical Ecocriticism* (2003), by Glen Love, considered the biological aspects of literature in connection with the environment, following a line of research that links literature studies more strongly to nature and the physical world. Nancy Easterlin has also followed this path, bridging ecocriticism and cognitive and evolutionary approaches to literature, while focusing on aspects such as gender and social context (2004, 2005, 2010).

Brian Boyd has recently published *On the Origin of Stories: Evolution, Cognition, and Fiction* (2009) where he also reminds us that we need to consider both biology and culture in order to formulate a comprehensive theory of literature. In a comparable effort, Marcus Nordlund (2007) advocates for "a biocultural fusion of evolutionary and cultural/historical explanation" (5), inviting us to consider Shakespeare both as a man of his time and a member of the human species, while Peter Swirski takes an analytic-philosophy approach to reflect on the implications of the neo-Darwinian paradigm for the literary-aesthetic study and literary theory (2010). In *Why Do We Care about Literary Characters?* (2010), Blakey Vermeule investigates our attachment to fictional beings from an evolutionary and socio-developmental perspective (see also "Literature and Human Development" section below). Further demonstration of how an evolutionary approach enriches our understanding of literature can be found in Joseph Carroll's *Literary Darwinism* (2004), David and Nanelle Barash's *Madame Bovary's Ovaries* (2005), William Flesch's *Comeuppance* (2007), and Jonathan Gottschall's *The Rape of Troy* (2008). In 2005, Gottschall and David Sloan Wilson edited *The Literary Animal*, featuring contributions from a variety of disciplines across the sciences and the humanities.

Gottschall has collaborated with both Boyd and Carroll to edit *Evolution, Literature, and Film: A Reader* (2010), a comprehensive volume that includes classic essays both from evolutionary psychology and evolutionary literary studies. Michelle Scalise Sugiyama focuses on folklore in hunter-gatherer and foraging societies, in order to investigate the adaptive function of storytelling and the use of narrative to transmit subsistence information (see 2001a, 2001b, 2003). She has also explored the dynamics between biological universals and cultural specifics and has called scholars' attention to context-sensitivity, arguing that while "we should expect to find literary universality at the macro-level (e.g., adaptive problems, cognitive adaptations)" (Scalise Sugiyama 2003, 383), "geographical, technological, economic, and demographic differences between cultures all affect local expression and solution of adaptive problems and, hence, narrative content" (387).

Patrick Colm Hogan has written extensively about literary universals (see 1997, 2005, 2008a, 2010), emphasizing the need for and complexity of taking a universalist perspective in our study of literature. He addresses the resistance that this approach has encountered, due to misconceptions such as the idea that universals are shared invariably by *all* literary works and traditions, or that the study of universals annuls the consideration of difference or opposes cultural and historical analysis. While reflecting on how a research program in literary universals can be articulated, Hogan reminds us that "the study of universals and the study of cultural and historical particularity are mutually necessary" (Hogan 2010, 40; see also "Culture, History, and Cognition" section below).

Finally, in connection with evolutionary approaches to verbal art it is important to mention the anthropological insights of Ellen Dissanayake on aesthetic response and early infancy (2001). In collaboration with English scholar David Miall she has explored "the poetics of babytalk" (Miall and Dissanayake 2003) to conclude that "the ability to respond to poetic features of language is present as early as the first few weeks of life and that this ability attunes cognitive and affective capacities in ways that provide a foundation for the skills at work in later aesthetic production and response" (353).

2. LITERATURE AND HUMAN DEVELOPMENT

During the last decade, spurred by the increased interest in theory of mind—our ability to recognize others' mental states as different from our own and to understand their beliefs, desires, and intentions[6]—some scholars have been taking a closer look at the relationship between fictional and real minds. They have examined how readers follow and make sense of literary characters and their social circumstances, and have revisited questions such as what these characters tell us about human emotions (Hogan 2011, this volume), why we get emotionally attached to them (Vermeule 2010), and whether our engagement in fictional worlds can educate us emotionally (Robinson 2005), influence our mind and self (Hakemulder 2000), sharpen our social skills (Mar et al. 2006; Mar and Oatley 2008; Mar, Djikic, and Oatley 2008; Oatley, Mar, and Djikic this volume), or lead us to be more empathetic and altruistic (Keen 2006, 2007).

The study of literature from a theory of mind perspective (see Leverage et al. 2011) opens an exciting line of research that may help us understand the literary phenomenon at both the ontogenetic (individual development) and the phylogenetic (species evolution) levels. Through our engagement in fiction, we work out our cognitive abilities to read minds (Zunshine 2006) and run simulations of social experience (Oatley 2008). Just as we would try to do in a real social scenario with real human beings, we attempt to guess the characters' intentions and to predict their behavior. While doing so, we go beyond understanding their circumstances theoretically, from the outside, and place ourselves in their situations. According to simulation theory (see note 6), we attempt "to replicate, mimic, or impersonate the mental life of the target agent" (Gallese and Goldman 1998, 497). As it happens in real life, the mimicking of literary characters is essentially emotional. By engaging in literary simulation, we share the emotions of characters, we feel with them, exhibiting what is known as empathy. The concept of empathy, shaped after Theodor Lipps' notion of *Einfühlung* ("feeling into"), points at the idea of projection into the observed individual. Empathy is fundamental to explain our emotional reactions to literature, the reasons why we are able to laugh and cry when we immerse ourselves in fictional worlds.

Theorizing about characters and trying to read their intentions on one hand, and simulating them and sharing their emotions on the other, may be at the core of our literary experience. Moreover, by exercising these important aspects of our social cognition, we may be preparing ourselves to face analogous situations that we might encounter in real life. In this sense, fictional characters and the narratives in which they are inserted have a clear pragmatic value. Stories may be viewed as a human adaptive strategy to maximize our chances for survival by allowing us to safely watch the experiences of others and extract valuable lessons, something that was already known to the ancient writers of didactic literature such as medieval exempla. This pragmatic hypothesis about the function of narratives has been articulated from an evolutionary perspective (see Scalise Sugiyama in section above) as well as a developmental one: Exposure to narratives "is responsible for the development of sophisticated folk psychological abilities and understanding; abilities which remain importantly in play in our adult life" (Gallagher and Hutto 2008, 35). The work of Oatley, Mar, and Djikic for this volume further illustrates how the functional value of literature may extend beyond individual development into wider social implications. In *The Moral Laboratory* (2000), Frank Hake-mulder reviews a series of psychological studies with the intention of exploring the relationship between literature and ethical reflection. His work invites us to further consider the role of literature in education. By providing students with different perspectives, fiction may play an essential role, for instance, in cross-cultural and gender discussion, where we aim at understanding "the other."

Another sociocognitive perspective on fiction focuses on the fact that literary characters, just like real people, are part of a social network and thus exhibit collective thought and behavior. As Alan Palmer reminds us in "Intermental Thought in the Novel: The *Middlemarch* Mind" (2005), "much of the mental functioning that occurs in novels is done by large organizations, small groups, work colleagues, friends, families, couples, and other intermental units" (427). The notion of intermental thought, "joint, group, shared, or collective, as opposed to intramental, individual, or private thought" (427), becomes particularly useful to explore novels heavily based on social cognition such as George Eliot's. Palmer's work takes the fictional mind debate from the interior material mind to the external and collective mental space, further emphasizing the contextual nature of the inquiry on literature and human development (see also 2004, 2010).

3. CULTURE, HISTORY, AND COGNITION

In recent years, humanists have stressed the need to consider not only cultural but also historical parameters, along with biological and evolutionary ones, in the study of literature and cognition. This endeavor has become especially important at a time when literary scholars are pondering and redefining their relationship with the sciences and with previous literary theory schools, while scientists increasingly turn to literary scholarship.

The importance of both acknowledging cultural complexity and historicizing (taking into account the specific synchronic and diachronic contexts that surround human cultural acts) has been claimed from perspectives known as cognitive materialism and cognitive historicism (see Richardson 2004, 19–26). In the context of Shakespearean studies, Mary Thomas Crane has argued that the brain is "the material site where biology engages culture to produce the mind and its manifestation, the text" (Crane 2001, 35). By reminding us that the universality of metaphor, as a product of the embodied mind, must always be considered in the context of cultural specificity, she not only contributed to the epistemological debate on human nature and cultural phenomena, but also to the emergence of cognitive historicism. Identified by Richardson and Steen in 2002 as "a new departure for cognitive literary criticism" (5), cognitive historicism soon transcended its status of historicized reading to develop into an investigation of the permeability between literary discourses and the discourses about the mind that existed in the cultural production of a given historical period. In addition to studies on early modern literature and culture (Crane 2001; Spolsky 2001, 2004, 2007; Hart 2011; Tribble 2011), we find examples of this path of inquiry in Leverage's study of reception and memory in medieval French literature (2010), Richardson's work on Romanticism and the mind (2001), and Sullivan (this volume), among others. The potential of cognitive historicism to provide us with powerful interpretations of mind and culture through the intersection of literary history and cognitive approaches has recently been revisited by Richardson (2010).

In the midst of the ongoing debate about what the relationship should be between cognitive approaches to literature and other critical theory schools, Lisa Zunshine invites us to consider the intrinsic cultural nature of cognitive literary studies (2010). Like Hart (2001) and Spolsky (2002), Zunshine believes that a cognitive outlook could mesh well with the theoretical corpus of cultural studies. Through a discussion on the work and ideas of Raymond Williams, founder of cultural studies, she seeks to demonstrate that by taking a cognitive turn, the cultural studies scholar is indeed getting closer to the cultural studies legacy. With this position, she aligns herself with previous claims of inclusiveness made by those literary critics who saw cognitive approaches to literature as a complement to post-structuralist literary theory. Her project, however, goes beyond these claims, as she hopes for a full blending of cultural and cognitive studies in literary criticism to the point that we will be able to comfortably drop the label "cognitive," since "cognitive" will be automatically included in our cultural approaches. Zunshine's project is yet another example of the current understanding—not only from within the literary academia, from where she speaks, but also from other more empirical and biological positions in the study of literature—that biology and culture, nature and nurture, human universals and historical and cultural specifics need to be equally considered in order to arrive at a coherent understanding of the human embodied mind and its cultural manifestations.

We find representative examples of the practice of (cognitive) cultural studies in Patrick Hogan's *Empire and Poetic Voice: Cognitive and Cultural Studies of Literary Tradition and Colonialism* (2004), *Understanding Indian Movies: Culture, Cognition, and Cinematic Imagination* (2008b), and *Understanding Nationalism: On Narrative, Cognitive Science, and Identity* (2009), as well as in

Frederick Aldama's "Race, Cognition, and Emotion: Shakespeare on Film" (2006), *A User's Guide to Postcolonial and Latino Borderland Fiction* (2009a), *Your Brain on Latino Comics* (2009b), *Multicultural Comics: From* Zap *to* Blue Beetle (2010a), and his recent special issue of *Image and Narrative* (2010b) on narrative and cognitive approaches to US ethnic and postcolonial film, comic books, animation, and art. These studies demonstrate the ongoing dialogue that the field of cognitive literary studies maintains with critical approaches and disciplines such as postcolonial theory and film studies. Over the next few years of cognitive literary studies we anticipate the emergence of a body of research that will integrate the historical, cultural, and biological coordinates of the study of literature more organically, crossing taxonomic borders and possibly dropping at some point, as Zunshine hopes, the "cognitive" label.

CONCLUSION

The last decade has been characterized by an increasing rapprochement between literary scholars and cognitive scientists, as well as an effort by these groups to consider human biological universals in relation to specific cultural and historical factors. A number of cognitive approaches to literature have become more inclusive and self-reflective, while remaining faithful to their original interests and research programs. New directions such as neurological approaches to literature demonstrate a willingness to embrace both the rigor of empirical methodology and the complexity of interpretation, while others such as (cognitive) cultural studies emphasize the importance of maintaining a healthy dialogue between cognitive approaches to literature and other literary theory traditions. We find ourselves at a decisive turn in cognitive literary studies, moving toward a more cooperative investigation of the cognition of literature. Researchers in a variety of disciplines are beginning to realize that a multilevel and multi-perspective approach to our engagement with fictional worlds is paramount to a better understanding of how we interact with other human beings, as well as how we develop as individuals and as a species.

NOTES

1. We are employing the term "literature" in a broader sense to refer to fictional phenomena not only across genres, but also across media (printed works, oral folktales, performances, films, etc.).

2. For previous surveys of cognitive literary studies, see Bizup and Kintgen (1993), Crane and Richardson (1999), Richardson (1999, 2004, 2006), Hart (2001), Richardson and Steen (2002).

3. For a discussion of the sources of cognitive narratology, see Jahn 2005.

4. Due to the interdisciplinary nature of this group, the IGEL project shows an impor-

tant degree of overlap with other lines of research presented in this chapter. Scholars whose work intersects with other branches of cognitive literary studies include Frank Hakemulder (see "Literature and Human Development" section in this chapter) and David Miall (see "Biology and Culture Reunited" section), among others.

5. For a review of prior neuroimaging research on story comprehension and production, see Raymond Mar (2004).

6. Two main theories have been proposed to account for theory of mind: 1) the "theory theory" (TT) (Baron-Cohen 1995; Gopnik and Meltzoff 1997), according to which *we know about*, we possess and employ a body of conceptual knowledge concerning the mental states of others, we theorize about their minds, and 2) the "simulation theory" (ST) (Gordon 1986; Goldman 1989, 2006), according to which *we know how*, our knowledge about others' mental states is achieved through pretense-play, we pretend to be in someone else's mental shoes and understand others by simulating being them. Recent investigations on mirror neurons, the alleged neurological underpinnings of simulation, have attracted scholars' interest in this theory (see "Neurological Approaches to Literature" section in this chapter). However, both TT and ST have been criticized for their shortcomings (see Ratcliffe 2007). One of the alternatives offered to these two canonical views has been "interaction theory": working from a phenomenological standpoint, philosopher Shaun Gallagher proposed that our capacity to understand others is an embodied practice based on our perceptual interpretations of others' movements, gestures, and facial expressions (see 2001, 2004, 2005).

WORKS CITED

Aldama, Frederick Luis. 2006. Race, cognition, and emotion: Shakespeare on film. *College Literature* 33, no. 1: 197–213.

———. 2009a. *A user's guide to postcolonial and Latino borderland fiction*. Austin: University of Texas Press.

———. 2009b. *Your brain on Latino comics: From Gus Arriola to Los Bros Hernandez*. Austin: University of Texas Press.

———, ed. 2010a. *Multicultural comics: From Zap to Blue Beetle*. Austin: University of Texas Press.

———, ed. 2010b. New horizons in the analysis of US ethnic and postcolonial film and animation narrative. Special issue, *Image and Narrative* 11, no. 2.

Barash, David P., and Nanelle R. Barash. 2005. *Madame Bovary's ovaries: A Darwinian look at literature*. New York: Delacorte Press.

Baron-Cohen, Simon. 1995. *Mindblindness: An essay on autism and theory of mind*. Cambridge, MA: MIT Press.

Bizup, Joseph M., and Eugene R. Kintgen. 1993. The cognitive paradigm in literary studies. *College English* 55, no. 8: 841–57.

Bortolussi, Marisa, and Peter Dixon. 2003. *Psychonarratology: Foundations for the empirical study of literary response*. Cambridge: Cambridge University Press.

Boyd, Brian. 2009. *On the origin of stories: Evolution, cognition, and fiction*. Cambridge, MA: Belknap Press of Harvard University Press.

Boyd, Brian, Joseph Carroll, and Jonathan Gottschall, eds. 2010. *Evolution, literature, and film: A reader*. New York: Columbia University Press.

Brône, Geert, and Jeroen Vandaele, eds. 2009. *Cognitive poetics: Goals, gains, and gaps*. Berlin: Mouton de Gruyter.

Bruner, Jerome Seymour. 1986. *Actual minds, possible worlds*. Cambridge, MA: Harvard University Press.

Burke, Michael. 2011. *Literary reading, cognition and emotion: An exploration of the oceanic mind*. London: Routledge.

Carroll, Joseph. 1995. *Evolution and literary theory*. Columbia: University of Missouri Press.

———. 2004. *Literary Darwinism: Evolution, human nature, and literature*. New York: Routledge.

———. 2008. An evolutionary paradigm for literary study. Special issue, *Style* 42, no. 2–3: 103–35.

Cook, Amy. 2007. Interplay: The method and potential of a cognitive scientific approach to theatre. *Theatre Journal* 59, no. 4: 579–94.

———. 2010. *Shakespearean neuroplay: Reinvigorating the study of dramatic texts and performance through cognitive science*. New York: Palgrave Macmillan.

Cooke, Brett, and Frederick Turner, eds. 1999. *Biopoetics: Evolutionary explorations in the arts*. Lexington, KY: ICUS Books.

Copland, Sarah. 2008. Reading in the blend: Collaborative conceptual blending in the *Silent traveller* narratives. *Narrative* 16, no. 2: 140–62.

Crane, Mary Thomas. 2001 [2000]. *Shakespeare's brain: Reading with cognitive theory*. Princeton, NJ: Princeton University Press.

Crane, Mary Thomas, and Alan Richardson. 1999. Literary studies and cognitive science: Toward a new interdisciplinarity. *Mosaic* (Winnipeg) 32, no. 2: 123–40.

Dissanayake, Ellen. 2001. Aesthetic incunabula. *Philosophy and Literature* 25: 335–46.

Easterlin, Nancy. 2004. "Loving ourselves best of all": Ecocriticism and the adapted mind. *Mosaic* (Winnipeg) 37, no. 3: 1–18.

———. 2005. How to write the great Darwinian novel: Cognitive predispositions, cultural complexity, and aesthetic evaluation. *Journal of Cultural and Evolutionary Psychology* 3, no. 1: 23–38.

———. 2010. Cognitive ecocriticism: Human wayfinding, sociality, and literary interpretation. In *Introduction to cognitive cultural studies*, 257–74. Edited by Lisa Zunshine. Baltimore: Johns Hopkins University Press.

Fabb, Nigel, and Morris Halle. 2008. *Meter in poetry: A new theory*. New York: Cambridge University Press.

Fauconnier, Gilles. 1997. *Mappings in thought and language*. New York: Cambridge University Press.

Fauconnier, Gilles, and Mark Turner. 2002. *The way we think: Conceptual blending and the mind's hidden complexities*. New York: Basic Books.

———. 2008. Rethinking metaphor. In *Cambridge handbook of metaphor and thought*, 53–66. Edited by Raymond Gibbs. New York: Cambridge University Press.

Ferstl, Evelyn C., and D. Yves von Cramon. 2007. Time, space and emotion: fMRI reveals content-specific activation during text comprehension. *Neuroscience Letters* 427, no. 3: 159–64.

Ferstl, Evelyn C., Mike Rinck, and D. Yves von Cramon. 2005. Emotional and temporal aspects of situation model processing during text comprehension: An event-related fMRI study. *Journal of Cognitive Neuroscience* 17, no. 5: 724–39.

Flaherty, Alice Weaver. 2004. *The midnight disease: The drive to write, writer's block, and the creative brain*. New York: Houghton Mifflin.

Flesch, William. 2007. *Comeuppance: Costly signaling, altruistic punishment, and other biological components of fiction.* Cambridge, MA: Harvard University Press.

Fletcher P. C., F. Happé, U. Frith, S. C. Baker, R. J. Dolan, R. S. J. Frackowiak, and C. D. Frith. 1995. Other minds in the brain: A functional imaging study of "theory of mind" in story comprehension. *Cognition* 57, no. 2: 109–28.

Fludernik, Monika. 2008. Narrative and drama. In *Theorizing narrativity*, 355–84. Edited by John Pier and José Ángel García Landa. Berlin: Walter de Gruyter.

Freeman, Margaret H. 2005. The poem as complex blend: Conceptual mappings of metaphor in Sylvia Plath's "The applicant." *Language and Literature* 14, no. 1: 25–44.

———. 2006. Blending: A response. *Language and Literature* 15, no. 1: 107–17.

———. 2007. Cognitive linguistic approaches to literary studies: State of the art in cognitive poetics. In *The Oxford handbook of cognitive linguistics*, 1175–1202. Edited by Dirk Geeraerts and Hubert Cuyckens. New York: Oxford University Press.

———. 2009. Minding: Feeling, form, and meaning in the creation of poetic iconicity. In *Cognitive poetics: Goals, gains, and gaps*, 169–96. Edited by Geert Brône and Jeroen Vandaele. Berlin: Mouton de Gruyter.

Gallagher, H. L., F. Happé, N. Brunswick, P. C. Fletcher, U. Frith, and C. D. Frith. 2000. Reading the mind in cartoons and stories: An fMRI study of "theory of mind" in verbal and nonverbal tasks. *Neuropsychologia* 38, no. 1: 11–21.

Gallagher, Shaun. 2001. The practice of mind: Theory, simulation, or primary interaction? *Journal of Consciousness Studies* 8, no. 5–7: 83–108.

———. 2004. Understanding interpersonal problems in autism: Interaction theory as an alternative to theory of mind. *Philosophy, Psychiatry, & Psychology* 11, no. 3: 199–217.

———. 2005. *How the body shapes the mind.* Oxford: Oxford University Press.

Gallagher, Shaun, and Daniel D. Hutto. 2008. Understanding others through primary interaction and narrative practice. In *The shared mind: Perspectives on intersubjectivity*, 17–38. Edited by Jordan Zlatev. Amsterdam: John Benjamins.

Gallese, Vittorio, and Alvin Goldman. 1998. Mirror neurons and the simulation theory of mind-reading. *Trends in Cognitive Sciences* 2, no. 12: 493–501.

Gavins, Joanna. 2007. *Text world theory: An introduction.* Edinburgh: Edinburgh University Press.

Gavins, Joanna, and Gerard Steen, eds. 2003. *Cognitive poetics in practice.* London: Routledge.

Geeraerts, Dirk, and Hubert Cuyckens, eds. 2007. *The Oxford handbook of cognitive linguistics.* New York: Oxford University Press.

Gerrig, Richard J. 1993. *Experiencing narrative worlds: On the psychological activities of reading.* New Haven: Yale University Press.

———. 2005. Psychological approaches to narrative. In *Routledge encyclopedia of narrative theory*, 470–74. Edited by David Herman, Manfred Jahn, and Marie-Laure Ryan. New York: Routledge.

Gerrig, Richard J., and Giovanna Egidi. 2003. Cognitive psychological foundations of narrative experiences. In *Narrative theory and the cognitive sciences*, 33–55. Edited by David Herman. Stanford, CA: Center for the Study of Language and Information.

Goldman, Alvin I. 1989. Interpretation psychologized. *Mind and Language* 4, no. 3: 161–85.

———. 2006. *Simulating minds: The philosophy, psychology, and neuroscience of mindreading.* Oxford: Oxford University Press.

Gopnik, Alison, and Andrew N. Meltzoff. 1997. *Words, thoughts, and theories.* Cambridge, MA: MIT Press.

Gordon, Robert M. 1986. Folk psychology as simulation. *Mind and Language* 1, no. 2: 158–71.

Gottschall, Jonathan. 2008. *The rape of Troy: Evolution, violence, and the world of Homer.* Cambridge: Cambridge University Press.

Gottschall, Jonathan, and David Sloan Wilson, eds. 2005. *The literary animal: Evolution and the nature of narrative.* Evanston, IL: Northwestern University Press.

Hakemulder, Frank. 2000. *The moral laboratory: Experiments examining the effects of reading literature on social perception and moral self-concept.* Amsterdam: John Benjamins.

———. 2001. How to make *alle Menschen Brüder*: Literature in a multicultural and multiform society. In *The psychology and sociology of literature: In honor of Elrud Ibsch*, 225–42. Edited by Dick Schram and Gerard Steen. Amsterdam: John Benjamins.

———. 2007. Tracing foregrounding in responses to film. *Language and Literature* 16, no. 2: 125–39.

———. 2008. Imagining what could happen: Effects of taking the role of a character on social cognition. In *Directions in empirical literary studies: In honor of Willie van Peer*, 139–53. Edited by S. Zyngier, M. Bortolussi, A. Chesnokova, and J. Auracher. Amsterdam: John Benjamins.

Hart, F. Elizabeth. 2001. The epistemology of cognitive literary studies. *Philosophy and Literature* 25, no. 2: 314–34.

———. 2011. 1500–1620: Reading, consciousness, and romance in the sixteenth century. In *The emergence of mind: Representations of consciousness in narrative discourse in English*, 103–31. Edited by David Herman. Lincoln: University of Nebraska Press.

Hasson, Uri, Ohad Landesman, Barbara Knappmeyer, Ignacio Vallines, Nava Rubin, and David J. Heeger. 2008. Neurocinematics: The neuroscience of film. *Projections* 2, no. 1: 1–26.

Hasson, Uri, Yuval Nir, Ifat Levy, Galit Fuhrmann, and Rafael Malach. 2004. Intersubject synchronization of cortical activity during natural vision. *Science* 303, no. 5664: 1634–40.

Herman, David. 1999. Introduction: Narratologies. In *Narratologies: New perspectives on narrative analysis*, 1–30. Edited by David Herman. Columbus: Ohio State University Press.

———. 2003. Introduction. In *Narrative theory and the cognitive sciences*, 1–30. Edited by David Herman. Stanford, CA: Center for the Study of Language and Information.

———. 2007. Storytelling and the sciences of mind: Cognitive narratology, discursive psychology, and narratives in face-to-face interaction. *Narrative* 15, no. 3: 306–34.

———. 2008. Narrative theory and the intentional stance. *Partial Answers* 6, no. 2: 233–60.

———. 2009a. *Basic elements of narrative.* Chichester, UK: Wiley-Blackwell.

———. 2009b. Narrative ways of worldmaking. In *Narratology in the age of cross-disciplinary narrative research*, 71–87. Edited by Sandra Heinen and Roy Sommer. Berlin: Walter de Gruyter.

———, ed. 2011. The emergence of mind: Representations of consciousness in narrative discourse in English. Lincoln: University of Nebraska Press.

Hogan, Patrick Colm. 1997. Literary universals. *Poetics Today* 18, no. 2: 223–49.

———. 2004. *Empire and poetic voice: Cognitive and cultural studies of literary tradition and colonialism.* Albany: State University of New York Press.

———. 2005. Literary universals and their cultural traditions: The case of poetic imagery. *Consciousness, Literature, and the Arts* 6, no. 2.

———. 2008a. Of literary universals: Ninety-five theses. *Philosophy and Literature* 32, no. 1: 145–60.

————. 2008b. *Understanding Indian movies: Culture, cognition, and cinematic imagination.* Austin: University of Texas Press.

————. 2009. *Understanding nationalism: On narrative, cognitive science, and identity.* Columbus: Ohio State University Press.

————. 2010. Literary universals. In *Introduction to cognitive cultural studies*, 37–60. Edited by Lisa Zunshine. Baltimore: Johns Hopkins University Press.

————. 2011. *What literature teaches us about emotion.* New York: Cambridge University Press.

Holland, Norman. 2009. *Literature and the brain.* Gainesville, FL: PsyArt Foundation.

Iacoboni, Marco. 2008. *Mirroring people: The new science of how we connect with others.* New York: Farrar, Straus, and Giroux.

Iacoboni, Marco, Istvan Molnar-Szakacs, Vittorio Gallese, Giovanni Buccino, John C. Mazziotta, and Giacomo Rizzolatti. 2005. Grasping the intentions of others with one's own mirror neuron system. *PLoS Biology* 3, no. 3: e79.

Jackendoff, Ray. 1987. *Consciousness and the computational mind.* Cambridge, MA: MIT Press.

Jahn, Manfred. 2001. Narrative voice and agency in drama: Aspects of a narratology of drama. *New Literary History* 32, no. 3: 659–79.

————. 2005. Cognitive narratology. In *Routledge encyclopedia of narrative theory*, 67–71. Edited by David Herman, Manfred Jahn, and Marie-Laure Ryan. New York: Routledge.

Jenkins, Adrianna C., and Jason P. Mitchell. 2010. Mentalizing under uncertainty: Dissociated neural responses to ambiguous and unambiguous mental state inferences. *Cerebral Cortex* 20 (February): 404–10.

Kauppi, Jukka-Pekka, Liro P. Jääskeläinen, Mikko Sams, and Jussi Tohka. 2010. Inter-subject correlation of brain hemodynamic responses during watching a movie: Localization in space and frequency. *Frontiers in Neuroinformatics* 4 (March): 1–10.

Keen, Suzanne. 2006. A theory of narrative empathy. *Narrative* 14, no. 3: 207–36.

————. 2007. *Empathy and the novel.* Oxford: Oxford University Press.

Kuiken, Don. 2008. A theory of expressive reading. In *Directions in empirical literary studies: In honor of Willie van Peer*, 49–68. Edited by S. Zyngier, M. Bortolussi, A. Chesnokova, and J. Auracher. Amsterdam: John Benjamins.

Kuiken, Don, Leah Phillips, Michelle Gregus, David S. Miall, Mark Verbitsky, and Anna Tonkonogy. 2004. Locating self-modifying feelings within literary reading. *Discourse Processes* 38, no. 2: 267–86.

Lakoff, George, and Mark Johnson. 1980. *Metaphors we live by.* Chicago: University of Chicago Press.

Langacker, Ronald W. 1987. *Foundations of cognitive grammar, volume 1: Theoretical prerequisites.* Stanford, CA: Stanford University Press.

————. 1991. *Foundations of cognitive grammar, volume 2: Descriptive application.* Stanford, CA: Stanford University Press.

Leverage, Paula. 2010. *Reception and memory: A cognitive approach to the "chansons de geste."* Amsterdam: Rodopi.

Leverage, Paula, Howard Mancing, Richard Schweickert, and Jennifer Marston William. 2011. *Theory of mind and literature.* West Lafayette, IN: Purdue University Press.

Love, Glen A. 2003. *Practical ecocriticism: Literature, biology, and the environment.* Charlottesville: University of Virginia Press.

Mar, Raymond A. 2004. The neuropsychology of narrative: Story comprehension, story production, and their interrelation. *Neuropsychologia* 42, no. 10: 1414–34.

Mar, Raymond. 2011. The neural bases of social cognition and story comprehension. *Annual Review of Psychology* 62 (January): 103–34.

Mar, Raymond A., and Keith Oatley. 2008. The function of fiction is the abstraction and simulation of social experience. *Perspectives on Psychological Science* 3: 173–92.

Mar, Raymond A., Maja Djikic, and Keith Oatley. 2008. Effects of reading on knowledge, social abilities, and selfhood: Theory and empirical studies. In *Directions in empirical literary studies: In honor of Willie van Peer*, 127–37. Edited by S. Zyngier, M. Bortolussi, A. Chesnokova, and J. Auracher. Amsterdam: John Benjamins.

Mar, Raymond A., Keith Oatley, Jacob Hirsh, Jennifer dela Paz, and Jordan B. Peterson. 2006. Bookworms versus nerds: Exposure to fiction versus non-fiction, divergent associations with social ability, and the simulation of fictional social worlds. *Journal of Research in Personality* 40: 694–712.

Massey, Irving. 2009. *The neural imagination: Aesthetic and neuroscientific approaches to the arts*. Austin: University of Texas Press.

McConachie, Bruce, and F. Elizabeth Hart. 2006. Introduction. In *Performance and cognition: Theatre studies and the cognitive turn*, 1–25. Edited by Bruce McConachie and F. Elizabeth Hart. London: Routledge.

Miall, David S. 2006. *Literary reading: Empirical and theoretical studies*. New York: Peter Lang.

———. 2008. Foregrounding and feeling in response to narrative. In *Directions in empirical literary studies: In honor of Willie van Peer*, 89–102. Edited by S. Zyngier, M. Bortolussi, A. Chesnokova, and J. Auracher. Amsterdam: John Benjamins.

Miall, David S., and Ellen Dissanayake. 2003. The poetics of babytalk. *Human Nature* 14, no. 4: 337–64.

Minsky, Marvin. 1975. A framework for representing knowledge. In *The psychology of computer vision*, 211–77. Edited by Patrick Henry Winston. New York: McGraw-Hill.

Nordlund, Marcus. 2007. *Shakespeare and the nature of love: Literature, culture, evolution*. Evanston, IL: Northwestern University Press.

Oatley, Keith. 2008. The mind's flight simulator. *Psychologist* 21, no. 12: 1030–32.

Pagán Cánovas, Cristóbal. 2010. Erotic emissions in Greek poetry: A generic integration network. *Cognitive Semiotics* 6 (forthcoming).

Palmer, Alan. 2004. *Fictional minds*. Lincoln: University of Nebraska Press.

———. 2005. Intermental thought in the novel: The *Middlemarch* mind. *Style* 39, no. 4: 427–39.

———. 2010. *Social minds in the novel*. Columbus: Ohio State University Press.

Ratcliffe, Matthew. 2007. *Rethinking commonsense psychology: A critique of folk psychology, theory of mind and simulation*. New York: Palgrave Macmillan.

Richardson, Alan. 1999. Cognitive science and the future of literary studies. *Philosophy and Literature* 23, no. 1: 157–73.

———. 2001. *British Romanticism and the science of the mind*. New York: Cambridge University Press.

———. 2004. Studies in literature and cognition: A field map. In *The work of fiction: Cognition, culture, and complexity*, 1–29. Edited by Alan Richardson and Ellen Spolsky. Aldershot, UK: Ashgate.

———. 2006. Cognitive literary criticism. In *Literary theory and criticism*, 544–56. Edited by Patricia Waugh. Oxford: Oxford University Press.

———. 2010. *The neural sublime: Cognitive theories and Romantic texts*. Baltimore: Johns Hopkins University Press.

Richardson, Alan, and Francis Steen. 2002. Literature and the cognitive revolution: An introduction. *Poetics Today* 23, no. 1: 1–8.

Rizzolatti, Giacomo. 2005. The mirror neuron system and its function in humans. *Anatomy and Embryology* 210, no. 5–6: 419–21.

Rizzolatti, Giacomo, and Corrado Sinigaglia. 2008. *Mirrors in the brain: How our minds share actions and emotions*. Translated by Frances Anderson. Oxford: Oxford University Press.

Robinson, Jenefer. 2005. *Deeper than reason: Emotion and its role in literature, music, and art*. Oxford: Oxford University Press.

Ryan, Marie-Laure. 2001. *Narrative as virtual reality: Immersion and interactivity in literature and electronic media*. Baltimore: Johns Hopkins University Press.

———, ed. 2004. *Narrative across media: The languages of storytelling*. Lincoln: University of Nebraska Press.

———. 2006a. *Avatars of story*. Minneapolis: University of Minnesota Press.

———. 2006b. From parallel universes to possible worlds: Ontological pluralism in physics, narratology, and narrative. *Poetics Today* 27, no. 4: 633–74.

Sarbin, Theodore R., ed. 1986. *Narrative psychology: The storied nature of human conduct*. New York: Praeger.

Scalise Sugiyama, Michelle. 2001a. Narrative theory and function: Why evolution matters. *Philosophy and Literature* 25, no. 2: 233–50.

———. 2001b. Food, foragers, and folklore: The role of narrative in human subsistence. *Evolution and Human Behavior* 22, no. 4: 221–40.

———. 2003. Cultural variation is part of human nature: Literary universals, context-sensitivity, and "Shakespeare in the bush." *Human Nature* 14, no. 4: 383–96.

Schank, Roger C., and Robert P. Abelson. 1977. *Scripts, plans, goals, and understanding: An inquiry into human knowledge structures*. Hillsdale, NJ: Lawrence Erlbaum Associates.

Semino, Elena. 2009. Text worlds. In *Cognitive poetics: Goals, gains, and gaps*, 33–71. Edited by Geert Brône and Jeroen Vandaele. Berlin: Mouton de Gruyter.

Semino, Elena, and Jonathan V. Culpeper, eds. 2002. *Cognitive stylistics: Language and cognition in text analysis*. Amsterdam: John Benjamins.

Sinding, Michael. 2005. *Genera mixta*: Conceptual blending and mixed genres in *Ulysses*. *New Literary History* 36, no. 4: 589–619.

Speer, Nicole K., Jeremy R. Reynolds, Khena M. Swallow, and Jeffrey M. Zacks. 2009. Reading stories activates neural representations of visual and motor experiences. *Psychological Science* 20, no. 8: 989–99.

Spolsky, Ellen. 2001. *Satisfying skepticism: Embodied knowledge in the early modern world*. Aldershot, UK: Ashgate.

———. 2002. Darwin and Derrida: Cognitive literary theory as a species of post-structuralism. *Poetics Today* 23, no. 1: 43–62.

———. 2004. Women's work is chastity: Lucretia, *Cymbeline*, and cognitive impenetrability. In *The work of fiction: Cognition, culture, and complexity*, 51–83. Edited by Alan Richardson and Ellen Spolsky. Aldershot, UK: Ashgate.

———. 2007. *Word vs. image: Cognitive hunger in Shakespeare's England*. Basingstoke, UK: Palgrave Macmillan.

Stockwell, Peter. 2002. *Cognitive poetics: An introduction*. London: Routledge.

———. 2009. *Texture: A cognitive aesthetics of reading*. Edinburgh: Edinburgh University Press.

Swirski, Peter. 2010. *Literature, analytically speaking: Explorations in the theory of interpretation, analytic aesthetics, and evolution*. Austin: University of Texas Press.

Talmy, Leonard. 2000a. *Toward a cognitive semantics, volume 1: Concept structuring systems*. Cambridge, MA: MIT Press.

———. 2000b. *Toward a cognitive semantics, volume 2: Typology and process in concept structuring*. Cambridge, MA: MIT Press.

Tobin, Vera. 2006. Ways of reading Sherlock Holmes: The entrenchment of discourse blends. *Language and Literature* 15, no. 1: 73–90.

Tribble, Evelyn B. 2011. *Cognition in the globe: Attention and memory in Shakespeare's theater*. New York: Palgrave Macmillan.

Tsur, Reuven. 1992. *Toward a theory of cognitive poetics*. Amsterdam: North Holland.

Turner, Mark. 1996. *The literary mind: The origins of thought and language*. New York: Oxford University Press.

Van Peer, Willie, Frank Hakemulder, and Sonia Zyngier. 2007a. Lines on feeling: Foregrounding, aesthetics, and meaning. *Language and Literature* 16, no. 2: 197–213.

———. 2007b. *Muses and measures: Empirical research methods for the humanities*. Newcastle, UK: Cambridge Scholars.

Vermeule, Blakey. 2010. *Why do we care about literary characters?* Baltimore: Johns Hopkins University Press.

Völlm, Birgit A., Alexander N. W. Taylor, Paul Richardson, Rhiannon Corcoran, John Stirling, Shane McKie, John F. W. Deakin, and Rebecca Elliott. 2006. Neuronal correlates of theory of mind and empathy: A functional magnetic resonance imaging study in a nonverbal task. *NeuroImage* 29, no. 1: 90–98.

Xu, Jiang, Stefan Kemeny, Grace Park, Carol Frattali, and Allen Braun. 2005. Language in context: Emergent features of word, sentence, and narrative comprehension. *NeuroImage* 25, no. 3: 1002–15.

Yarkoni, Tal, Nicole K. Speer, and Jeffrey M. Zacks. 2008. Neural substrates of narrative comprehension and memory. *NeuroImage* 41, no. 4: 1408–25.

Young, Kay, and Jeffrey L. Saver. 2001. The neurology of narrative. *SubStance* 30, no. 1–2: 72–84.

Zacks, Jeffrey M., Nicole K. Speer, Khena M. Swallow, and Corey J. Maley. 2010. The brain's cutting-room floor: Segmentation of narrative cinema. *Frontiers in Human Neuroscience* 4 (October): 1–15.

Zunshine, Lisa. 2006. *Why we read fiction: Theory of mind and the novel*. Columbus: Ohio State University Press.

———. 2008. *Strange concepts and the stories they make possible: Cognition, culture, narrative*. Baltimore: Johns Hopkins University Press.

———. 2010. What is cognitive cultural studies? In *Introduction to cognitive cultural studies*, 1–33. Edited by Lisa Zunshine. Baltimore: Johns Hopkins University Press.

Zyngier, Sonia, Marisa Bortolussi, Anna Chesnokova, and Jan Auracher, eds. 2008. *Directions in empirical literary studies: In honor of Willie van Peer*. Amsterdam: John Benjamins.

THE COGNITIVE SCIENCES AND
LITERARY THEORY IN DIALOGUE

The essays included in this section exhibit the ongoing dialogue about the exchange between the cognitive sciences and literary research. How can cognitive scientists benefit from the work of literary scholars? How might the study of readers' responses and interpretations enrich our understanding of narrative processes? What are the issues and steps to consider in building a model of narrative comprehension that relies both on neuroanatomical research and developmental psychology? Gerrig and Murphy amplify the volume's interdisciplinary motif, laying the ground for further discussion on the advantages of combining humanistic and scientific approaches and methods to obtain a more coherent picture of how we experience literature.

CHAPTER 2

WHY LITERATURE IS NECESSARY, AND NOT JUST NICE

RICHARD J. GERRIG

AS AN ACADEMIC DISCIPLINE, cognitive science aspires to understand the full range of human experience. To do so, its practitioners draw upon a variety of domains, including psychology, linguistics, philosophy, and neuroscience. The thesis of this chapter is that literary scholars should also play a critical role in achieving the goals of cognitive science. When cognitive scientists began to study story comprehension in earnest, they recognized the broad value of this enterprise. Consider the words of a pioneering researcher, Gordon Bower (1978, 212):

> I think story comprehension gives us a way to illuminate cognitive processes, because the procedures people use to understand and remember stories are very general. In fact, in understanding stories, we seem to use much the same principles and procedures that we use when we are interacting with people in real settings, trying to interpret or explain why some person acts the way he does . . . . Therefore, story understanding provides an experimental microcosm or small test tube in which psychologists can isolate and study how people understand the social-behavioral world around them.

I embrace Bower's assertion that insights from the study of stories resonate far beyond the bounds of story comprehension itself. In that context, I claim that the products of literary studies—literary scholars' insights about readers' responses to narratives—have important implications for cognitive science theories. That's the sense in which literature is necessary, and not just nice: without a keen appreciation of the full scope of literary experiences, cognitive science theories will remain incomplete or incorrect.

In this chapter I provide two case studies that illustrate the value of literary analyses for cognitive science. For each case study I provide a brief sketch of insights that have emerged from close analyses of literary experiences. I then describe psychological research, chiefly from my own laboratory, which has flowed from those insights, and explore the implications for theories in cognitive science. The first case study focuses on circumstances in which readers experience suspense with respect to outcomes that are already known to them. This phenomenon has implications for how memory processes function in the context of narrative experiences. The second case study focuses more broadly on readers' responses to narratives. This latter example questions the completeness of cognitive science accounts in the domain of narrative.

Before I proceed, I wish to acknowledge the allusion in my title to Ortony's (1975) essay "Why Metaphors Are Necessary and Not Just Nice." In his essay, Ortony presents a strong case that metaphors are essential to language function: "Metaphors are necessary as a communicative device because they allow the transfer of coherent chunks of characteristics—perceptual, cognitive, emotional and experiential—from a vehicle which is known to a topic which is less so" (53). An important implication of Ortony's essay is that researchers who wish to provide a theory of language use cannot succeed if they do not involve metaphor at the core of their enterprise. In this chapter I engage the similar claim that any account of human cognition that excludes consideration of literary experiences will be inherently flawed.

I. ANOMALOUS SUSPENSE

Researchers in cognitive science have devoted an extraordinary amount of attention to the vicissitudes of human memory. Much of that research has focused on circumstances in which people fail to call information to mind that has, in fact, been represented in memory. However, in this first section, I explore the implications of a memory phenomenon that falls outside the bounds of traditional memory research. An excerpt from the novel *Swim to Me* (Carter 2007, 197–98) exemplifies the phenomenon that is an unusual type of suspense:

Chuck [Varne] opened the broadcast with these words: "Last evening, we witnessed an extraordinary act of courage by a member of our own WGUP news team. Sent out to cover the damage caused by Hurricane Claudia, weathergirl Delores Taurus was standing oceanside at Belleair Beach when she spotted a little boy being dragged out into the roiling ocean. Without hesitation, Ms. Taurus threw down her mike and swam after the helpless child, all the while fighting against the forces of nature. Tonight, we will show you the footage of those frightening and treacherous moments that, fortunately for everyone, culminated in a victory at sea."

Again, they watched Delores's rescue and even though they all knew how it would end, Hanratty and Roy put down their food and Rex blew a whoosh of relief through his cheeks when Delores and the boy finally landed on the shore.

The text asserts that the three characters watching the newscast (Hanratty, Roy, and Rex) were all well aware of how the story would end. Still, as they become immersed in the newscast, that perfect knowledge of the outcome does not apparently present itself to consciousness. The experience of the narrative appears to render the characters' memories inaccessible; suspense occurs where none should be possible. Given the ubiquity of narratives in everyday life, it seems critical that memory theorists understand exactly what processes are at work here.

Fortunately, literary scholars and philosophers have provided a framework for research on this phenomenon through their discussions of "the paradox of suspense." I call the phenomenon "anomalous suspense" because that provides a better fit for cognitive science (Gerrig 1989, 1993). I made my first acquaintance with anomalous suspense in an article by Kendall Walton (1978), who observed that "suspense may remain a crucial element in our response to a work almost no matter how familiar we are with it" (26). Walton's solution to the paradox emerged from his larger account of texts as props for games of make-believe (Walton 1990). Each new experience of a narrative initiates a new game of make-believe; within each new game, readers do not know an outcome and thus suspense remains. Other theorists have argued against Walton's account to articulate their own views. For example, Carroll (1996) focused his account on the types of thoughts readers entertain as they experience a narrative. Yanal (1996) argued that readers do not actually experience suspense upon rereading. Rather they misidentify some other emotion as suspense (see Gerrig 1997 for a rebuttal). Prieto-Pablos (1998) expounded on the variety of reading experiences that may lead to experiences of suspense of different intensity. Each of these accounts has made provocative claims with respect to the theoretical framework of cognitive science.

In my own research, I sought to establish how easily readers can be made to experience suspense in the absence of uncertainty. My goal was to demonstrate, in a sense, the reality of the phenomenon with respect to its impact on the accessibility of information in readers' memory. The general hypothesis is that when readers are transported to narrative worlds some types of information external to that world become less accessible. In particular, anecdotal reports of anomalous suspense suggest that information about particular outcomes fails to penetrate into consciousness during narrative experiences. Consider what *might* have happened while Hanratty, Roy, and Rex watched the news account of Delores's daring rescue. Their memory processes could have presented to them the information that "everything turns out fine" and even particular information about how events unfolded. Memory processes *often* provide information in such an automatic fashion, without any conscious search of memory. That is true, for example, when we see close friends and greet them by name. However, this appears not to happen in circumstances of anomalous suspense.

To test this property of anomalous suspense, I wrote a series of stories based on well-known facts from the real world (Gerrig 1989). I chose the facts to be unambiguous and uncontroversial:

* Cheerios is a brand of breakfast cereal.
* Hawaii is one of America's fifty states.
* Geraldine Ferraro was nominated for vice president.

For each fact I wrote a story that I intended to create suspense. Consider this example, which is centered on the statement "John Belushi died of an overdose of drugs":

> John Belushi was one of the hottest young stars in Hollywood. Belushi had become extremely popular on TV's Saturday Night Live. The police were shocked to find him dead in a hotel room. The detective at the scene thought that Belushi had been murdered. Bruises on Belushi's body suggested a lengthy struggle.

Although the statement "John Belushi died of an overdose of drugs" is true, this *suspense* story suggests otherwise.

Participants in the study read a series of thirty-two brief stories. As exemplified by the Belushi story, the experimental materials likely did not inspire intense suspense. Still, to the extent that readers were transported to these narrative worlds, we would expect outcome knowledge from the real world to become less accessible. Specifically, in the face of this mild suspense, we would expect that readers would find it harder to confirm that "John Belushi died of an overdose of drugs" or to disconfirm that "John Belushi did not die of an overdose of drugs." To test that prediction, I recorded participants' latencies to respond "true" or "false" to one of those statements.

As a baseline, I also had control, *no suspense* stories:

> John Belushi was one of the hottest young stars in Hollywood. Belushi had become extremely popular on TV's Saturday Night Live. The police weren't

surprised to find him dead in a hotel room. The last few months of his life were almost one long party. He mixed drugs and alcohol like someone who wished to die.

To assess the impact of the suspense, I compared readers' latencies to respond to the target statements (for example, "John Belushi died of an overdose of drugs") after they read the *suspense* versus *no suspense* stories. The data confirmed the impact of anomalous suspense: participants took about 260 milliseconds longer to respond to the target statements after having read stories that created suspense.

These data support the importance of anomalous suspense as a genuine memory phenomenon. However, one objection might be that although participants knew the relevant facts, those facts were not particularly accessible as they read the stories. To provide even stronger evidence for anomalous suspense, the experiment included versions of both the *suspense* and *no suspense* stories that provided *prior warning*. Each of those stories had as its first sentence the precise statement that later served as the target for verification. For example, the first sentence of the John Belushi story was "John Belushi died of an overdose of drugs" rather than "John Belushi was one of the hottest young stars in Hollywood."

When participants read the *prior warning* stories they made their judgments more quickly overall. That is, having read "John Belushi died of an overdose of drugs" just six sentences earlier, participants found it easier to verify the truth of that assertion than they did when the story began with the alternative statement. Even so, suspense still wielded an impact. Without the prior warning, participants took, on average, 238 milliseconds longer to respond correctly to the target statements in the presence of suspense (versus the *no suspense*, control stories). With the prior warning, participants took 260 milliseconds longer to make the judgments with suspense. Thus, even when participants read correct information at the story's outset, they became sufficiently transported by the suspense stories to make that information somewhat less accessible.

My initial research on anomalous suspense asked participants to make explicit judgments about outcomes. Rapp (2008) extended the results to circumstances in which participants read the outcomes as a continuous part of the narrative. Participants' reading times provide an index of the difficulty they experience assimilating outcome information into their discourse representations. All other things being equal, we would expect readers to find it difficult to accept outcomes that are discordant with their background knowledge. However, Rapp's prediction was that suspense would ameliorate some of that difficulty. That is, Rapp predicted that readers would find it relatively less difficult to assimilate discordant outcomes in the presence of suspense.

To test that prediction, Rapp contrasted unambiguous (*no suspense*) and suspenseful contexts (with texts modified from Gerrig 1989). The outcomes appeared as sentences within the larger stories. Consider this suspense story, focused on the making of *The Wizard of Oz*:

> L. Frank Baum was the author of the book "The Wizard of Oz." The popularity of the book led MGM Studios to purchase the movie rights. To ensure the movie's success, MGM wanted a big star in the lead role of Dorothy. Judy Garland made the list of qualified candidates. However MGM wanted Shirley Temple to star in the film. Shirley Temple was the biggest child star at the time. Temple's agent quickly negotiated and a contract was drafted. Shirley Temple starred in the movie "The Wizard of Oz." "The Wizard of Oz" ended up both a commercial and critical success. It was also one of the first movies to appear in full color.

Readers should know that Shirley Temple did not, in fact, star in the movie. The question at hand is whether they nonetheless found it somewhat easier to assimilate that untrue outcome in the presence of suspense. Thus, there were four versions of each experimental text, with unambiguous or suspenseful contexts followed by outcomes that were accurate or inaccurate with respect to historical truth.

Rapp correctly anticipated that participants would find it more difficult to assimilate the inaccurate statements: They took, on average, 522 milliseconds longer to read outcomes that contradicted the historical record. However, the presence of suspense attenuated some of the impact of this discrepancy. In unambiguous contexts, participants took 693 milliseconds longer to read the inaccurate statements (versus the accurate statements); in suspense contexts, they only took 410 milliseconds longer to do so. This difference suggests that readers of the suspense stories found it relatively easier to assimilate the statement asserting that Shirley Temple starred in *The Wizard of Oz*.

In a second experiment, Rapp asked participants to stop before they read each story to retrieve two facts about the topic of the story. He asked them, for example, to write "two different facts that each describe something you know about *The Wizard of Oz*." Rapp intended this exercise to provide an even stronger type of prior warning (cf. Gerrig 1989). If participants expend effort to retrieve information from memory relevant to a particular fact, we might expect suspense to have less of an impact. However, Rapp replicated his original results. Participants took 655 milliseconds longer to read the historical untruths. However, in unambiguous contexts, participants took 755 milliseconds longer to read the inaccurate statements whereas in suspenseful contexts they only took 555 milliseconds longer to do so.

This body of research provides strong evidence that theorists of memory and text processing should pay close attention to anomalous suspense. At the same time, this focus on anomalous suspense as a memory phenomenon does not expend its value on cognitive science. As I noted in my brief review, theorists have used "the paradox of suspense" as a touchstone for discussions of how readers experience and understand emotions in the context of narrative. Cognitive scientists would do well to follow some of those other leads, to add nuance to their accounts, for example, of interactions between cognition and emotion (see Hogan 2003).

II. READERS' RESPONSES TO NARRATIVES

Most cognitive science theories of narrative processing make the assumption that, at least tacitly, what readers largely do is extract meanings from texts (for several examples, see McNamara and Magliano 2009). These approaches embody what Reddy (1979) called "the conduit metaphor"—the idea that words, utterances, and texts *contain* ideas. However, Reddy made the strong case that there is danger inherent in this metaphor: "There are of course no ideas in the words, and therefore none in any books, nor on any tapes or records. There are no ideas whatsoever in any libraries" (309).

> We do not preserve ideas by building libraries and recording voices. The only way to preserve culture is to train people to rebuild it, to "regrow" it, as the word "culture" itself suggests, in the only place it can grow—within themselves. (310)

The strong assertion that meaning does not reside within a text but rather emerges through readers' interaction with a text will be familiar to scholars from the humanities. In fact, much literary scholarship points to ways in which people's distinctive responses to narratives bring about quite different understandings of what a particular narrative "means." The various approaches, for example, joined under the title "reader-response criticism" (Suleiman and Crosman 1980; Tompkins 1980) provide an enormous number of ideas cognitive sciences might pursue to understand how readers construct—rather than extract—the meanings of texts (see Gerrig 1993).

In our own research, my students and I have taken the concept of readers' responses rather literally by studying how narratives prompt readers to encode particular preferences about narrative events. Literary narratives quite regularly provide circumstances in which readers' preferences could have an impact on how they experience a narrative. Consider a compelling scene from *The Abstinence Teacher* in which Maggie, the daughter of the novel's main character Ruth and her ex-husband Frank, takes possession of the ball in the last few seconds of a tied soccer game (Perrotta 2007, 65):

> Maggie took control of the ball near midfield, with nothing but grass between her and the goal. It looked to Ruth like one of those scenarios from a wish-fulfillment dream—one player way out front, everyone else stampeding behind, unable to catch up. When it became clear that help would arrive too late, the Comets' goalie began moving away from the net, hoping to force a bad shot. Maggie just kept charging forward as if the goalie weren't even there, and it looked to Ruth for a second like another collision was inevitable.
> "Shoot!" Frank was shouting. "Bang it in!"

It's hard to imagine that people could read this passage without encoding some mental responses that reflect their preferences: They might think "Shoot!" or "Score!" or, if they prefer Maggie to fail, "Trip!" or "Miss!"

We call the mental contents that embody readers' preferences *participatory responses* (Gerrig and Jacovina 2009; Polichak and Gerrig 2002). When readers encode "Shoot!" or "Miss!" those thoughts parallel the types of responses they might have were they actual participants in the unfolding scene. Readers have opportunities to encode other types of participatory responses: When they find a particular plot turn disagreeable, they might attempt to undo it mentally; when they experience suspense about an outcome, they might engage problem-solving processes to offer the hero mental advice. In all these circumstances, the participatory responses will become part of the totality of the readers' narrative experience. To the extent that readers encode different participatory responses, they will have different experiences of the same narrative.

To demonstrate the impact of participatory responses on readers' narrative experiences, David Rapp and I carried out a pair of projects that focused on readers' preferences. Our first project (Rapp and Gerrig 2002) focused on readers' preferences in the context of time shifts. Consider this brief text (one of the twenty-four we used):

> Billy was waiting outside the St. Louis Cardinals' baseball stadium, with a baseball card for Mark McGwire to sign. Billy stood in a large group of fans waiting to meet the future hall of fame player. McGwire's fans were holding

all types of baseball memorabilia. One child was holding a baseball. Another fan was holding a large framed photo of McGwire. Billy looked at his perfect condition card. He really wanted to get that autograph. McGwire appeared and said hello to the fans.

At this juncture, readers know that Billy wishes to get McGwire's autograph. The story had two different endings; each one was read by half the participants:

A minute later McGwire got into his limo and rode off.
An hour later McGwire got into his limo and rode off.

In our initial experiment, we provided participants with an outcome statement and asked them to respond yes or no to whether they thought the sentence accurately conveyed what would happen next in the story. Again, there were two possibilities, each one of which half the participants read:

Billy didn't get the autograph.
Billy got Mark McGwire's autograph.

Suppose readers are able to make appropriate use of the information about the time shift. We would expect those who had read that McGwire left in a minute would be more likely to agree that Billy didn't get the autograph; we would expect those who read that McGwire left in an hour would be more likely to agree that he had gotten the autograph. Participants' responses confirmed those expectations. When there was a match between the time shift and the outcome, participants agreed that the outcome "would happen next" 85 percent of the time; with a mismatch they agreed only 28 percent of the time.

In a second experiment, we asked participants to read the stories through to the end—including the sentence stating the time shift (for example, "A minute later McGwire got into his limo and rode off") and the sentence stating the outcome (for example, "Billy got Mark McGwire's autograph"). We measured how long participants took to read each sentence. Participants' reading times provide an indication of how much difficulty they experienced assimilating new information into their representations of prior parts of the narrative. We expected participants to take longer to read sentences when there was a mismatch between the time shift and the outcome. The data bore out that prediction: participants took 140 milliseconds longer to read outcomes that mismatched expectations based on the stated time shift.

We chose to study preferences in the context of time shifts exactly because we believed that participants would respond to the shifts in this appropriate fashion. Prominent theories of text processing, such as the *event-indexing model*, suggest that readers are diligent about encoding the passage of time as narratives unfold (Zwaan, Langston, and Graesser 1995; Zwaan, Magliano, and Graesser 1995). This claim has an empirical basis. For example, Zwaan (1996) demonstrated that the size of a time shift (for example, *a moment later*, *an hour later*, or *a day later*) had an impact on the relative accessibility of concepts from parts of the text that preceded the time shift. After a longer time shift, such concepts were relatively less accessible. Results of this sort make it unsurprising that participants in our experiment would demonstrate reasonable sensitivity to which outcomes could obtain after a minute versus an hour passage of time.

However, against that background, we predicted that readers' preferences would create a context in which they would be less attentive to the realities of time shifts. To manipulate readers' preferences, we inserted new material into our experimental texts just after the initial sentence that established the setting:

> Billy was waiting outside the St. Louis Cardinals' baseball stadium, with a baseball card for Mark McGwire to sign. Billy was a dishonest collectibles dealer who would overcharge children when they bought sports cards from him.

We would expect the second sentence to produce a reader preference that Billy not obtain McGwire's autograph. We intended different material to produce the opposite preference:

> Billy had been diagnosed with terminal cancer, and his lifelong dream was to meet his baseball idol.

We pretested these additions to ensure that the majority of participants agreed that, after reading one or the other, they would prefer that Billy obtain or not obtain McGwire's autograph. With the inclusion of preference information, we now had eight versions of each experimental story. Each story had one of two outcome preferences, one of two time shifts, and one of two final outcomes.

How might preferences wield an impact on readers' narrative experiences? Consider what might happen when participants read that Billy "really wanted to get that autograph" in the context of his being a dishonest collectibles dealer. We'd expect readers to encode participatory responses that expressed the preference that he not obtain the autograph: We'd expect some mental content similar to "I hope you don't." Such responses provide part of the context for readers' considerations of the actual outcomes. Thus, an outcome that readers should ordinarily find hard to assimilate (for example, Billy's lack of success in the context of a one-hour shift) should become easier to assimilate if readers had encoded a preference for that outcome.

Once again, we carried out an experiment that asked participants to indicate yes or no as to whether they thought that a particular outcome accurately captured what was likely to happen next. Even with preferences in place, participants continued to respect the constraints of time shifts. When an outcome matched a preceding time shift they were 35 percent more likely to embrace the outcome than in circumstances of a mismatch. However, readers' preferences also had a consistent impact. When an outcome matched readers' preferences, they were 17 percent more likely to accept the outcome than in circumstances of a mismatch. Consider versions of the story that ended with a minute time shift (for example, "A minute later he got into his limo and rode off"). In the absence of preference information, participants agreed with an outcome consistent with that time shift (for example, "Billy didn't get the autograph") 86 percent of the time. However, when participants read a version of the story that created a preference for the outcome consistent with an hour shift (for example, when they read that Billy had been diagnosed with terminal cancer), they endorsed the minute-shift consistent outcome only 69 percent of that time.

The same pattern obtained when we recorded reading times for the outcome sentences. Even in the face of preferences, participants' reading times respected the bounds of reality: They took 220 milliseconds longer to read outcome sentences that mismatched the time shifts. However, we also found a robust effect of readers' preferences: they took 302 milliseconds longer to read outcomes that were inconsistent with their preferences. Preferences had their biggest impact when a time shift was consistent with a preference (for example, readers preferred that Billy not get the autograph and Mark McGwire left "a minute later") but the outcome contradicted both the preference and the time shift (for example, Billy got the autograph).

Recall that Rapp and I chose the domain of time shifts because we had good reasons to believe that readers would be successful at appreciating what types of outcomes were possible in a given period of time. We didn't expect readers to let loose from the reality of time in the face of preferences. Rather we suggested that preferences—and the participatory responses that followed from those preferences—created a context in which it was easier or harder to accept an outcome. When, for example, readers knew that Billy had cancer it was just that much harder to accept the outcome that he didn't get an autograph, whatever the passage of time.

For a second project on readers' preferences, Rapp and I (2006) turned our attention to readers' expectations about likely outcomes. Recall the scene from *The Abstinence Teacher* in which Maggie is charging downfield. We can ask how likely it is that, in the moment, readers would encode the expectations "Maggie will shoot" or "Maggie's team will win." Readers with sufficient background understanding of how soccer games unfold should be able to draw upon that knowledge to make some reasonable guesses about what might happen next.

In any particular narrative situation, readers have the opportunity to encode any number of expectations. However, readers avail themselves of some opportunities but not others. We would be surprised, for example, if readers encoded an expectation that Maggie would weep with joy should she score a goal, although that's been known to happen to some soccer players at some times. A relevant dimension here is between those *predictive inferences* that readers would generate automatically, without any conscious intervention, versus those that require strategic, conscious intervention. Research in psychology has been directed toward defining the contexts and content for automatic inferences (for example, Casteel 2007; Lassonde and O'Brien 2009; Peracchi and O'Brien 2004). Consider this brief text (McKoon and Ratcliff 1986):

> The director and cameraman were ready to shoot close-ups when suddenly the actress fell from the 14th story.

Using texts of this sort, McKoon and Ratcliff demonstrated that readers are likely to encode predictive inferences automatically, but that the content of those inferences was somewhat abstract. For example, with respect to the falling actress, participants were likely to encode "something bad will happen" rather than, more specifically, "the actress will die."

Against this background of research on readers' expectations about future narrative events, Rapp and I asked a different question: do readers' preferences have an impact on what they expect? If they know that the actress is a paragon of virtue, would they find it more difficult to predict that she will die? If they know that she is a blackmailing harridan, would they find it more difficult to accept a miraculous survival? Our previous research with time shifts supported our predictions that readers' preferences would affect their expectations for narrative outcomes. Once again we expected that such an effect would be brought about by the types of participatory responses that readers encode as a narrative unfolds. If, for example, readers encode the thought "Don't die!" while the actress plummets, they should find it more difficult to accept her death (if it comes).

To test this prediction, Rapp and I (2006) once again wrote a series of brief stories. For these stories, we provided background information that we expected readers to interpret as the "reality" of the situation. Consider this example:

Charles was running for a seat on the Senate. The *New York Times* put his efficient campaign several points ahead in its final poll. Today was Election Day, and people were coming out to vote. At the end of the day, the ballots were tabulated and the outcome declared.

We intended the story's second sentence to create a *success bias*: the information suggests that Charles is likely to succeed in his efforts to become a senator. We intended a contrasting sentence to create a *failure bias*:

The *New York Times* put his lackluster campaign several points behind in its final poll.

Before we carried out our main experiments, we had a group of participants read the biasing information for the full set of twenty-four stories to confirm that the two sentences succeeded at foreshadowing success or failure outcomes. As with the project on time shifts, the stories had two possible outcomes:

Charles was successful in his bid to become senator.
Charles had failed in his bid to become senator.

Thus, participants read one of four versions of each story that either matched or mismatched with respect to the outcome suggested by the context (that is, a bias toward success or failure) and the actual outcome (that is, success or failure). As before, we conducted separate experiments with different measures: One set of participants made explicit judgments with respect to the likelihood of each outcome; a second set of participants provided reading times for the outcome sentences. For explicit judgments, participants were 59.7 percent more likely to agree that an outcome would obtain when it matched the contextual bias. For reading times, participants took 203 milliseconds less to read outcome sentences that were consistent with the contexts.

These data strongly suggest that the contextual information was constraining readers' expectations about possible outcomes. Note, however, that we could not make any precise statements about time course. For example, it could be the case that, after participants read "The *New York Times* put [Charles's] efficient campaign several points ahead in its final poll," they encoded the inference "Charles will win." It could also be the case that participants read all the way to the outcome before they assessed the extent to which it fit with the contextual information. As I noted earlier, past researchers who studied readers' expectations about outcomes have focused largely on automatic inferences. Although we cannot make any claims about a precise time course, and therefore about the conscious versus unconscious nature of these inferences, the data strongly suggest that readers are using the contextual information to encode expectations. These initial results provide the context in which we could turn our attention to readers' preferences.

To create preferences, we wrote contrasting sentences for each story. For example, we intended that one text would prompt readers to hope for Charles's success:

Charles worked hard to help the underprivileged and underrepresented have a voice in government.

We intended a second text to prompt the opposite preference:

Charles was corrupt, taking bribes and giving favors to companies that polluted the environment.

We obtained ratings from an initial group of participants who confirmed that the sentences for the full set of twenty-four stories created the preferences we intended. The preference sentences functioned as introductions to the full stories. Consider the first two sentences of one version of Charles's story:

Charles worked hard to help the underprivileged and underrepresented have a voice in government. Charles was running for a seat on the Senate.

For the pair of preference experiments, there were eight versions of each story, that contrasted on the preference (for success or failure), the contextual bias (toward success or failure), and the outcome (success or failure).

As with the time-shift experiments, we expected that the inclusion of preference information would not cause readers to let loose of the constraints of reality. In fact, when they provided explicit judgments, participants were still 44 percent more likely to agree that an outcome would obtain when it matched the previous contextual bias. However, participants were also 19 percent more likely to agree with the outcome that matched their preferences. Consider stories in which participants judged the likelihood of successful outcomes in the presence of success-biasing outcomes. When participants had a preference for the success outcome, they agreed that the successful outcome would likely happen about 95 percent of the time. However, when participants had a preference for the failure outcome, they only agreed that the successful outcome was likely (despite the success-bias in the context) about 69 percent of the time. Participants' reading times for the outcomes demonstrated much the same patterns. Participants were 184 milliseconds slower to read outcomes when they mismatched the contextual bias. However, they also took 96 milliseconds longer to read outcomes that mismatched their preferences.

The results of these two projects point to the strong conclusion that readers' preferences have an impact on their narrative experiences. To make this point experimentally, we needed to create circumstances in which we could expect readers' preferences to be reasonably uniform: to detect the impact of mismatches between readers' preferences and actual outcomes we needed to be reasonably certain of what would count as a "match" and what would count as a "mismatch."

However, we believe our results generalize to narrative circumstances in which readers would have a variety of preferences. Consider a scene from *The Abstinence Teacher* in which Tim needs to make an important decision (Perrotta 2007, 291):

> Tim glanced at the clock above the sink.
> "Yikes," he said, startled to see that it was already ten fifteen. "I'm gonna be late for church."
> "It won't take long," [Ruth] said. "I cleaned the coffeemaker, like you said. It's working a lot better."
> "Cool." Tim grinned, oddly gratified that his diagnosis had panned out. "But I really should go."
> "Come on," she said, her voice suddenly flirtatious. "Just one cup. I got this really nice French Roast."

Should Tim stay or should he go? It seems quite likely that different readers will bring different preferences to bear on this moment as a function of their own personal experiences (and also, perhaps, as a function of their aesthetic preferences). As it turns out, Tim opts to leave:

> "Ruth," he said, rising abruptly from his chair, sounding more serious than he'd meant to. "Please don't tempt me like this."

Our experimental results suggest that readers will respond quite differently to this outcome depending on whether it matches or mismatches their preferences. Thus, we can make a claim about a process that is uniform across readers: readers' preferences exercise control over their narrative experiences. However, because those preferences will vary in content and strength, it is impossible to identify a single "meaning" at which all readers would arrive.

These experiments on preferences emerged from an empirical approach to narrative processing that embraces some of the fundamental concepts of reader-response criticism—most importantly, the concept that readers construct their own understanding of a narrative. The projects illustrate only one example of the type of research that flows from this perspective. Cognitive scientists would likely achieve a much more complete account of readers' narrative experiences if they followed up the observations literary scholars have made about readers' interpretive processes.

CONCLUSION

In this chapter, I have offered two case studies that illustrate how the products of literary scholarship can yield empirical research that adds nuance to cognitive science theories. Literary treatments of anomalous suspense established it as a phenomenon that provided new mysteries for extant theories of memory processes. Laboratory research on the phenomenon demonstrated its generality in readers' narrative experiences. The broad perspective of reader-response criticism suggests how cognitive science researchers might overcome the (at least tacit) error of assuming that meanings reside within texts. Scholarship associated with that approach vastly expands the range of hypotheses that cognitive scientists might consider as elements of their theories. Laboratory research confirmed that readers respond to texts by encoding preferences with respect to potential outcomes. Those preferences affect the ease with which readers accept outcomes when they ultimately arrive. With these case studies in hand, I repeat the claim that it is necessary, and not just nice, for cognitive scientists to incorporate the products of literary studies into their enterprise. To use story understanding as an "experimental microcosm" to "isolate and study how people understand the social-behavioral world around them," cognitive scientists must have a finely honed understanding of the full range of processes that apply as readers experience literary narratives.

WORKS CITED

Bower, Gordon H. 1978. Experiments on story comprehension and recall. *Discourse Processes* 1: 211–31.

Carroll, Noël. 1996. The paradox of suspense. In *Suspense: Conceptualizations, theoretical analyses, and empirical explorations*, 71–91. Edited by Peter Vorderer, Hans J. Wulff, and Mike Friedrichsen. Hillsdale, NJ: Erlbaum.

Carter, Betsy. 2007. *Swim to me*. Chapel Hill, NC: Algonquin Books of Chapel Hill.

Casteel, Mark A. 2007. Contextual support for predictive inferences: What do readers generate and keep available for use? *Discourse Processes* 44: 51–72.

Gerrig, Richard J. 1989. Suspense in the absence of uncertainty. *Journal of Memory and Language* 28: 633–48.

———. 1993. *Experiencing narrative worlds*. New Haven: Yale University Press.

———. 1997. Is there a paradox of suspense? A reply to Yanal. *British Journal of Aesthetics* 37: 168–74.

Gerrig, Richard J., and Matthew E. Jacovina. 2009. Reader participation in the experience of narrative. In *The psychology of learning and motivation, volume 51*, 223–54. Edited by Brian H. Ross. Burlington, MA: Academic Press.

Hogan, Patrick C. 2003. *Cognitive science, literature, and the arts*. New York: Routledge.

Lassonde, Karla A., and Edward J. O'Brien. 2009. Contextual specificity in the activation of predictive inferences. *Discourse Processes* 46: 426–38.

McKoon, Gail, and Roger Ratcliff. 1986. Inferences about predictable events. *Journal of Experimental Psychology: Learning, Memory, and Cognition* 12: 82–91.

McNamara, Danielle S., and Joe Magliano. 2009. Toward a comprehensive model of comprehension. In *The psychology of learning and motivation, volume 51*, 298–384. Edited by Brian H. Ross. Burlington, MA: Academic Press.

Ortony, Andrew. 1975. Why metaphors are necessary and not just nice. *Educational Theory* 25: 45–53.

Peracchi, Kelly A., and Edward J. O'Brien. 2004. Character profiles and the activation of predictive inferences. *Memory & Cognition* 32: 1044–52.

Perrotta, Tom. 2007. *The abstinence teacher*. New York: St. Martin's Press.

Polichak, James W., and Richard J. Gerrig. 2002. "Get up and win!": Participatory responses to narratives. In *Narrative impact: Social and cognitive foundations*. Edited by Melanie C. Green, Jeffrey J. Strange, and Timothy C. Brock, 71–95. Mahwah, NJ: Erlbaum.

Prieto-Pablos, Juan A. 1998. The paradox of suspense. *Poetics* 26: 99–113.

Rapp, David N. 2008. How do readers handle incorrect information during reading? *Memory & Cognition* 36: 688–701.

Rapp, David N., and Richard J. Gerrig. 2002. Readers' reality-driven and plot-driven analyses in narrative comprehension. *Memory & Cognition* 30: 779–88.

———. 2006. Predilections for narrative outcomes: The impact of story contexts and reader preferences. *Journal of Memory and Language* 54: 54–67.

Reddy, Michael J. 1979. The conduit metaphor—a case of frame conflict in our language about language. In *Metaphor and thought*, 284–324. Edited by Andrew Ortony. Cambridge: Cambridge University Press.

Suleiman, Susan R., and Inge Crosman, eds. 1980. *The reader in the text*. Princeton, NJ: Princeton University Press.

Tompkins, Jane P., ed. 1980. *Reader-response criticism*. Baltimore: Johns Hopkins University Press.

Walton, Kendall L. 1978. Fearing fictions. *Journal of Philosophy* 75: 5–27.

———. 1990. *Mimesis as make-believe*. Cambridge, MA: Harvard University Press.

Yanal, Robert J. 1996. The paradox of suspense. *British Journal of Aesthetics* 36: 146–58.

Zwaan, Rolf A. 1996. Processing narrative time shifts. *Journal of Experimental Psychology: Learning, Memory, & Cognition* 22: 1196–1207.

Zwaan, Rolf A., Mark C. Langston, and Arthur C. Graesser. 1995. The construction of situation models in narrative comprehension: An event indexing model. *Psychological Science* 6: 292–97.

Zwaan, Rolf A., Joseph P. Magliano, and Arthur C. Graesser. 1995. Dimensions of situation model construction in narrative comprehension. *Journal of Experimental Psychology: Learning, Memory, & Cognition* 21: 386–97.

CHAPTER 3

THEORY OF MIND IN RECONCILING THE SPLIT
OBJECT OF NARRATIVE COMPREHENSION

JOSEPH A. MURPHY

I

A central point of Chomsky's 1959 critique of Skinner's *Verbal Behavior* is that, when dealing with complex, human behavior, it is important to form a judgment on the *relative importance* of external conditions (inputs and outputs) and internal structure:

> One's estimate of the relative importance of external factors and internal
> structure in the determination of behavior will have an important effect on
> the direction of research on linguistic (or any other) behavior, and on the
> kinds of analogies from animal behavior studies that will be considered rele-
> vant or suggestive. (27)

Chomsky demonstrates that the behaviorist assumption that external factors are of exclusive importance leads to incoherence and absurdity in considering complex, higher-level functions. His readjustment of the ratio to reflect the importance of the internal structure of the organism had not just an important but a revolutionary effect on the subsequent direction of research in linguistics.

Inferences about internal structure, by which Chomsky means "a complicated product of inborn structure, the genetically determined course of maturation, and past experience" (27), can be arrived at in a variety of ways. For Chomsky, "insofar as independent neurophysiological evidence is not available, it is obvious that inferences concerning structure of the organism are based on observation of behavior and outside events." That is to say, within that project there are two main lines of evidence, events and externally observable behavior, and neurophysiological evidence. However, Chomsky, writing in 1959, limits himself to the former. The dramatic rise in availability of neurophysiological evidence in the intervening fifty years, however, has opened the second line of inquiry to practical research, and linguistics now reflects this, with thriving schools of inquiry based both on external evidence (language in the world), and on new neurophysiological techniques (Pinker 1994; Kaan and Swaab 2002).

Contemporary literary studies, by contrast, have shown a marked reluctance to use evidence of any kind to make inferences about internal structure, and have tended to see the forms and instances of literary behavior as historically contingent, or determined by linguistic, class, gender, or local social structures understood to be external to finite, individual beings. Insofar as contemporary linguistics begins with Chomsky's revision of the estimate of the relative importance of internal structure, the consistent reliance in literary theory on Saussure, that is to say pre-Chomskyan linguistics, is symptomatic of this deep commitment, rather than a modest disinclination to speculate about psychology when evidence is restricted to observable events and behavior, a constraint Chomsky shared.

Neurophysiological techniques are equally available for the study of literature. In this essay I would like to participate in the adjustment of the estimate of the relative importance of internal structure in the study of literature recently opened by cognitive literary studies by advocating for a specifically neuroanatomical line of evidence. Versus the more common cognitive scientific approach, with its ties to AI and the problem of instantiation in machine language, the advantages of adopting such an approach are twofold: the possibility of elaborating a causal, physical basis for the experience of literature, and a greater suppleness in handling emotion. The question in contemplating an experimental program for elaborating a material basis for narrative forms, then, becomes a strategic question of pursuing controlled, lab-based experiments into the neurophysiological basis of adult cognition, or clinical and psychological investigation into the developmental psychology of these capacities. This article attempts to think through this strategic choice, and finds a field of possibilities in each.

II

Literature is a complex, higher-order process involving beliefs, desires, and aesthetic questions. Cognitive neuroscience understands higher-order mental phenomena to be in a causal relation to physical processes in the brain, specifically the topology and dynamics of impulse propagation in the net of nerve cells or neurons, and the more general purpose raising and lowering of the system by emotional and physical processes (Wiener 1948; Rosenblatt 1962). In this regard, a neuroanatomical approach to literary studies will necessarily be first interdisciplinary, and then reductive.

"Reductive" carries a negative connotation in the humanities, but what does it mean? According to David Chalmers' account in relation to the problem of consciousness, reductive explanation characterizes the experimental sciences, and involves the explanation of phenomena wholly in terms of simpler entities. When an appropriate account of lower-level processes is given, the explanation of the higher-level phenomenon falls out (Chalmers 1996, 43–51). A reductive explanation, however, "is not the be-all and end-all of explanation" (49). There are also historical explanations, which explain "the genesis of phenomena, such as life, where a reductive explanation only gives a synchronic account of how living systems function." There are, further, "all sorts of high-level explanations, such as the explanation of aspects of behavior in terms of beliefs and desires," that still have a strong place in cognitive literary studies, marked by the emphasis on practice and interpretation. "Even though this behavior might be in principle explainable reductively, a high-level explanation is often more . . . enlightening" (43).

Hence, a move to constitute literature reductively, as a natural scientific object, is never meant to displace or invalidate other types of explanation. However, in the context of literary theory, a reductive explanation is always and necessarily a *mystery-removing* explanation:

> Its chief role is to remove any deep sense of mystery surrounding a high-level phenomenon. It does this by reducing the bruteness and arbitrariness of the phenomenon in question to the bruteness and arbitrariness of lower-level processes. (Chalmers 1996, 48–49)

"Interdisciplinarity" is a buzzword nowadays in both the sciences and the humanities. Cognitive studies of literature would seem by their very nature to be interdisciplinary undertakings, but one must notice that participants in conferences and edited volumes tend to be overwhelmingly from departments of humanities. The converse tends to be the case in scientific studies. A recent volume in the MIT Press Social Neuroscience series includes contributions from psychology, psychiatry, neurology, radiology, and neuroscience, but none from humanists, and an fMRI study of brain activity in popular movie spectators involves specialists in neurobiology, computer science, and neural computation, but they did not think to consult a film studies expert (Blakemore 2006, 60; Hasson et al. 2004). Hasson, for one, has progressed to include a film specialist in recent work (Hasson et al. 2008), but it will be worthwhile to define what is meant by "interdisciplinary," to continue to chip away at this dissymmetry in the future.

I take my understanding of the term from Norbert Wiener's *Cybernetics* (1948), a text that remains a key for the current century. The central insight in cybernetics is that there is an essential unity to the problems of communication and control in the machine and in living tissue, a unification of formerly separate domains on the order of the accomplishments of Newton, Maxwell, and DuBois-Reymond. In the introduction to the original edition, Wiener describes the interdisciplinary environment, the tentative reading and discussion groups and collaborative work involving mathematicians, physiologists, electrical engineers, physicists, etc., out of which this insight came. In the context of the specialization of knowledge in the university, the key to real interdisciplinary work is not each becoming an expert in another's field, but a process of acculturation whereby one learns to pose questions in a form that those in another discipline can understand:

> If a physiologist who knows no mathematics works together with a mathematician who knows no physiology, the one will be unable to state his problem in terms that the other can manipulate, and the second will be unable to put the answers in any form that the first can understand . . . . A proper explanation of these blank spaces on the map of science [can] only be made by a team of scientists, each a specialist in his own field but each possessing a thoroughly sound and trained acquaintance with the fields of his neighbors; all in the habit of working together, of knowing one another's intellectual customs, and of recognizing the significance of a colleague's new suggestion before it has taken on full formal expression. The mathematician need not have the skill to conduct a physiological experiment, but he must have the skill to understand one, to criticize one, and to suggest one. The physiologist need not be able to prove a certain mathematical theorem, but he must be able to grasp its physiological significance and to tell the mathematician for what he should look. (Wiener 1948, 2–3)

Hence the interdisciplinary task for the humanist is to be able to put relevant questions in a way that a scientist, particularly a neuroscientist, can recognize. For example, while a humanist faced with a spaghetti western might raise all sorts of questions about identification, plot, and perspective, about genre theory and history, the question a scientist raises in the fMRI study mentioned above is: "As you watch Clint Eastwood in the 1966 movie classic *The Good, the Bad, and the Ugly*, what is happening in your brain?" (Pessoa 2004, 1617). That is a reductive, interdisciplinary question.

III

Steps to achieve a "sound and trained acquaintance" with the field of neuroscience were taken during a three-year period of participation in the CNS (Central Nervous System) seminar of the Neurology Department of my university's medical school. Here is what I learned about their intellectual customs.

Neuroscience recognizes two basic kinds of result, corresponding roughly to a clinical and a research setting. The first is a walk-in or referral patient with localized brain trauma accompanied by sharply diminished capacity of some particular mental or social behavior, and the second is a controlled experiment. In the first case, particular to hospitals, patients are assigned a label consisting of some permutation of Greek roots and prefixes, such as aphasia, akinesia, amusia, aprosodia, prosoplegia, prosopagnosia (respectively, loss of language ability, failure to move or initiate movement, inability to sing, inability to understand emotional language, inability to make emotional faces, inability to recognize familiar faces) and so on, the permutations of which are matched with existing models of the brain and its functional subsets, to see if any predict the observed functional deficit. Frequently they don't, and as ambivalent as the circumstances are for clinical doctors committed to healing, the resulting modification of models is one of the primary ways our understanding of the brain has evolved over the last 150 years. The second is a controlled experiment using behavioral techniques, and a variety of image-producing techniques such as ERP (event-related potentials), PET (positron emission tomography) and fMRI (functional magnetic resonance imaging) scans. The development of imaging technologies over the last half-century has been revolutionary in that for the first time it is possible to make noninvasive, noncatastrophic observation of the brain at work. Experiments are often modest, involving small data sets, poor resolution, and equivocal interpretations. Flaws are realized afterward; researchers disagree sharply among themselves when presenting data. However, the point is always to put some data on the table, and in this sense researchers display confidence that their work contributes to a project that is cumulative in richness, precision, and effectiveness, a situation in poignant contrast with the humanities.

In posing the question of a causal relation of any kind of mental phenomenon to processes in the brain, the point is never to come to an immediate, totalizing account. It is rather to develop a model—based on the best knowledge we have right now about the phenomenon and about the brain—that will allow one to propose experiments. Wiener states, "[T]he science of today is operational; that is, it considers every statement as essentially concerned with possible experiments or observable processes" (125). If you cannot propose an experiment, or generate testable hypotheses, neuroscientists simply do not care. But what this commitment allows is for one to step in somewhere and begin to disentangle the strands.

IV

Arguments similar to those made to establish the universality of language can be made for narrative. All known human societies process information in terms of stories, and no known other animal species do. In evolutionary terms, stories are one of the key methods for imprinting systems of values on large target audiences.[1] It is reasonable to believe that the processes of narrative comprehension are: a) universal, b) unique to humans, and c) simple enough to admit of study. However, unlike primary processes such as perception, memory, and attention, these are not likely to reside in any single region or subsystem of the brain. There will, in other words, be no narrative module. The capacity to comprehend narrative, universal across cultures, is likely to be found rather in the exploitation of particular biases in the heterogeneous architecture of the brain.

The first step in enabling hypotheses is to produce a model of the phenomenon in question, here comprehension of stories, that can then be compared to the heterogeneous architecture of the brain.

The broadest distinction to be made is between the computational operations required to understand plot, story space, and the relations of spectator or reader to that space, and the less-defined tonal or affective qualities of character identification. I. A. Richards (1971) refers to the former as states of affairs, but writes that "we also, as a rule, have some feelings about these items." A feeling for Richards is an "attitude toward things, some special direction, bias or accentuation of interest, some personal flavor or coloring" (848). Walton further argues that while there is a sharp distinction in how we treat information about fictional space and events from information about the real world (we do not act on the former), there is no sharp distinction between the experience of identification with real people and with fictional characters (1991). This difference, between affective processes of identification and the more computational relations of plot and story space and time, is captured with particular clarity in a recent ad campaign for a US television network with an extensive library of TV series and classic Hollywood movies. The campaign consisted of a series of full-page color advertisements, each featuring a single high-resolution photograph of an adult face in extreme close-up and one-quarter profile over a pitch-black background, registering a particular, stereotyped emotion. Superimposed over each photograph is a pair of options separated by a question mark.

The first features a man covering his face, but staring out from between his fingers in fascination or horror, with the caption:

CAN'T LOOK
—?—
CAN'T LOOK AWAY

The second features a woman biting her lip in suspense and anticipation, with the caption:

DOUBLE OVERTIME
—?—
DOUBLE JEOPARDY

The third features a woman with a round, open expression and a tear running down her cheek, with the caption:

HERO LIVES
—?—
HERO DIES

The copy at the bottom reads, "[Network Initials]: We Know Drama."

What is figured in this intuition from the field with a rare clarity and concision is the idea that the dramatic or narrative act is composed of two parts that are heterogeneous to each other. One is a computational process of choosing between binary alternatives, represented by the text, and the second is an emotional process of identification, represented by the image. This allows us to take a first step in correlating a model of narrative with what we know about the structure of the nervous system, namely that it is constituted by computational and emotional processes that are both different in kind, and reside in physically different parts of the brain.

Wiener achieved this insight in *Cybernetics*, well before the details on the chemical processes and neurophysiology were known. Because cybernetics is concerned with the possibility of the physical combination of computers and the nervous system, he is also closely attentive to their differences:

> [A] point of considerable interest is that [an affective] mechanism involves a certain set of messages which go out generally into the nervous system, to all elements which are in a state to receive them. . . . Now such messages "to whom it may concern" may well be sent out most efficiently, with a smallest cost in apparatus, by channels other than nervous. (129)

By "nervous" here Wiener means "neuron-based"—that is, a system based on serial processing of discrete bits of information through the neural net. In this sense, an affective system operating through a gross raising and lowering of the system by chemical messages in the bloodstream, cerebrospinal fluid, etc., operates on principles heterogeneous to the binary, sequential logic of neural information. Because cybernetics seeks to combine nervous systems, which have an affective component, and computers, which do not, this is highly significant. What I would like to argue is that narrative is universal be-cause it is the most fundamental activity that integrates these two aspects of the nervous system.

Wiener's insight can better be translated into neuroscientific terms fol-lowing Solms and Turnbull (2002, 28–35). For Solms and Turnbull, because computational processes involve getting from A to B based on neural relays where the state of one neuron (at rest or firing) depends on the state of neu-rons earlier in the process, these are "path-dependent." By contrast, because affective processes raise and lower the general system level based on flooding the system, they are called "state-dependent." Hence narrative comprehension would be said to combine state-dependent emotional processes, which con-vey information about the internal states of the organism and are physically associated with the limbic system, with path-dependent cognitive processes associated with receiving sensory and linguistic input in the occipital, parietal, and temporal lobes, and higher-level information processing associated with the prefrontal cortex. This would make it a midlevel process involving "zones of convergence" associated with the binding problem, and associational areas of the cortex. Robeck and Wallace (1990) identify as areas of the brain that are phylogenetically recent and markedly developed compared with other mam-mals the prefrontal cortex (higher-level intellectual functions, particularly time sequencing), and tertiary association areas of the cortical areas posterior to the central fissure (overlap and integration among the lobes). What is par-ticular to the comprehension of narrative will likely emerge in the exploitation of biases found in these two areas, as well as in the ventromedial frontal brain, involved in integration of the emotional limbic system and reasoning systems in the frontal lobe, and tectum and dorsal tegmentum at the core of emotion-generating systems.

V

Drawing on more detailed component models of narrative allows one to suggest experiments. Experiments in neuroscience tend to take the following form: given higher-order mental phenomenon X, what are the cognitive and neural mechanisms underlying A, B, or C processes in X? For example: What are the cognitive and neural mechanisms underlying recovery from ambiguity in sentence comprehension (Kaan 2000)? In this example from neurolinguistics, the larger phenomenon X is sentence comprehension, and one of the component processes is recovery from ambiguity. This provides the researcher with a point in time that can be tested, in this case by the superior time-resolution of ERP. The initial problem then, for literary theory, would appear to be to draw on existing knowledge of literary form to break down the process of understanding a story into simpler component processes, such that one can design an experiment of the X: A, B, C form. Component parts can then be tested as localized nervous system activity, mapped in their relation to better understood processes of language, perception, memory, and emotion, and distinguished from cognition of the physical world.

Elements for an initial model will of necessity be simple, and can be drawn from any point in the history of poetics. Plot-driven possibilities for what Todorov calls the Ur-narratives include:

- The stranger comes to town
- The hero goes on a journey (Todorov 1977)

A model legendary among aspiring screenwriters is attributed to Julius Epstein, author of the script for *Casablanca* (1939). A bunch of young directors were energetically discussing Barthes and ambiguity and all the things they had learned in film school, and Mr. Epstein, an old man from Brooklyn, leaned back in his chair and said, "You're wasting your money. I'll tell you how to write a screenplay."

- You get your guy up a tree.
- You throw rocks at him.
- Then you get your guy down out of the tree. (Sassone 2000)

One may also look at formal structures. All stories may be said to have a beginning, a middle, and an end, or to pass through complications to denouement (Aristotle, 682–84, 691; Sec. 2–3, 13), or to consist of the following:

- Equilibrium state 1
- Something disturbs equilibrium
- Equilibrium state 2 (Todorov 1977)

Narrative may be defined in terms of sites of identification and sites of personification. A narrative may contain a protagonist, an antagonist, and a witness who learns (Miller 1995, 69–72). Characters may be above us in their level of virtue, below us, or the same (Aristotle, 692; Sec. 2, 13, 15). And so forth.

All narratives of whatever complexity are formed from combinations of these basic plots and elements. These provide simple, component-rich models that collectively grasp the two heterogeneous aspects of narrative, and provide points in time at which a developing narrative is comprehended, hence at which an experiment can be constructed.

VI

It would appear, then, that narratives confer beginnings and endings on events, personify actors in causal relation to events in space and time, and involve a process of identification with personified positions. As basic cognitive elements, narrative comprehension appears to involve:

1. *Closure* (narratives inevitably confer beginnings and endings on events)
2. *Time sequencing* (judgments of causality require before–after determinations)
3. *Personification* (normal children and adults attribute independent mental states to others in order to explain and predict behavior)
4. *Identification* (narrative involves sympathy for, or loss of differentiation with, personified positions, that is to say fictional characters)
5. *Situational cues* (narrative relies on ritualistic cues to effect a shift in attention from the physical world to an artistic and imaginative world, "Once upon a time," the rolling of credits in a film, the click when a needle is dropped onto an analog recording).

Recalling the general form of the neuroscientific question developed earlier, this results in the following experimental program: to use behavioral techniques (ERP, PET, and fMRI) to study cognitive and neural mechanisms underlying A, B, C processes in narrative comprehension, where A, B, C (et al.) are provisionally closure, time-sequencing, personification, identification, and situational cuing—for example, to use PET scans to study the cognitive and neural mechanisms underlying closure processes in narrative comprehension; to use ERP to study cognitive and neural mechanisms underlying ambiguities in time sequence in narrative comprehension; to use fMRI to examine the difference in brain activity between a person who hears a short, well-constructed narrative with a surprise at the end, and a subject who is informed of the surprise ending prior to hearing the story; to use fMRI to study the transition effected by the dimming of lights in a movie theater. Additional steps in a systematic experimental program, then, would involve investigating the changes in sense-ratio when different media activate different input modules in absorbing narrative information—for example, to use ERP to study the difference in emotional processing of faces in animation and live-action film.

VII

This provides a systematic, articulated experimental program to identify what parts of the brain are recruited in various aspects of story comprehension, to separate out computational and affective processes, and to begin a provisional map of their relation to primary processes such as perception, affect, memory, language processing, and attention, whose functions in the brain are localized and relatively well understood. The problem is that, when analyzed like this, the object seems to disappear, as any experimental program concerned with controlling variables will tend to test one or the other, that is to say either the computational, path-dependent processes or the emotional, state-dependent processes, in which I have argued the identity of narrative lies. Because we are concerned with a midlevel process rather than a primary process, that is to say, a process that exploits the biases in the relation between systems rather than being a module itself, their combination will appear simply as the global operation of the brain. One is left at the stage of experiment with two halves that are not essentially integrated, and no rationale for positing the larger object as something more than the sum of its parts. This initial experimental program has in other words "reduced" the problem, and it will be necessary to step up an interpretive level to regain its unity.

We receive a hint again from Chomsky, recalling that internal structure is not strictly a physical matter of the topology and dynamics of impulse propagation in the net of nerve cells or neurons, and the more general purpose raising and lowering of the system by the emotions, but "a complicated product of inborn structure, the genetically determined course of maturation, and past experience." The problem may be that a strictly neuroanatomical model only gets the first element of the picture. In the final part of this essay, I would like to use a concept from developmental psychology to produce a model that, because it incorporates the second part of the definition—the genetically determined course of maturation and past experience—may yield clues to integrating narrative as a phenomenon determined by internal structure. Narrative is posited not as emotional identification plus time and space computation. Narrative is rather the means by which perception of *this kind of object* in a trajectory is enabled.

VIII

Quine (1995) gives an account of the acquisition by the human species of a responsible theory of the world based on "our meager contacts with it: from the mere impacts of rays and particles on our surfaces and a few odds and ends such as the strain of walking uphill" (16). He agrees with the classic British empiricists Locke, Berkeley, and Hume that our complex sense of a physical world is a fabric of ideas built up from sense impression. However, the empiricists seemed to regard the mind as an undifferentiated medium, hence "regarding the structured details of the fabric and its fabrication, all three were at a loss for the rudiments of an account."

> [Locke] wrote of association of ideas by contiguity, succession, and resemblance, but this is the barest beginning of what goes on in the most primitive report on the material world around us. What of our identification of an intermittently observed body as the same body? An identical body can look different over time, and different bodies can look alike. Much remained to be explained. (4–5)

What Quine seeks to do, with the benefit of 250 years' accumulation of scientific knowledge, is to sketch in more of the details of the fabric of that acquisition, and the centrality of language in this story.

Because he is engaged in a "rational reconstruction" of humans' conceptual development, the tale has a "just so" quality, but his version is committed to constraint by the sciences that deal with cognitive, psychological, social, and linguistic development, and is in a sense simply filling in blanks lost in the mists of prehistory and trimming the models logically. Quine first lays out the physiological conditions for the puzzle of shared experience when stimuli are private, and locates an initial reification of bodies as a primitive cognitive process. What defines a body? "Typically, a body contrasts with its visual surroundings in color and in movement or parallax, and typically it is fairly chunky and compact. If it is animate and seen full face, it is bilaterally symmetric . . . . It is merely such traits, at first, that distinguish bodies . . . from other details of the passing show" (24). What is interesting about Quine's "rational reconstruction" is that it is the acquisition of language, by the species and recapitulated in the infant, that enables further conceptual development, from simple expression of expectations, to the more clean-cut reification of objects through the substitution of pronouns, to the momentous step of "transcending of the specious present" which requires "acquisition of our whole schematism of space and time and the unobserved trajectories of bodies within it" (36). The story continues through the reification of properties, on to truth, logic, and mathematics; however, for Quine this acquisition, in the earliest stages of language and by the infant in the first years of life, is a key point in the emergence of a primitive natural scientific conception of the world embodied in propositional language.

Perception of trajectory is a fundamental activity in all higher vertebrates, essential to tracking food and avoiding predators, and to developing object permanence, for it is the perception of an abstract trajectory, not available to the senses, that allows the vertebrate to see, for example, that a predator disappearing behind a tree is continuous. In Quine's simulation, speculation about the trajectory of bodies becomes a metaphor for all subsequent scientific knowledge and provides the adaptive rationale. However, in the physical world a body in motion can only be perceived as an object. The only subject one knows is oneself, stationary within one's coordinate field (the task of which abstract notions of space and time is to build). I would argue that, given an abstract conception of space and time and the trajectory of bodies through it that is in place by age two, and a conception of what it is like to be oneself, it is the cognitive task of the story form to put that *subject* in motion. The repetitive imagining of characters' movement through time in the story form functions to introduce *subjects* into the abstract environment of trajectories through space, preparing the way for social being. This perspective will add further detail to the fabric of the conceptual development of our species sketched out by Quine.

IX

Theory of mind (ToM) is a concept from developmental psychology that refers to "the ability of normal children and adults to attribute independent mental states to self and others in order to explain and predict behavior" (Fletcher et al. 1995, 109). It is important to notice the second condition. Children of age one distinguish biological and inanimate objects, and attribute mental states to others, but they attribute the same mental state as their own, hence cannot predict, and are constantly surprised and frustrated by the inexplicable actions of others. The developmental sequence from the perception of certain patterns of movement in terms of physical causation by the age of one and the perception of behavioral interaction in terms of intention between the ages of two and five appears to be "culturally invariant and relatively independent of the level of intelligence, with little individual variation and a strikingly narrow time window" (Fletcher et al. 1995, 110; Cassidy et al. 1998).

The coincidence of the most intense period of exposure to stories in children and the acquisition of theory of mind (from age two to five) puts this in the right place in both empirical psychological accounts and in Quine's simulation, and suggests the adaptive function of narrative, and a necessity to its form. The specialist literature carries an assumption that ToM is prior to complex, higher-order functions that use it, that there is something about the brain that enables ToM capacity, which is then *used*, for example, in narrative comprehension. Fletcher et al. (1995) consider the ability to be "biologically based": "In light of its apparent evolutionary advantages, it is plausible that mentalizing is performed by an innately determined cognitive mechanism" (110). However, if narrative is strongly correlated with acquisition of ToM, it is also possible to suggest that the intense social circulation of narrative is involved in *instantiating* ToM. In analogy to the role of language in Quine, and in light of the hypothesis arrived at in the first part of this essay that narrative is a midlevel phenomenon combining computational, path-dependent brain processes and emotional, state-dependent brain processes, the implication is that theory of mind as a human faculty was put in place by an interaction between the emerging story form and certain integrational biases in the architecture of the brain.

The investigation of this aspect of internal structure has mixed implications for experiment. Like the question of the evolution of language, the burial in Paleolithic times of the genesis of the story form presents serious evidentiary obstacles (Bolhuis 2008). Further, while work on emotional behavior prior to neocortical feedback (Panksepp 2003) draws analogies from animal experimentation, there is much less scope for this in narrative. One will likely have to seek answers rather in the recapitulation of this process in child development. One can't do controlled experiments on the role of rate and intensity of childhood exposure to stories on development of ToM, for obvious ethical reasons, but one could envision longitudinal studies on enriched story environments, suggestive both in relation to normal development and autism. Recalling the two types of result recognized by neuroscience, current research on autism suggests the possibility of defining this disorder as a kind of dysnarrativia (inability to comprehend or produce stories), and researchers are already investigating deficits in the ability to place oneself or others in a narrative context in high-functioning children with autism (Losh and Capps 2003). One of the most promising new lines of inquiry is that "autism results from abnormal communications between brain regions rather than a broken part of the brain" (Wickelgren 2005, 1856). Further, recent challenges to the entire field of ToM, such as Hutto's *Folk Psychological Narratives* (2008), raise the question of ToM as an effect, not a cause, of early childhood discursive practices. While I suggested a limitation in the ability of the earlier, lab-based experimental program to grasp the object, both lines of inquiry, controlled physiological experiment and clinical and developmental psychology, are necessary to grasp Chomsky's notion of internal structure as being composed of "inborn structure" (the synchronic object of experiment) and the "genetically determined course of maturation and past experience" (the diachronic object of developmental and evolutionary psychology). That hypotheses about narrative along both lines independently arrived at a model involved in integrating heterogeneous parts of the brain stands as some confirmation of the potential of literary studies to contribute to organizing this problem.

CONCLUSION

The purpose of this essay has been to propose a model of narrative comprehension as a midlevel cognitive process that *puts the perceiving subject* in motion outside the origin of its own coordinate field. It is speculative but informed by long acquaintance with the techniques and intellectual customs of practicing neuroscientists. Like any interdisciplinary statement it is addressed in two directions. Toward colleagues in the sciences, I would argue that the contribution of literary criticism at the stage of experimental design should be considered indispensable. Toward colleagues in the humanities, I argue that a reductive experimental program is needed to begin disentangling the problem of the relation of literary and artistic experience to physical processes in the brain, and will occur whether we participate or not. Although there are important differences between a cognitive psychological approach and a neuroanatomical approach, in the context of literary studies they share the implication that a basic change in our estimation of the relative importance of external conditions and internal structure is necessary for the field of literary studies to begin to participate in work on the cognitive basis of social forms.

The restriction of literary experience to narrative and accounts of narrative experience here may strike humanists as reductive. According to Forceville and Hamilton, though, "in order to secure reliable results, testable hypotheses must be relatively simple . . . [and] probe these works from a limited perspective only" (2003). Conversely, scientists may feel they are doing fine on their own. A number of studies have appeared since 2000 in experimental psychology that raise the question of the mechanisms by which narratives are processed by the brain or mind, and the relation of those mechanisms to learning and social development (Magliano et al. 2001; Mar 2004; Ferstl et al. 2005). However, Mar and Oatley still need to write in 2008 that "[f]iction literature has largely been ignored by psychology researchers because its only function seems to be entertainment" (173), suggesting a certain Platonism that would still banish literature from the Republic. Implicit in this simple beginning is that a properly elaborated scientific program will eventually move to humanist concerns of aesthetics, style, and ideology, the effect of different delivery media (oral, print, comic/manga, film, animation, computer gaming) on the mechanisms underlying narrative comprehension, and the key clinical problem of production of self-narratives. Though the details of such a program are far into the future, I see no reason to believe in principle that it is not possible to come to a complete, closed account of the neuroscientific underpinnings of literary experience, even if the details elude us now. The point in science is not to produce at the outset a complete and adequate account, but to step in somewhere, and begin untangling the threads.

NOTES

AUTHOR'S NOTE: The author would like to acknowledge the support and advice of Norman Holland, Steve Nadeau, Tianna Leonard, and other members of the weekly CNS Seminar in the University of Florida Medical School, at which an early version of this essay was presented in 2003. This weekly seminar, directed by Dr. Richard Heilman, involves clinical neurologists, research neuroscientists, therapists, and academic researchers in the sciences and linguistics. Research presentations on rotating topics followed by discussion were instrumental in forming my understanding of the approach and methodology of research on the physiological basis of behavior.

1. Studies on the adaptive function of literature include Scalise Sugiyama 2001a, 2001b; Carroll 1995; Boyd et al. 2010; and Gottschall and Wilson 2005.

WORKS CITED

Aristotle. 1952. Poetics. In *Aristotle II*, 681–99. Chicago: Britannica Press.
Blakemore, Sarah. 2006. How does the brain deal with the social world? *Science* 314: 60–61.
Bolhuis, Johan J. 2008. Piling on the selection pressure. *Science* 320: 1293.
Boyd, Brian, Joseph Carroll, and Jonathan Gottschall, eds. 2010. *Evolution, literature, and film: A reader.* New York: Columbia University Press.
Carroll, Joseph. 1995. *Evolution and literary theory.* Columbia: University of Missouri Press.

Cassidy, K. W., et al. 1998. Theory of mind concepts in children's literature. *Applied Psycholinguistics* 19: 463–70.

Chalmers, David J. 1996. *The conscious mind: In search of a fundamental theory.* New York: Oxford University Press.

Chomsky, Noam. 1959. Review of *Verbal behavior*, by B. F. Skinner. *Language* 35, no. 1: 26–58.

Ferstl, Evelyn C., et al. 2005. Emotional and temporal aspects of situation model processing during text comprehension. *Journal of Cognitive Neuroscience* 17: 724–39.

Fletcher, P. C., et al. 1995. Other minds in the brain: A functional imaging study of theory of mind in story comprehension. *Cognition* 57: 109–28.

Forceville, Charles, and Craig Hamilton. 2003. A testable or detestable hypothesis? Literary research as an empirical science. Language, Literature and Science Workshop, Université de Limoges, France.

Goodby, Silverstein, and Partners. 2001. TNT: We know drama. Time-Warner, press release, June 5.

Gottschall, Jonathan, and David Sloan Wilson, eds. 2005. *The literary animal: Evolution and the nature of narrative.* Evanston, IL: Northwestern University Press.

Hasson, Uri, et al. 2004. Intersubjective synchronization of cortical activity during natural vision. *Science* 303: 1634–40.

Hasson, Uri, et al. 2008. Neurocinematics: The neuroscience of making movies. *Projections: The Journal for Movies and Mind* 1, no. 2: 2–26.

Hutto, Daniel D. 2008. *Folk psychological narratives: The sociocultural basis of understanding reasons.* Cambridge, MA: MIT Press.

Kaan, Edith. 2000. The P600 as an index of syntactic integration difficulty. *Language and Cognitive Processes* 15, no. 2: 159–201.

Kaan, Edith, and Tamara Swaab. 2002. The brain circuitry of syntactic comprehension. *Trends in Cognitive Sciences* 6, no. 8: 350–56.

Losh, Molly, and Lisa Capps. 2003. Narrative ability in high-functioning children with autism or Asperger's syndrome. *Journal of Autism and Developmental Disorders* 33, no. 3: 239–51.

Magliano, Joseph P., et al. 2001. Indexing space and time in film understanding. *Applied Cognitive Psychology* 15: 533–45.

Mar, Raymond A. 2004. The neuropsychology of narrative. *Neuropsychologia* 42: 1414–34.

Mar, Raymond A., and Keith Oatley. 2008. The function of fiction is the abstraction and simulation of social experience. *Perspectives on Psychological Science* 3: 173–92.

Miller, J. Hillis. 1995. Narrative. In *Critical terms for literary study*, 66–79. Edited by Frank Lentricchia. Chicago: University of Chicago Press.

Panksepp, Jaak. 2003. At the interface of the affective, behavioral, and cognitive neurosciences: Decoding the emotional feelings of the brain. *Brain and Cognition* 52: 4–14.

Pessoa, Luiz. 2004. Neuroscience: Seeing the world in the same way. *Science* 303: 1617–18.

Pinker, Steven. 1994. *The language instinct: How the mind creates language.* New York: William Morrow.

Quine, William V. 1995. *From stimulus to science.* Cambridge, MA: Harvard University Press.

Richards, I. A. 1971. Practical criticism. In *Critical theory since Plato.* Edited by Hazard Adams. New York: Harcourt.

Robeck, Mildred, and Robert Wallace. 1990. *The psychology of reading: An interdisciplinary approach.* Hillsdale, NJ: Erlbaum.

Rosenblatt, Robert. 1962. *Principles of neurodynamics.* Washington, DC: Spartan Books.

Sassone, Vincent. 2000. Screenwriting: The ABC's, letter to the editor, *New York Times*, January 23.

Scalise Sugiyama, Michelle. 2001a. Narrative theory and function: Why evolution matters. *Philosophy and Literature* 25, no. 2: 233–50.

———. 2001b. Food, foragers, and folklore: The role of narrative in human subsistence. *Evolution and Human Behavior* 22, no.4: 221–40.

Solms, Mark, and Oliver Turnbull. 2002. *The brain and the inner world*. New York: Other Press.

Todorov, Tzvetan. 1977. *The poetics of prose*. Ithaca, NY: Cornell University Press.

Walton, Kendall. 1991. *Mimesis as make-believe*. Cambridge, MA: Harvard University Press.

Wickelgren, Ingrid. 2005. Autistic brains out of synch? *Science* 308: 1856–58.

Wiener, Norbert. 1948. *Cybernetics: Or communication and control in the animal and the machine*. Cambridge, MA: MIT Press.

NEUROLOGICAL APPROACHES TO LITERATURE

The growing interest in the neural underpinnings of literature is exemplified by the following essays, which contribute to the discussion introduced by Murphy in the preceding section. They represent three different approaches to the neuroanatomy of our engagement with fictional stories. Holland's examination of the effects of metafictional narratives on our embodied minds resonates with Gerrig's research on readers' responses, while elucidating from a neuropsychoanalytic viewpoint the uncanny feeling and anxiety that such narratives can produce on us. His essay is followed by Hogan's neurologically informed account of emotion in literature, which considers what *Hamlet* reveals about how humans experience attachment and mourning. Hogan explores how Shakespeare's play portrays the social contexts and ideologies that shape feeling, demonstrating how a neurological approach to literature can help us understand the complex dynamics of emotion. The section ends with Mishara's investigation of the creative mind in connection to anomalous states of consciousness. In illustrating how Kafka's writings reflect the neural mechanisms involved in phenomena such as the projection of an imaginary double, he also advocates for the use of literary data in clinical neuroscience, strongly supporting the argument initiated by Gerrig and echoed throughout the volume that the cognitive sciences may be informed by literature and literary theory.

CHAPTER 4

DON QUIXOTE AND THE NEUROSCIENCE
OF METAFICTION

NORMAN N. HOLLAND

WHAT IS METAFICTION? Originally coined by William Gass in 1970 (4), in the 1970s this term came to mean "a fiction that both creates an illusion and lays bare that illusion" (Waugh 1984, 6). But the term has since expanded and expanded, becoming ever more grandiose, until it now includes any fiction that even mentions the idea of fiction. That can cover a lot of things, starting with the Bible and the Iliad. I want to be more specific.

I would like to go back to the original idea, both because I think it is more precise and because it better fits the brain operations involved. By my definition, metafiction tells a story in which *the physical medium of the story becomes part of the story.*

Ordinarily we are clear in our minds as to what is the fictional part of a story and what is the physical part in the real world. So-and-so is a character and such-and-such is an event in the story we are reading (or perhaps the movie or play we are watching). They are fictions. That is, someone else is making them up, and I cannot act to change them. By contrast, here is the physical book. I can act on the book, pick it up or put it away. Or here is the play or movie, eleven rows in front of me in a theater—I could kick up a rumpus and interrupt it. The physical work of literature and the fictions it represents differ fundamentally in whether we can act to change them. And that difference translates into the brain's inhibition of action which in turn leads to what we have traditionally called (in Coleridge's phrase) the willing suspension of disbelief.

In metafiction, though, the physical medium of the story becomes part of the story. As a result, we seem to be able to act on what a moment before we could not act on. That alters the systems in our brains for reality testing, systems that come into play only when we are acting or planning to act.

I. METAFICTIONS, METATHEATER, METAFILM

Among contemporary authors who create metafiction, one could list my erst-while colleagues, John Barth, Donald Barthelme, and Ray Federman. Others are Borges, Calvino, Nabokov, Umberto Eco, John Fowles, Salman Rushdie, and on and on. Metafiction has become extremely popular in our question-ing centuries, the twentieth and twenty-first. From previous times, one could point to Diderot's *Jacques le fataliste* or Sterne's *Tristram Shandy*. The blank pages and marbled pages of *Tristram Shandy*, for example, become part of the story of *Tristram Shandy*.

Metafictions lead to some of the more dizzying effects possible in litera-ture. I am thinking of those novels which are novels about writing the novel which is the novel. In Doris Lessing's *The Golden Notebook*, for instance, one of the notebooks tells about a novelist trying to write a novel. A friend asks her to give him the first sentence, and the novelist rattles off the first sentence of *The Golden Notebook* itself. Somehow the novel has stopped being a fiction and become something physically "real" to my motor systems. I become puzzled. Is the story as solid and nonfictional as the book I am physically holding? Am I reading fiction or fact? I start fretting about the status in reality of what I am reading.

Drama gets this effect and becomes metadrama or metatheater, for ex-ample, in Pirandello's *Six Characters in Search of an Author*. The six characters wander about the stage looking for an author to write the play which is, of course, the play we are watching. In Pirandello's *Henry IV*, the play we are watching is also the mad fantasy of the main character. At such a play, I get tense—slightly anxious.

We also have metafilm with examples as far back as the silent era. In 1924, Buster Keaton's *Sherlock Jr.* (1924) had the projector projecting the hero's fan-tasies appear in the very film that embodies those fantasies. Probably the most striking metafilmic moment in movies occurs in Ingmar Bergman's *Persona* (1966). Midway through this film, at a point where one of the characters be-comes violently angry, the film apparently starts to burn. What we see on the screen is a burning hole in a film frame with light shining through it as if some-thing had gone wrong with the projector. So realistic is the effect that some of the projectionists showing the film ran for their fire extinguishers. But the film is not burning in fact. In fact, we are seeing a fictional film of its own cel-luloid burning.

Brevity is the soul of wit, and my briefest example of this kind of thing in movies comes in the Marx Brothers' *Horse Feathers*. Groucho turns to the cam-era, that is, the audience—us—and comments on the film he is in: "I've gotta stay here, but there's no reason you folks shouldn't go out in the lobby till this thing blows over." When the meta- in whatever genre is brief, it becomes a joke, as in Groucho's remark or John Barth's often-quoted exclamation, "Oh God comma I abhor self-consciousness" (Waugh 1984, 149).

Spike Jonze's 2002 movie *Adaptation* shows us Charlie Kaufman (a real-life screenwriter, *Being John Malkovich*) trying to write a screenplay. A gloomy, self-doubting obsessive-compulsive, Charlie is suffering from writer's block as he tries to write a movie based on a factual article and book about orchid stealing, a book that exists in real life. (Why would writing a movie about orchid stealing lead to writer's block? Our word "orchid" comes from the Greek word *orchis* which means testicle, but that leads to another kind of paper, not a neuroscientific one.) Real-life Charlie Kaufman, who is a character in the movie, is outdone as a screenwriter by his devil-may-care twin brother Donald (who is totally fictitious, but played by the same actor, Nicolas Cage, who plays Charlie). Incidentally, both real-life Charlie and fictitious Donald appear in the credits for the film. In the course of the film, the writer who wrote the article becomes involved with the real-life orchid thief. And all the writers get into the film's action, particularly the bizarre ending. It comes from both following and systematically violating the strictures of a screenwriting course both the brothers attend. And at the very end of the film, after all the screen credits and copyright notices have rolled, we get an excerpt from Donald Kaufman's fictitious screenplay, and a last title card says, "In loving memory of Donald Kaufman." To top the joke, in 2003, both Charlie *and Donald* were nominated for the Oscar for best screenplay based on an "adaptation" of previously published material.

I mention this film in detail because we have a useful statement about its emotional effect. *Adaptation*, writes its *New York Times* reviewer, A. O. Scott (2002), "is . . . a movie about its own nonexistence." Then Scott describes his reaction in terms like "panic," "frantic anxiety," or "paranoid." Like Scott, I too feel dizzy and uncertain—but delighted at this playing with levels of reality. Most reviewers thought the film's playing with reality was a big joke, but Scott and I got nervous. That's what I'd like to explore and explain. Why "panic"? Why "anxiety"? And why a joke?

II. *DON QUIXOTE*

Surely the genial granddaddy who sired all these effects is that first and greatest of metafictions, *Don Quixote*. Although it is the earliest of the great novels, *Don Quixote* already plays metafictional games.

The book begins in uncertainty, for we are not sure where Don Quixote comes from or what his name is or who is writing the book. What are we to believe? This fictional lunatic accepts from his squire Sancho the sobriquet "Knight of the Sad Countenance"—why? Not from a fictional impulse from his fictional brain, but because the (real?) writer of his history makes him do so (Part I, chap. XIX). Is this then a "real" history or just something the writer (whoever he may be) imposes?

The book turns fully metafictional when Part I (published in 1605) is followed by Part II (published in 1615). In one chapter of Part II (chap. IV), a roguish scholar starts toying with Don Quixote's fancies. The scholar tells us that the author of Part I, the Moor Cide Hamete Benengeli (or perhaps Berenjena), is an Arab whose narrations therefore cannot be trusted. (But Benengeli swears like a Christian they are true, although he is an Arab.) This fictional author, says the scholar, will produce a Part II, which, of course, we are reading at that very moment. The fictional characters of Part II go on to discuss errors and distortions in Part I and even the sales figures for Part I.

Don Quixote finds, as he proceeds through Part II, that everybody knows about him and his goofy knight-errantry because so many people have read Part I. These readers—are they real readers or are they fictional readers?—go on to have discussions and play tricks on Don Quixote motivated by Part I.

There's more. One Avellaneda has written a false sequel to Part I (and there was in reality such a book). Don Quixote makes a point of discrediting it: its knight and squire are not at all like the "real" Don Quixote and Sancho. The "real" author of the novel (Benengeli? Cervantes?) then causes a reader of the fake *Don Quixote*, Part II, to swear an oath before a notary that the "real" Don Quixote and Sancho are not a bit like the ones in the plagiarist's novel (Part II, chap. LXXII). (For a fuller discussion of metafictional elements in *Don Quixote*, see Mancing 2006, 109–17.)

In short, Cervantes' metafiction gives us a madman's illusions within the reality known to fictional others within a fiction which is itself physically real because it is the book we are holding in our hands at that moment. I am as confused about fictional knight-errantry as the confused knight-errant himself. And when I experience the novel, even though it is a comic novel, these metafictional episodes have a peculiarly disconcerting effect, as do other examples of the genre. Sometimes they are funny, sometimes eerie.

To all these metafictional works, in my experience, people have two kinds of response, sometimes both at once. If the effect is very short, like Groucho's remark or John Barth's quip, we laugh; it's a joke. If the effect goes on for a while, as in the metafilm *Adaptation* or the play *Six Characters in Search of an Author*, people can get tense, edgy, a little dizzy, the way the *New York Times* critic felt "panic" and "frantic anxiety" while watching *Adaptation*. I would not go so far, but I do feel as though I am in a hall of mirrors. And slightly anxious. Why?

III. WHY DOES METAFICTION MAKE US NERVOUS?

In all these metafictional works, I am getting that strange feeling Freud called the "Uncanny." It is the feeling we get from reading stories about doubles, ghosts, or the undead. It is the vertigo we get when something familiar suddenly seems strange and unfamiliar, like unexpectedly seeing yourself in a mirror. Freud describes and explains the uncanny this way: "An uncanny experience occurs either when infantile complexes which have been repressed are once more revived by some impression, or when primitive beliefs which have been surmounted seem once more to be confirmed" (Freud 1919, 246). I can understand why the return of fears and fantasies repressed in childhood, when they return, should evoke the same anxiety that led to their repression in the first place. But why should "primitive *beliefs*" inspire fear? Beliefs (*Überzeugungen*) are intellectual, not emotional. They should not elicit anxiety. Freud goes on to explain the anxiety with the claim that primitive beliefs are intimately connected with infantile complexes. I wonder.

Freud goes on to discuss the uncanny in literature. He argues that fairy tales and other nonrealistic narratives involving wish-fulfillments, secret powers, animation of inanimate objects, and so on, can have no uncanny effect, because the writer and reader have abandoned everyday reality from the start. Therefore, he says, we do not submit such fictions to reality testing. In realistic literature, however, he claims that "we react to [the writer's] inventions as we would have reacted to real experiences," and the writer can produce exaggerated effects (Freud 1919, 250–51). Again, I doubt that this is an accurate statement of readers' responses either to literature or to film. But I also think Freud is right in suggesting that the issue of belief is crucial.

Does our anxiety come from some primitive belief that any story—be it realistic like those in *Dubliners* or fanciful like Jack and the Beanstalk—that any story you view or read or hear may describe a physical reality? May be true? And does the uncanny feeling, the anxiety, come from the belief that something untoward is happening? That I can and perhaps should act on that story? The question becomes: what do we believe when we are experiencing a story in fiction or drama?

IV. "POETIC FAITH"

Coleridge stated the answer that has stood pretty well unchallenged since 1817, when he asked in *Biographia Literaria* (chap. XIV) that the readers of *Lyrical Ballads* grant his poems about the supernatural "that willing suspension of disbelief for the moment that constitutes poetic faith." In the 1980s and 1990s, however, Richard Gerrig conducted some remarkable experiments that bear on this question (Gerrig 1989, 1998). They suggest that Coleridge's second phrase, "poetic faith," describes our state of mind better than his first, the more famous "willing suspension of disbelief."

Gerrig had his subjects (Yale students) read (on a computer, sentence by sentence) a little story. And at the end of the story Gerrig would ask the subject to say whether a certain sentence was true or false. One version was called the *no suspense* version. Here is one of them:

> George Washington was a famous figure after the Revolutionary War. Washington was a popular choice to lead the new country. Few people had thought that the British could be defeated. The success of the Revolutionary War was attributed largely to Washington. His friends worked to convince him to go on serving his country. Washington agreed that he had abundant experience as a leader.

The other version of the story was designed to create a little uncertainty about the outcome. In other words, this second version was designed to create suspense. Here is one of those:

> Washington was a popular choice to lead the new country. Washington, however, wanted to retire after the war. The long years as general had left him tired and frail. Washington wrote that he would be unable to accept the nomination. Attention turned to John Adams as the next most qualified candidate.

Gerrig then asked his subjects to say whether a sentence, "George Washington was elected first president of the United States," was true or false.

What Gerrig found was that the response time was significantly longer for subjects who had read stories that created some suspense, some uncertainty, as to whether Washington would be our first president or not. Gerrig called this phenomenon "anomalous suspense." The suspense is anomalous because all his subjects knew perfectly well that in fact George Washington was elected our first president. So why the slight hesitation? Gerrig concluded that the answer came more slowly because the suspense, the uncertainty in response to the narrative, made the subjects believe in some temporary way that maybe George Washington *didn't* become America's first president.

You can see the same phenomenon in children. They have heard the story of Jack and the Beanstalk a zillion times, but every time, when the giant chases Jack, they get excited: Will the giant catch him? Will he escape? You experience the same phenomenon when you see a movie like *Casablanca* for the umpteenth time. Will Rick put Ilsa on the plane with Laszlo? You know at one level of your mind that he will, but you still feel suspense. As Gerrig says, *you have to actively construct disbelief*.

Notice too that the stories Gerrig used were *nonfiction*. They were factual stories about American history and pop culture and other things his Yale subjects would know. What Gerrig's experiments imply is: if you subject yourself to *any* narrative, you believe it for the time of the experience, whether you think it fiction or nonfiction. Anomalous suspense happens with both. You have to construct disbelief actively, deliberately, and usually after the story is over.

Gerrig's results agree with a well-known psychological phenomenon, the "truth effect" or "lie blindness." People are not good at rejecting stories that they have comprehended. Science writer Natalie Angier summarizes this line of research: "In more than 100 studies, researchers have asked participants questions like, is the person on the videotape lying or telling the truth? Subjects guess correctly about 54 percent of the time, which is barely better than they'd do by flipping a coin. Our lie blindness suggests to some researchers a human desire to be deceived, a preference for the stylishly accoutred fable over the naked truth" (Angier 2008; see for example, Ekman and O'Sullivan 1991).

"Lie blindness" tends to confirm Gerrig's results, but does not explain the emotional effect. Why do these meta-genres—metafiction, metadrama, metafilm—sometimes make people edgy? Why do they sometimes seem like a joke? Freud and Gerrig tell us that the effects come from conflicting beliefs. But the emotion, the anxiety or the mirth, tells me that these reactions have to do with more than just an intellectual issue.

V. MOTOR SYSTEMS

The conflicting beliefs have to do with action on the events portrayed in the literary work, and action is fundamental. Ultimately a brain has only one function: to move its organism through the world so that that organism can survive and reproduce (Kalat 2001, 224). All the other fancier functions of the brain—belief, memory, learning, and particularly the executive function in the prefrontal cortex—all serve that one purpose, moving us around.

We can imagine the system that moves us as a long feedback loop in our brains and bodies. The executive system in the prefrontal cortex decides on some general plan of action and that impulse travels backward through the frontal lobe, activating more and more specific elements of the action. The cortical impulse innervates the basal ganglia in the middle of the brain. That is an earlier (prehuman) part of the brain, where we store programs for relatively fixed actions like walking or grasping. The impulse to act, having been spelled out in detail, as it were, by these relatively advanced systems, travels to the primitive (or reptilian) brain stem and on to the cranial nerves or through the spinal cord to particular motor neurons in the lower body. The body moves. Then other nerves feed back what has happened. Impulses in the musculature send data up to the sensory regions in the posterior lobes of the brain. The information goes particularly to the parietal lobe, which monitors proprioceptive activity. Systems there tell the rest of the brain what happened with the body's movement.

The keystone of this loop, the crucial initiator of it all, is the prefrontal cortex, and, within the prefrontal cortex, probably the dorsolateral prefrontal cortex (Brodmann areas 46 and 9). "It is clear," writes Oxford psychologist Richard Passingham, "that the dorsolateral prefrontal cortex plays an important role in the spontaneous generation of movements" (1993, 125–153, 152). Patients with prefrontal damage suffer from an inability to generate coherent representations of alternate or counterfactual realities (Young and Saver 2001). They have deficits in generating and evaluating counterfactual scenarios.

VI. INHIBITION

Frontal lobe patients also have deficits in inhibitory control, the do-not-act, that is based in the prefrontal cortex (Knight and Grabowecky 1995, Table 90.1). They suffer from what neurologists call "utilization behavior." If you put a pencil in front of them, for example, they will pick it up and begin to doodle or write. "The patients' behavior was striking, as though implicit in the environment was an order to respond to the situation in which they found themselves" (Passingham 1993, 25–153, 152). In short, "Confidently monitoring and adjusting . . . one's behavior is a key component of human cognition. Evidence from neurological patients suggests that this capacity is dependent on the evolution of the dorsolateral prefrontal cortex" (Knight, Grabowecky, and Scabini 1995, 21–22). Frontal lobe specialist Joaquin Fuster locates inhibitory control of motor action in the prefrontal cortex. It is in the prefrontal cortex that we do our most complex planning, and *planning entails waiting, not acting on impulse* (1999, 191–93). Importantly for literature and other media, it is there that we start the cognitive inhibition of action, as when we know we are not going to act on the situations represented in a play, movie, or story. (Specifically, Fuster assigns this inhibiting to the part of your brain just above your eyebrows, the orbital prefrontal cortex, and extending back toward the brain stem at the base of your skull. He diagrams Brodmann areas 10, 11, 13, and 47.) It may be that the right hemisphere plays more of a role in this inhibition than the left (Aron et al. 2007).

In brief, prefrontal cortex is essential for planning, choosing among, and executing *or inhibiting* actions, like not acting on the people or events in a fiction. It is in systems receiving information from the dorsolateral prefrontal cortex that sensory and cognitive information becomes translated into a decision whether we are going to act or not.

In the case of literature, at least, that is a decision based partly on social appropriateness: we have to behave a certain way in theaters and libraries. Probably, then, the right prefrontal cortex (more sensitive to context and interpersonal situations) plays more of a role in this brain activity than the left. "The right hemisphere has a greater capacity for dealing with informational complexity and for processing many modes of representation within a single task, whereas the left hemisphere is superior at tasks requiring detailed fixation on a single, often repetitive, mode of representation or execution" (Springer and Deutsch 1998, 310; see Goldberg 2001). Responding to metafiction is surely a task with informational complexity.

There may be another source of inhibition, the famous "mirror neurons" found by Giacomo Rizzolatti, Vittorio Gallese, and others on their team based at the University of Parma. (For reviews, see Iacoboni and Dapretto 2006; Iacoboni 2008.) This group recorded individual neurons from the ventral premotor area in the frontal lobes of macaques. They found that specific motor neurons fire when a monkey performs one particular action with its hand. Different neurons fire in response to different actions: pulling, pushing, tugging, grasping, or picking up and putting a peanut in the mouth.

Obviously these motor neurons make muscles do certain specific things. In fact, however, these neural assemblies also include "mirror" neurons. Any given mirror neuron will *also* fire when the subject monkey watches another monkey (or even the experimenter) perform an action like grasping a peanut. The Parma group also believes it has located the brain region in which the observed action and the copy of the action are compared, the superior temporal sulcus (Iacoboni et al. 2001). Another experiment suggests that mirror neurons enable subjects to infer goals. Subjects watched a hand's movements in the context of a full or emptied tea setting. The subjects' mirror neurons lit up as they inferred the intention, either to drink tea or to clean up (Iacoboni et al. 2005). Two Harvard psychologists offer evidence that when we think about the future actions of another person, we project ourselves into that person's situation (Buckner and Carroll 2007). Still more remarkably, *listening to action-related sentences modulates the motor system* through mirror neurons, particularly those in Broca's area, specialized for speech movements (Buccino et al. 2005; Tettamanti et al. 2005). This implies that, in a literary setting, while watching or reading about actions, the motor regions of the brain experience an impulse to imitate the action (mirror response) *but then the brain inhibits at lower levels that musculoskeletal expression*, the "inverted mirror response" (Baldissera et al. 2001; Rizzolatti et al. 2006, 142). In effect, this experiment links Kant's high-level, cognitive disinterestedness in our enjoyment of works of art to a low-level, unconscious motor inhibition of action.

Generally when we watch someone else doing something, our mirror neurons fire as if we ourselves were doing the same thing. Because we are acting (in imagination) like the other person, we will feel the same emotions as the person in the situation we are watching. In an emotional sense, now, we are empathic. We identify.

Thus, watching a movie in which a character hurtles through space, we will feel in our own bodies that sensation and the emotions that go with it. My students write of such a situation: "I can almost feel the sensation of hurling [*sic*] through space—my stomach may lurch." "I react as if I am hurtling through space alongside the movie character." "I would most likely cover my eyes in fear." "I find myself suspending my natural breathing patterns until that character lands safely." Indeed, a recent experiment confirms that one's brain responds to others' fearful body expressions. Seeing a person recoil, say, with fearful feelings might lead to impulses to move one's own body, perhaps to flee (de Gelder et al. 2004).

VII. ACTION AND BELIEF

To move, to plan actions, we imagine situations. Suppose I want to push aside the book on the table in front of me. In order to tell my arms and legs to make the necessary moves, I have to imagine where I want that book to be. *I have to imagine something that is not actually the case*. Neuroscientists call this something a "counterfactual."

Neuropsychology has long established that we assess the reality of a stimulus only if we act or plan to act in response to that stimulus (Chelazzi et al. 1998; Hobson 1995, chap. 6; Rolls 1995; Knight and Grabowecky 1995; Kahneman and Miller 1986). We know that the counterfactual goals we imagine are not real. We know that the physical state of things as they are is real. To change the way things are to the way we want them to be, we have to be clear about what is real and what is imagined. We have to test reality.

Reality testing thus depends on action or possibilities of action. "Perception," according to cognitive scientist Andy Clark, "is itself tangled up with specific possibilities of action—so tangled up, in fact, that the job of central cognition often ceases to exist" (1997, 51). Neuroscientist Rodolfo Llinás writes, "What I must stress here is that the brain's understanding of anything, whether factual or abstract, arises from our manipulations of the external world, by our moving within the world and thus from our sensory-derived experience of it" (Llinás 2001, 58–59). And two specialists in frontal lobe function, Robert T. Knight and Marcia Grabowecky, put the principle this way: "Reality checking involves a continual assessment of the relation between behavior and the environment" (Knight and Grabowecky 1995, 1360). In short, *reality testing in our brains depends on our acting or intending to act.*

When we enjoy aesthetic pleasure, however, we are not desiring to possess or use the work of art. We are not taking up any purposeful or other attitude toward it. We are not behaving like critics—that is an activity and altogether different from simply enjoying our feeling of pleasure. This is Kant's basic thesis about the arts which, so far as I know, is accepted by just about everybody before and after Kant, going back to Aristotle: we do not act; we are, in Kant's term, "disinterested" (Kant 2000, sec. 6; see Hospers 1967).

Now that means that art and literature occupy a special, paradoxical place among human activities. *We have a brain designed for the sole purpose of action that enables us to enjoy works of art precisely because we know we are not going to act on them.*

In general, we humans simulate counterfactuals in order to arrive at the best, the most appropriate, physical actions. Ultimately, emotions guide our choices. We act out what feels good and right. We obey Freud's "pleasure principle" or, more accurately, his "unpleasure principle." We avoid unpleasure, especially anxiety. But, oddly, we feel anxiety in the middle of a book or movie or play that we are enjoying if it turns metafictional.

Since we are not planning to act when we respond to fictional events, we are not generating counterfactuals. We are not imagining the world as we would like it to be. We may be filling in the story, visualizing things not described, adding in a background for one of the characters, or working out cause and effect, but we are not imagining ourselves acting on the events of the story. Instead, the story itself is giving us a constant stream of counterfactuals in place of the ones we would normally imagine for ourselves. Whatever imagining we do simply fits in with the imagining the writer has already done for us. What we imagine has nothing to do with action in the real world of survival.

But I *can* act toward this book in front of me, I can turn its pages, I can pick it up, I can put it down—it's real therefore. But when I am absorbed in a literary work, getting pleasure from it, I have agreed in my mind that *I will not act* on the events or situations represented in the work. I will not try to deter Don Quixote or Sancho from their foolishness. Without movement or the intention to move or some plan to move or some thought about moving, I need not check the reality of the events I perceive, *and I don't*. As Gerrig's experiments show, I will believe a story, at least temporarily, until I have some reason not to.

The brain is an economical creature. If I can't act toward something, it doesn't matter whether it's real or not real. My brain doesn't waste energy testing it.

VIII. THE META- IN METAFICTION

To sum up, I turn off a system (governed probably by the right dorsolateral prefrontal cortex) that had been using the total literary context to make predictions about my bodily relation to what I was perceiving in the literary work. I was not going to act on what I was perceiving. I was not even contemplating the possibility of action. I was not imagining counterfactuals. I had suspended the testing of reality or probability.

But now that system has been fooled, and (so to speak) it knows it has been fooled. Suddenly the fiction about a deluded reader of chivalric romances isn't just a fiction—it includes a physical fact to which I am motor-connected, namely the book in my hand. In my experience of *Don Quixote*, the narrative has acquired a different kind of reality from the narrative I was temporarily believing. The physical reality of the novel being dealt with in the story makes me realize that my temporary belief in the story was mistaken. The story was "only a story," but this new thing I am perceiving is "real." Or, alternatively, it suggests that the story I am believing in is as real as the book I am holding (Berns, Cohen, and Mintun 1997). I begin to substitute my own counterfactuals for those that I had been getting from the book, the play, or the movie. I start concerning myself with the reality or unreality of the story I had been passively enjoying. I suddenly feel a contradiction in my perceptions. Is what I am perceiving just a story or is it something real? I will begin to feel a vague sense of perhaps having to do something, but at the same time I know that part of what I am perceiving is a fiction.

Your brain is wired, as all animals' brains are wired, so that, whenever any new thing pops into your environment, you have to pay attention to it. This novelty could be a threat or an opportunity for sex or maybe just food, and you have to pay attention to ensure survival and reproduction. In your brain, this new conflict in which the same thing (the events of the story) has become both real and fictional mobilizes your systems for attention. What should I be doing about this new thing? How will I cope with this? How will I act toward it? What will I *do*? And, because I am contemplating action, I test reality.

In psychoanalytic terms, this confusion of the two levels leads to what Freud (1926) called a "signal of anxiety." Such a signal mobilizes your defenses and adaptations, that is, your characteristic way of coping with inner and outer reality. You will begin to feel a vague sense of having to do something, but at the same time you know that what you are perceiving is a fiction.

The fictional events portrayed may be the same kind of thing as the book I am holding or the theater I am in. Do I need to test these events for reality, probability, and truth preparatory to acting on them? Do I need to bring those frontal lobe reality-testing systems into play? For a given piece of the world, the story, the executive function of my brain is getting two inconsistent signals. One says, "Get ready to act." The other says, "Don't act." In effect, I am asking the dorsolateral prefrontal cortex to set my brain both for nonaction and action (Passingham 1993, 222–37). I become uncertain about my own status in reality as well as that of the story.

The writer's mingling reality with unreality, the possibility of action with the ongoing impossibility of action, gives me the slightly anxious feeling that Freud called the uncanny. The metafictional effect rests on a childish belief that fiction might be true or real, a belief that Gerrig's experiments show persists in adults (or at least Yale students). And I can have this false belief because I am not going to act. Now I have a book (or play or movie) that is open to action. The inconsistency grabs my attention, and my uncertainty about this thing I am paying attention to becomes a call to possible action. My "poetic faith," my being "transported" because I was not going to act, comes to an end. And that is how a puzzle about belief created by the writers of metafiction, metadrama, and metafilm leads to Freud's "signal of anxiety" (Holland 2007b).

That is the case if the metafiction goes on for a while. One feels edgy and tense as the *New York Times* critic did with *Adaptation*. If the metafiction is short, like Groucho Marx's remark or John Barth's mot, then it's a joke. We suddenly and playfully dissolve the incongruity between the physically real and the purely imaginary, and that is the standard neuropsychological account of jokes (Holland 2007a). And that, to sum up, is how neuroscience can explain the two metafictional effects, signal anxiety or joke.

IX. *DON QUIXOTE* ONCE MORE

Cervantes' masterpiece, however, goes even farther into this hall of mirrors than other metafictions. This novel builds on the very premise that metafictional uncertainties are playing with. And that, to me, makes for one of the brilliances of this great novel.

That is, metafictions play with the fact that the events in fictions are unreal and we are not going to act on them. But what is this book about? It's about a man who *does act* in response to fictions. It's about a man who reads silly chivalric stories but thinks they are not make-believe but histories. It's about a man who reads fictions, but instead of *not* acting like a normal reader, he goes out and does things, tilting at windmills, chasing sheep, and all his other glorious antics.

It's a book about a man who is a fictional character who denies he is a fictional character. It's about a fictional man who is really a metafictional man, who even—particularly in Part II—seems to know that he is metafictional. That is why *Don Quixote* is such a wonderfully funny trick on readers like us. The novel violates the essential neuropsychological nature of its own metafiction. *Don Quixote* becomes perhaps the greatest of metafictions, because it not only uses, but ultimately transcends, the very brain mechanisms of metafiction.

I too would like to transcend. In talking about the role of the brain in metafiction, I am obviously hinting at a much larger issue. How do we do "a cognitive approach to literature"? I am saying that we need to get beyond purely philosophical or ratiocinative or introspective approaches or evolutionary hopes about the adaptive virtues of literature. We need to look at actual feelings and emotions. And to do that we need seriously to learn about what is in fact doing literature, namely, our brains. But perhaps in making such a demand, I too am doomed to crash into a windmill.

WORKS CITED

Angier, Natalie. 2008. A highly evolved propensity for deceit. *New York Times*, December 23, D1.

Aron, Adam R., et al. 2007. Triangulating a cognitive control network using diffusion-weighted Magnetic Resonance Imaging (MRI) and functional MRI. *Journal of Neuroscience* 27 (April 4): 3473–752.

Baldissera, Fausto, Paolo Cavallari, Laila Craighero, and Luciano Fadiga. 2001. Modulation of spinal excitability during observation of hand actions in humans. *European Journal of Neuroscience* 13, no. 1: 190–94.

Berns, Gregory S., Jonathan D. Cohen, and Mark A. Mintun. 1997. Brain regions responsive to novelty in the absence of awareness. *Science* 276 (May 23): 1272–75.

Buccino, Giovanni, et al. 2005. Listening to action-related sentences modulates the activity of the motor system: A combined TMS and behavioral study. *Cognitive Brain Research* 24: 355–63.

Buckner, Randy L., and Daniel C. Carroll. 2007. Self-projection and the brain. *Trends in Cognitive Science* 11, no. 2: 49–57.

Chelazzi, Leonardo, John Duncan, Earl K. Miller, and Robert Desimone. 1998. Responses of neurons in inferior temporal cortex during memory-guided visual search. *Journal of Neurophysiology* 80, no. 6: 2918–40.

Clark, Andy. 1997. *Being there: Putting brain, body, and world together again*. Cambridge, MA: MIT Press.

de Gelder, Beatrice, et al. 2004. Fear fosters flight: A mechanism for fear contagion when perceiving emotion expressed by a whole body. *Proceedings of the National Academy of Science* 101 (November 23): 16701–6.

Ekman, Paul, and Maureen O'Sullivan. 1991. Who can catch a liar? *American Psychologist* 46 (September): 913–20.

Freud, Sigmund. 1919. The "Uncanny." In *The Standard Edition of the Complete Psychological Works*, 17: 217–56. Translated and edited by James Strachey. In collaboration with Anna Freud, assisted by Alix Strachey and Alan Tyson. London: Hogarth Press, 1953–74.

———. 1926. Inhibitions, symptoms, and anxiety. In *The Standard Edition of the Complete Psychological Works*, 20: 75–175. Translated and edited by James Strachey. In collaboration with Anna Freud, assisted by Alix Strachey and Alan Tyson. London: Hogarth Press, 1953–74.

Fuster, Joaquin M. 1999. Cognitive functions of the frontal lobes. In *The human frontal lobes: Functions and disorders*, 187–95. Edited by Bruce L. Miller and Jeffrey L. Cummings. New York: Guilford Press.

Gass, William H. 1970. Philosophy and the form of fiction. In *Fiction and the figures of life*, 3–26. Boston: David R. Godine.

Gerrig, Richard J. 1989. Suspense in the absence of uncertainty. *Journal of Memory and Language* 28 (December): 633–48.

———. 1998. *Experiencing narrative worlds: On the psychological activities of reading*. Boulder, CO: Westview Press. (Orig. pub. by Yale University Press 1993)

Goldberg, Elkhonon. 2001. *The executive brain: Frontal lobes and the civilized mind*. Oxford: Oxford University Press.

Hobson, J. Allan. 1995. *The chemistry of conscious states: How the brain changes its mind*. Boston: Little, Brown.

Holland, Norman N. 2007a. Tickled rats and human laughter. *Neuropsychoanalysis* 9, no. 1: 41–57.

———. 2007b. The neuroscience of metafilm. *Projections* 1 (Summer): 59–74.

Hospers, John. 1967. Aesthetics, problems of. In *The encyclopedia of philosophy, volume 1*, 35–56. Edited by Paul Edwards. 8 vols. New York: Macmillan/Free Press.

Iacoboni, Marco. 2008. *Mirroring people: The new science of how we connect with others*. New York: Farrar, Straus and Giroux.

Iacoboni, Marco, and Mirella Dapretto. 2006. The mirror neuron system and the consequences of its dysfunction. *Nature Reviews Neuroscience* 7 (December): 942–51.

Iacoboni, Marco, et al. 2001. Reafferent copies of imitated actions in the right superior temporal cortex. *PNAS (Proceedings of the National Academy of Sciences)* 98 (November 20): 13995–99.

———. 2005. Grasping the intentions of others with one's own mirror neuron system. *PLoS Biology* 3 (March): e79.

Kahneman, D., and D. T. Miller. 1986. Norm theory: Comparing reality to its alternatives. *Psychological Review* 93, no. 2: 136–53.

Kalat, James W. 2001. *Biological psychology*. Belmont, CA: Wadsworth/Thomson Learning.

Kant, Immanuel. 2000. *Critique of the power of judgment: The Cambridge edition of the works of Immanuel Kant*. Translated and edited by Paul Guyer and Eric Matthews. Cambridge: Cambridge University Press. (Orig. pub. 1790)

Knight, Robert T., and Marcia Grabowecky. 1995. Escape from linear time: Prefrontal cortex and conscious experience. In *The cognitive neurosciences*, 1357–71. Edited by Michael S. Gazzaniga. Cambridge, MA: MIT Press.

Knight, Robert T., Marcia Grabowecky, and Donatella Scabini. 1995. Role of human prefrontal cortex in attention control. *Advances in Neurology* 66: 21–34.

Llinás, Rodolfo R. 2001. *The I of the vortex: From neurons to self*. Cambridge, MA: MIT Press.

Mancing, Howard. 2006. *Cervantes' "Don Quixote": A reference guide*. Westport, CT: Greenwood Press.

Passingham, Richard. 1993. *The frontal lobes and voluntary action*. Oxford Psychology Series 21. New York: Oxford University Press.

Rizzolatti, Giacomo, et al. 2006. The inferior parietal lobule: Where action becomes perception. In *Percept, decision, action: Bridging the gaps*, 129–45. Novartis Foundation Symposium 270. Chichester: Wiley.

Rolls, Edmund T. 1995. A theory of emotion and consciousness, and its application to understanding the neural basis of emotion. In *The cognitive neurosciences*, 1091–106. Edited by Michael S. Gazzaniga. Cambridge, MA: MIT Press.

Scott, A. O. 2002. Forever obsessing about obsession. Review of *Adaptation*, by Spike Jonze. *New York Times*, December 6, E1.

Springer, Sally P., and Georg Deutsch. 1998. *Left brain, right brain: Perspectives from cognitive neuroscience*. 5th ed. New York: W. H. Freeman.

Tettamanti, Marco, et al. 2005. Listening to action-related sentences activates fronto-parietal motor circuits. *Journal of Cognitive Neuroscience* 17, no. 2: 273–81.

Waugh, Patricia. 1984. *Metafiction: The theory and practice of self-conscious fiction*. London: Methuen.

Young, Kay, and Jeffrey L. Saver. 2001. The neurology of narrative. *SubStance* no. 94/95: 72–84.

CHAPTER 5

THE MOURNING BRAIN: ATTACHMENT, ANTICIPATION, AND HAMLET'S UNMANLY GRIEF

PATRICK COLM HOGAN

WHEN I THINK OF MOURNING, a complex of ideas and memories comes to mind. One prominent memory concerns my mother's response to her own mother's death. One day, my mother repeatedly telephoned my grandmother throughout the morning, but no one answered. One of the attendants at the retirement home went to my grandmother's room and found that she had died during the night. My mother got through the events of the following week well enough. But I came downstairs one morning, a few days after the burial, and found her weeping piteously.

When she was able to control her breath, my mother explained what had happened. It seemed a triviality. She had the television on and there was some announcement. "I thought Mama would like to know about that," she explained. So she picked up the telephone and dialed the number. It was only when the phone began to ring that she remembered no one would be there to answer. Perhaps something about the sound, a peculiar crackling when the call passed through the switchboard, reminded her of her calls a week before.

Another thing that comes to mind when I think of grief is not personal but literary. It is Claudius's admonishing of the bereaved prince, Hamlet—"'Tis sweet and commendable in your nature, Hamlet, / To give these mourning duties to your father. . . . / But to persever / In obstinate condolement is a course / Of impious stubbornness. 'Tis unmanly grief" (1.2.88–89, 92–94). Perhaps the first thing that strikes many of us about the passage is the way it links grief with gender. In an age of culture studies, we are likely to see this as part of the "cultural construction" of emotion. In this view, societies make emotions in much the way they make tools or clothes. Shakespeare's society made grief, and it made that grief feminine. But this blunts the fine point of the passage. Claudius has lost a brother. His identification of grief as unmanly serves a purpose. It explains and justifies the brevity of his own mourning.

It also takes up a theme that is of central concern to anyone in a position of power, including a monarch—authority. Claudius brands Hamlet's mourning "impious," going on to explain that "[i]t shows a will most incorrect to heaven" (2.2.95). Claudius recognizes in Hamlet's mourning a threat to his own position and rule. Like many rulers, he invokes God against that threat. Finally, the mere fact that Claudius needs to justify his own lack of mourning, and that he needs to chide Hamlet in terms of both gender and religion, tells us something. It tells us that this is not a matter of social construction. The emotions have not been socially made. If they had been made, then Claudius's manly lack of grief would seem entirely ordinary. There would be no reason to rationalize it. Hamlet's inky cloak would be met with astonishment by the God-fearing Danes. What we are faced with in Claudius's speech is not the social making of emotion, but the invocation of a partially flexible ideology that tries to characterize and evaluate emotion in the service of political, familial, and gender hierarchies. Of course, this still indicates that cultural practices and ideas play a key role in emotion—but more in its understanding and assessment than in its constitution.

These two incidents—one from personal memory, the other from a literary work—suggest two crucial issues facing any cognitive account of human emotion in general, and any account of grief in particular. The first is just how one might explain a complex emotion such as grief, an emotion that relies on absence, rather than presence—an emotion of nothingness, as we might call it, using the term in its Sartrean sense. The second issue is just how one might reconcile an understanding of the common neurobiology of emotion with an understanding of the sociology of emotion.

APPRAISAL AND SUBCORTICAL
AROUSAL ACCOUNTS OF EMOTION

The predominant cognitive theories view emotion as the result of appraisal—the evaluation of events or situations in light of goals and interests. However, the appraisal account is problematic in several ways. Two are crucial. First, it is not clear that an appraisal account is algorithmically specifiable in terms of cognitive architecture. In other words, it seems to rely on our intuitive sense of what it means to evaluate situations in terms of likely outcomes. Second, appraisal accounts seem to make some false predictions. For example, appraisal theory would seem to suggest that two events or situations should have the same emotional impact if they are evaluated as having the same facilitating or inhibiting effect on goal achievement. But, in fact, this is simply not the case. Many people rightly evaluate automobile travel as far more dangerous than air travel. However, almost no one fears automobile travel more than air travel.

The most common alternative account of emotion is broadly summarized by Panksepp in the following terms: "the driving forces behind the fundamental feeling tones and autonomic/behavioral/cognitive tendencies that we commonly recognize as distinct types of emotional arousal arise primarily from the neurodynamics of specific types of subcortical circuits" (2000, 137). In connection with this, we might argue that emotions are, first of all, the result of genetically predetermined sensitivities connected with various subcortical brain regions. For example, fear, in this account, is first the result of certain perceptual sensitivities, connected via the thalamus to the amygdala (see LeDoux and Phelps 2000, 159). As Damasio put it:

> We are wired to respond with an emotion, in a preorganized fashion, when certain features of stimuli in the world or in our bodies are perceived, alone or in combination. Examples of such features include size (as in large animals); large span (as in flying eagles); type of motion (as in reptiles); certain sounds (such as growling). (1994, 131)

Crucially for students of literature, these perceptual sensitivities bear not only on our experience of the external world and of our own bodies; they bear also on imagination. Anything that affects imagination may, within limits, affect one's emotional response to particular events or situations.

Innate triggers are not the only sources of emotional arousal in this account. The eliciting conditions of our emotions may be altered through emotional memories (see LeDoux 1996, 200–204). Emotional memories are memories of emotionally arousing experiences; when activated, they produce an emotion. They are "implicit"—that is, they do not introduce representational content into working memory. However, they are usually linked with explicit episodic memories, which do introduce representational content. Explicit episodic memories are what we ordinarily think of as memories—for example, a recollection of my last trip to a particular building. If my last trip there was happy, I may experience joy on entering the building. The joy is due to the emotional memory. My ability to understand my joy is due to the episodic memory.[1]

Elaborating on this approach, I would distinguish three levels of a neurobiological account of emotion. The first may be derived in part from research regarding such systems as motion and vision. In those systems, we find a high degree of fragmentary specialization at the level of particular neurons. We do not find neurons that are specialized for walking, but for a particular sort of muscle contraction, for example. These fragmentary specializations are co-ordinated to produce particular motions. Similarly, as Barlow (1999) explains, "Neurons in the *primary visual cortex* . . . are selectively responsive to edge, orientation, direction of motion, texture, color, and disparity" (112). The general idea is well expressed by Pulvermüller (2002) when he points out that most "neurons usually fire at a low rate of a few action potentials per second. They become more strongly active only in response to specific stimuli and are not much affected by the rest" (77).

In the case of emotions, then, it seems likely that there are neurons with fragmentary functions contributing to particular emotions. For example, there should be emotion system neurons that are activated only for particular perceptual fragments—or configurations of fragments signaled by firings of populations of sensory neurons. However, these functions are not emotions themselves. They are components of the elicitation, expression, or other aspects of emotion. Only when combined and coordinated do they become emotions. Of course, neurons bearing on particular emotions do tend to cluster together in particular regions. As Pulvermüller explains, for example—speaking more generally and in another context—there are differences between "local and long-distance" neuronal connections (12). He goes on to point out that "the high probability of local . . . links suggests local clusters of neurons that exchange information intensely and therefore show similar functional characteristics" (17). Thus neuronal specificity and regional functional neuroanatomy are closely interrelated, forming the first level of explanation in this account.

Local connections among specialized neurons are far from the whole story. Long-distance projections are important as well. This leads us to the second component of emotion systems—synaptic circuits. I have been speaking of neurons that are crucial for triggering cascades of emotional response. These include, for example, neurons in the nuclei of the amygdala. We might refer to these as "emotion neurons" (though they may have other functions as well). Such neurons do not operate on their own. They operate with other neurons in patterned sequences of activation and inhibition. We may distinguish very simply between incoming and outgoing synaptic pathways relative to such emotion neurons. Incoming or afferent pathways serve to activate (or inhibit) the emotion neurons. Outgoing or efferent pathways are activated (or inhibited) by the emotion neurons.

The afferent pathways directly or indirectly projecting into emotion neurons serve to transmit the eliciting conditions for emotion. By my account, these include the "low road," rough-sketch perceptual features isolated by

LeDoux, and the relevant perceptual triggers from imagination, as well as emotional memories. It is important to stress that these features are fragmentary and the triggers or eliciting conditions are somewhat loose and variable configurations of (fragmentary) features. Consider, by way of illustration, some patterns in visual perception and their emotional effects. As Hoffman (1998) explains, when a blackbird nestling is faced with "two adjacent disks, one having a diameter about a third that of the other," it responds with something akin to attachment behavior, as if it is seeing Mom (8). When faced with "a cross moving in the direction of its short end," chickens and ducks respond with fear, presumably because of the very rough resemblance of the figure to a hawk (9). Though Hoffman does not discuss the data in this way, he is isolating emotional responses triggered by rough configurations of fragmentary perceptions through the activation of emotion circuits.

The references to attachment behavior and fear responses lead us from the incoming synaptic connections to the outgoing synaptic connections. The outgoing or efferent pathways lead to other areas, eventually affecting musculature, blood pressure, hormone release, and so forth (see LeDoux and Phelps 2000, 160).

My contention is that the triggering of emotions is, in the first place, confined to particular sorts of innate feature detection. However, there are several ways in which plasticity enters. Our perceptual skills are not all equally developed, nor are they the simple product of genetic instructions. In other words, we do not all encode perceptual features in the same degree. Similarly, innate propensities will at most determine general structures for actional outcomes. However, the details of the action rely on motor skills, including acquired procedural schemas, ongoing calculation of one's location and movement, and so forth. In other words, they recruit separate systems that have a degree of plasticity. Moreover, pleasure and pain are not constrained to innate features. Consider a person who experiences severe spasms on eating butter. Even though we have no preset pain emotion sensitivity to butter, the experience of pain from such a reaction produces an emotional memory with the usual consequences for subsequent emotional experiences.

But there is a puzzle here. I just stated that the experience of pain produces the usual consequences for subsequent emotional experiences. For example, Smith learns that he has just inadvertently eaten butter. He is suddenly overwhelmed with emotion. The puzzle here is that the emotion is something new. The emotion now is fear. But he did not feel fear when he ate butter for the first time. Initially he felt nothing. Then he unexpectedly felt terrible stabs of pain. So the emotional memory of the pain produces not pain but fear. Note that this seems like a prime case of appraisal. Smith judges that he is likely to experience pain due to the butter and therefore experiences fear. By my account, in contrast, the fear does not result from appraisal. Rather it results from the activation of the emotional memory. But just how does this happen?

I will return to the problem of emotional memories below. However, I should first mention the third component in the account I am developing. Functionally this is a more sustained inclination toward certain sorts of emotional response. Neurobiologically, it is roughly a matter of neurochemistry that facilitates or inhibits certain sorts of neuronal firing, thus neurochemistry that facilitates or inhibits the activation of certain synaptic circuits. Generally, neurochemical processes are slower than the activation of specific circuits. As a very rough phenomenological approximation, we may say that lingering propensities toward certain sorts of emotional response are more closely connected with neurochemistry. In contrast, spikes of emotion correspond with the activation of specific synaptic pathways involving emotion neurons in emotionally functional regions.

As already indicated, the neurobiological components of emotion provide the material, explanatory substrate for the usual functional components of emotion, such as eliciting conditions, actional and expressive outcomes, and mood or emotional receptivity. One functional component of particular importance for our purposes is attentional focus.

Both incoming and outgoing circuits link emotion neurons and regions with the system for attention (for example, the reticular formation). The result of emotion-based attentional arousal is not generalized. It is selective, feature-oriented. Emotionally aroused attention is directed to emotion-relevant aspects of the world, our bodies, and our memories. One does not attend to the same aspects of the world if one is sexually aroused, afraid, or hungry.

Consider the advertisement where an adolescent male looks up with a vaguely confused expression and an undirected gaze. Suddenly his eyes focus and wonder spreads across his face. We cut to a nubile young woman in scanty clothing. She holds out her hand, beckoning him seductively. Returning to the youth, we see him transfixed by the sight. He can barely control the overwhelming urges that, we infer, result from powerfully aroused circuits feeding into the hypothalamus. Suddenly the circuit reaches a threshold. The pathway for an actional outcome is activated. He moves closer. His lips open slightly. He reaches out toward the woman's extended hand, plucks the peanut butter cup from her palm, and tosses it into his mouth. Despite his age and chemical propensity toward the easy arousal of sexual desire, and despite the presence of salient environmental triggers for such arousal, his attentional focus was governed by hunger (or, more exactly, the desire to eat—presumably result-ing in part from emotional memories of past experiences with other peanut butter cups that had similar perceptual properties). Thus his attentional focus filtered out all distractions and concentrated his encoding of experience on a limited set of relevant triggers.

Now suppose for a moment that the youth bites into the chocolaty nugget of goodness and tastes pork. The romantic music scratches to a halt. He spits out the fatty sinews and feels a powerful spike of disgust. This is likely to occur even if he is a regular consumer of pork chops and barbecue ribs. What has just happened? It is not the taste of the pork per se that triggered his disgust. It is rather the difference from what he anticipated. Until the moment that he tasted pork, he may not have been aware that he had any specific antici-pation at all. But here and elsewhere anticipation is crucial to our emotional responses.

This leads us to another system, or perhaps set of systems, which are cru-cially involved with emotion—the systems bearing on expectation. Expecta-tion is of central importance for the human brain. Indeed, Barlow maintains that the cells of the neocortex have a single "common function," which is "prediction." Despite Barlow's emphasis, expectation or prediction is not by any means confined to the neocortex. Indeed, one of the most widely studied forms of expectation is primarily cerebellar. Moreover, anticipation has its emotional effects through the operation of subcortical, anticipatory circuits, as LeDoux and Phelps explain, for example.

Expectation systems bear on both experience and action and they are cru-cial for inputs to and outputs from emotion neurons. Thus some of our emo-tional responses have complex anticipatory calculations in their eliciting con-ditions. To take a very simple example, I do not find a truck frightening if it is parked a few yards from me. However, I may find it very frightening if I see a truck thirty yards from me, look away, then look back and see it a few yards from me. The calculation of the truck's trajectory is what frightens me. In fact, we calculate such trajectories swiftly and implicitly all the time (see van Leeu-wen 2002, 272).

This already suggests a solution to the problem of emotional memories. Emotional memories serve, first of all, to guide expectations. Indeed, this makes sense in evolutionary terms. The function of emotional memories should be to orient our future action toward opportunities and away from threats, not simply to make us re-experience feelings. Thus it is not quite right to say that emotional memories, when activated, lead us to re-experience past emotions. Rather they partially guide our expectations. In some cases that means that we will, more or less, re-experience the emotion in question. Expectation of joy makes us feel roughly a species of joy. However, our expectation of pain makes us feel fear.

But just how does expectation work in these cases and what precisely is its relation to emotion? There has certainly been research dealing with expectation. For example, the extensive work on the vestibulo-ocular reflex is in part research on expectation, for it is research on the ways in which our visual focus maintains smoothness in perception by anticipating object movement. Ivry (1997) points out that "in order to generate an appropriate saccade, it is necessary to have an accurate representation of the future position of a moving stimulus" (563). However, as far as I am aware, this research has not been organized under the rubric of expectation and it has not been developed systematically in relation to emotion.

It seems likely that there are at least three sorts of expectation (for a fuller discussion, see Hogan 2007). The longest-term expectations are cases of what might be called "situational prototyping." These are a matter of what we expect from extended sequences of events. The range of temporal *reference* here is quite broad. It extends from eating at a restaurant to engaging in a war. However, the range of temporal *experience*—the actual cognitive processing of the situational prototype—is usually limited to tens of seconds. Situational expectations are primarily a matter of long-term semantic memory, with prototypes and related structures being recruited to organize one's imagination of extended trajectories. For the most part, they are probably a matter of cortico-cortical connections.

The second set of expectations might be called "working anticipations." While situational prototyping might unfold over tens of seconds, a working anticipation involves ongoing inferential particularizations governing our response to currently changing situations. Thus it unfolds over seconds. Examples would include our ongoing, changeable responses to entering a restaurant (for example, looking to see if there is a stand for a host or hostess). Though bound up with working memory, these may also be involved with subcortical connections bearing on periodicity.

Finally, there is perceptual and motor projection. Our temporal experience here is less than a second and we are likely to find a substrate of cortico-cerebellar interconnections, though very short-term perceptual memory systems may be involved as well. Akshoomoff, Courchesne, and Townsend (1997) explain that, as "sequences of external and internal events unfold, they elicit a readout of the full sequence in advance of the real-time events. This readout is sent to and alters, in advance, the state of each motor, sensory, autonomic, attentional, memory, or affective system which . . . will soon be actively involved in the current real-time events. So, in contrast to conscious, longer time-scale anticipatory processes mediated by cerebral systems, output of the cerebellum provides moment-to-moment, unconscious, very short time-scale, anticipatory information" (593).

It seems clear that working anticipations and perceptual/motor projections give rise to emotions (as in my fear of the suddenly approaching truck). It also seems clear that the fulfillment or violation of working anticipations and perceptual/motor projections produces emotions. Violations may be particularly consequential. Indeed, as Oatley points out, several theorists have "stressed that emotions occur when . . . an expectancy is violated" (Oatley 1999, 274). The emotional force of violations is greatest when the initial expectation is itself an emotion trigger. One important factor in these cases is the gradient of change from the first emotion to the second. This change itself produces a second-order emotion. For example, if a working anticipation or perceptual projection gives rise to joy, the violation of that expectation—even through a change to emotional neutrality—will give rise to disappointment.

Here we begin to see how we may account for emotions of nothingness. They are not emotions that have a direct presence as trigger. Rather they are emotions that rely on the activation and violation of expectation systems. Specifically, experience generates anticipation and projection. Anticipation and projection generate emotion—joy, for example. The new experience differs from anticipation and projection and it has distinct emotional consequences (for example, neutrality). The gradient of emotional change generates a second-order emotion. In a particular set of cases, for particular sorts of anticipated emotion, such a violation gives rise to grief.

GRIEF

Returning to the case of my mother, we see that her spike of emotion fits the analysis given thus far. She anticipated talking with her mother, giving her the news of whatever she had seen on the television. That anticipation—along with related perceptual projections—gave my mother some degree of joy. The sudden realization of her mother's death violated that anticipation and projection. This was an emotion trigger for a circuit related to grief. It was no doubt enhanced by an ongoing mood, itself partially specifiable in neurochemical terms. My contention is that spikes of grief are always of this sort. They are violated short-term expectations—a combination of working anticipations and perceptual projections—relating to the person who has died. Note that this is very different from the long-term expectations that are emphasized by proponents of appraisal theories. In the view developed here, long-term expectations are emotionally important only insofar as they generate short-term expectations through concrete imagination and the activation of emotional memories.[2]

But to say that such frustrated anticipation occurs in grief—perhaps is even a necessary condition for grief—clearly does not explain grief. After all, the frustration of an emotionally positive projection is clearly not a sufficient condition for grief. Thus far I have not distinguished between my mother's feeling about her mother's death and some banal case of disappointment. Why is my mother's experience on the telephone different from, say, my disappointing discovery that I have run out of pretzels? Both involve working anticipation and perceptual projection giving rise to a sense of happiness—as when I walk into the kitchen thinking, "Pretzels—yum!" But, however much I like pretzels, we would be disinclined to say that I experience grief when I discover that the last bag of pretzels has only a residue of salt and a few crusty flakes. Part of this is a matter of emotional memories. My mother had seen her mother's dead body, gone through a funeral where her younger of two sons had become seriously ill, and so on. I have had no such experiences with pretzels. But that is not all there is to it.

What then is the difference between these two violations of expectancy? It is a matter of the initial emotion system engaged by the anticipation. In all emotions of nothingness, there is some emotion system that is activated in the initial anticipations. The violated expectation inhibits that system suddenly. When I feel certain sorts of relief, anticipations had first engaged the fear system. The relief is the result of the sudden inhibition of the fear system. The imagination of pretzels engaged the system governing my desire to eat. The question then is what emotion system produces grief when its satisfaction is inhibited.

Once one asks the question, the answer seems straightforward: attachment. Stabs of grief result from anticipations that pleasurably activate the attachment system. The fundamental difference between my mother's response to her telephone call and my response to my empty cupboard is that the thought of pretzels does not engage my attachment system.

One could understand attachment—in a preliminary and very simplified way—in terms of its relation to a few subcortical areas and their related emotion systems, particularly the corpus striatum, the amygdala, and the hypothalamus. Attachment seems likely to involve the activation of areas in the corpus striatum that bear on trust (see King-Casas et al. 2005), the establishment of a home place (see Oatley 2004, 64), and mirth (see Goldin et al. 2005, 34). The presence of an attachment figure would appear to involve the partial inhibition of the areas of the amygdala that bear on fear. It also seems likely that there is some relation between attachment and systems bearing on hunger and thermal regulation, thus including the hypothalamus. Hunger and cold turn our attentional focus not only to such features of the world as food and fire but also to features of the world that bear on attachment. Put in the most basic and obvious way, a hungry child looks for food by looking for Mom; a cold child looks for warmth by looking for Mom.

Given this account of attachment, one might expect the violation of positive attachment expectations to produce the following sequence of feelings: a sudden loss of security of place or being "at home" and a disinhibition of fear, thus a response not unrelated to panic. Indeed, Panksepp has argued that panic is precisely a separation-distress emotion. One might also expect one's longer-term mood to inhibit mirth and the feeling of trust (which allows confidence in secure action), and to affect aspects of hunger or wanting to eat and perhaps thermal regulation. These predicted effects are largely what we find in grief—a sense of being out of place, a sense of anxiety, a loss of mirth, a lack of confidence in secure action, a lack of interest in food, and a sense of cold (or lack of warmth). As to the last, Panksepp explains that at least some young mammals show "decreases in body temperature" when isolated (1998, 262).

This leads us to the question of what is involved in the joy-inducing anticipations and projections based on attachment. Attachment is somewhat peculiar among emotions in that it is particularistic. We may fear a particular individual. But our fear is triggered by general features, even in particular cases. If I am afraid of mean Billy, I am afraid because he punches me in the face and steals my pretzels whenever he sees me on the playground. Thus my fear is ultimately a response to a general property. In contrast, if baby is attached to Mom, that is not because Mom has breasts or is warm. I would fear anyone who kept punching me in the face and stealing my pretzels. Baby is not attached to everyone who has breasts and is warm.

On the other hand, even this particularity of attachment is inflected by innate feature sensitivities. Put differently, not every aspect of the mother is of equal importance to the child. At least three aspects seem particularly significant. As Schore (2000) notes, "the attachment system" seeks "not just proximity but access to an attachment figure who is emotionally available and responsive" (26). All three aspects serve to signal the presence, accessibility, and emotional attitude of the attachment figure, generally the mother. The mother's emotional attitude is particularly important because the child's sense of security in a given environment is bound up with the mother's emotional reaction to both the child and to that environment. The three features are facial expression (including identifying features of the face itself), voice, and touch (particularly the encompassing touch of an embrace). If this is correct, we should expect particularly intense spikes of grief to come from working anticipations and perceptual projections bearing on the responsive facial expression, voice, and touch of the attachment figure.

Now we may recur one last time to my mother's case. This account explains her stab of grief in the following way. When telephoning her mother, even about a trivial topic, her attachment system was engaged. This was connected to working anticipations of a conversation with her mother and perceptual projections of hearing her mother's voice in particular. The violation of that expectation produced an inhibition of security and a disinhibition of anxiety, both facilitated by the neurochemically based mood that resulted from recent events. In addition it undoubtedly gave rise to the imagination of future telephone calls, all leading to the same result. It also triggered a series of emotional memories bearing specifically on attachment losses—from the recent memories of her unanswered calls a week earlier, calls that led to the discovery of her mother's dead body, to much older memories, stretching back to the time when she was a girl and a telephone call came with the news that her father had died.

Finally we may return to Claudius. I indicated earlier that his statements bear more on gender ideology than on the cultural construction of emotion. The preceding analysis indicates why gender ideology might label grief as unmanly. In a broad range of societies, masculinity is bound up with war. The most definitively male traits are the traits that make a soldier. Grief is tied to two things that are anathema to a soldier—fear and attachment. Any society that wishes its men to be warriors is likely to mark grief as feminine. Indeed, there is a specific emotion system that opposes both the calm trust of attachment and the anxiety of grief. It is also the emotion system that is crucial for war. That is the system of anger. The point bears directly on Hamlet. The prince spends a great deal of the play trying to make himself act like a soldier. He compares himself unfavorably to Fortinbras, a paradigmatic fighter who will engage in battle over a mere straw. Contrasting himself with Fortinbras, he anguishes over his own lack of military virtue, confessing to himself, "I do not know / Why yet I live to say, 'This thing's to do,' / Sith I have cause, and will, and strength, and means / To do't" (4.4.43–46). Critics have shared Hamlet's bafflement, perennially wondering why he does not act. But I do not believe there is any problem here. There is never a question of Hamlet acting. The motivation for an action is an emotion—not an objective reason ("cause"), cortical choice ("will"), physical ability ("strength"), or circumstantial opportunity ("means"). For revenge, Hamlet would need to be motivated by that manly emotion of anger. But, with only momentary exceptions, Hamlet does not feel anger. He feels grief. A martial act is not what we would expect from a soul in grief, which is to say, from a mourning brain.

Indeed, the puzzle with Hamlet is not why he fails to act, but why he does act in some instances. The preceding analysis suggests an explanation. Hamlet is spurred by temporary spikes of anger. These spikes have a particular type of cause, a type related to Hamlet's ongoing condition of grief and the disturbances in attachment relations that are part of this grief. Anger is prototypically triggered by the blocking of one's acts or expectations. In Hamlet's case, anger occurs when particular sorts of acts and expectations are blocked—specifically, acts and expectations of forming a substitute attachment relation, something to take the place of what he has lost. Generally, *Hamlet* is a play about the loss of attachment relations and the attempt to repair that loss through new attachments. Indeed, as is typical with literature, these central concerns—attachment concerns that extend even to warmth and food—spread out beyond Hamlet himself, saturating other aspects of the play. Thus it is, I believe, no accident that the play begins with an isolated guard's apparently superfluous complaint, "'Tis bitter cold / And I am sick at heart" (1.1.7–8). Nor is it an accident that Hamlet expresses his distress over losing his mother as an attachment object by reference to his distaste for food, explaining to Horatio that "[t]he funeral baked meats / Did coldly furnish forth the marriage tables" (1.2.180–81).

In keeping with the play's pervasive focus on grief and attachment, Hamlet responds with a sort of rage just when he feels trust and a sense of home have been violated in a direct and concrete way. He never feels this with Claudius. He has no memory or hope of an attachment there. His emotions regarding Claudius are all abstract, things he should feel but does not. One might say that they are a matter of appraisal. In contrast, he responds directly to the inhibition of attachment—to home, security, trust—posed by his childhood friends, Rosencrantz and Guildenstern; his remarried mother, Gertrude; Polonius (who should have been a second father, but who cuts him off from Ophelia just when he is most in need of home and security); and to Ophelia herself. Indeed, there is something not entirely foolish in Polonius's idea that frustrated love is at the core of Hamlet's madness.

We may conclude with a particularly telling moment of such rage. It occurs in the first scene of the third act, immediately following Hamlet's famous "To be, or not to be" soliloquy, in which he contemplates suicide. His sense of homelessness, his lack of any real attachment figures, has intensified his grief to such an extent that he can no longer see any point in living. Then suddenly he sees "[t]he fair Ophelia!" (3.1.88), her fairness contrasting with his dark grief. His anticipatory imagination of the future is a blank absence, peopled only by ghosts. But Ophelia is something else, a possibility, something visible, palpable—a person one can hold onto and be held by. She greets him, asking, "How does your honor for this many a day?" (3.1.90). What would anyone think of these words? Clearly Ophelia must have missed his company; the time dragged out its tedious course without his companionship "this many a day." He responds enthusiastically, "I humbly thank you; well, well, well" (3.1.92). He repeats the affirmation, not once, but twice—this from the person who, seconds before, contemplated making his quietus with a bare bodkin. The happy state is inseparable from anticipation. He cannot help but expect that she will ask why he has kept away, perhaps even confess that she missed him—perhaps even respond favorably to his poems and his assertions of love. She begins, "My lord, I have remembrances of yours." What will she say? "Remembrances of yours that moved my heart"? "That made me recognize my own love"? No. "My lord," Ophelia says, "I have remembrances of yours / That I have longed long to re—" To reciprocate, perhaps? A momentary projection gives rise to anticipatory joy. At his most desperate moment, when Hamlet had the least sense of trust or home, the possibility of a new, more lasting attachment now faces him. "I have remembrances of yours / That I have longed long to redeliver. / I pray you now, receive them" (3.1.92–94). The sharp gradient of change from hope to frustration of hope, and from a feeling of trust and shared security of place to a feeling of betrayal, predictably triggers Hamlet's intense anger. First, he denies ever giving her such tokens. He then questions her honesty. Questioning her honesty may seem to make no sense. But it follows directly from Hamlet's shattered sense of trust. His harangue culminates in the famous admonition "Get thee to a nunnery" (3.1.121). It is a way of denying her a home and a family. It is a way of subjecting her to a complete and enduring loss of attachment relations, a sort of grief.

Such grief, again, afflicts Hamlet himself. It in effect defines his character. That character both fascinates and puzzles us. Perhaps this is because, despite its grand setting in the palace of a king, the play does indeed hold the mirror up to nature, reflecting for us our own puzzling relation to attachment and mourning, and to the ideologies through which those feelings are filtered and distorted in our ordinary lives.

CONCLUSION

The preceding analyses indicate that grief is a function of attachment and the small, recurring hopes that go along with it. Specifically, the grieving person generates short-term expectations—working anticipations and perceptual projections—regarding the attachment object, despite that person's death. These expectations relate most intensively to individuating, emotionally expressive features of the attachment object, such as facial expression, voice, and touch. Moreover, they are bound up with expectations of security, warmth, and mirth. Spikes of grief occur when these anticipations are violated by the realization of the person's death. Intense moments of grief are due not only to the gradient of change from strongly positive imaginations; they result also from the sudden disinhibition of anxiety. These spikes (thus activations of particular neuronal circuits) are facilitated by sorrowful or anxious moods (involving specific neurochemistry) and related emotional memories. At the same time, the spikes foster such moods and make relevant emotional memories more readily accessible. This account indicates that grief will occur most forcefully in situations where short-term expectations operate automatically and will not necessarily arise through the longer-term evaluations predicted by appraisal theory. This account also suggests why grief sometimes has an ideological function, being viewed—as in parts of *Hamlet*—as unmanly.[3]

NOTES

1. For simplicity, I am leaving aside some other factors that would enter into such an account of emotion, such as short-term and long-term habituation to potential emotion elicitors and critical period experiences that may affect the scope and specification of such elicitors.

2. To illustrate the difference between long-term and short-term expectations, which some readers have found confusing, we might take an example from outside grief. People may be aware that smoking is far more risky in the long term than flying. However, that long-term appraisal is likely to have no force in eliciting actual fear in a smoker. In contrast, the short-term anticipation of take-off in an airplane may produce a great deal of anxiety— due not to an appraisal of the situation, but, for example, due to the anticipated experience of being physically unsupported. Note that "long-term" and "short-term" here do not necessarily refer to distance in real time. They concern distance in imagined time. If someone has very strong imaginative capacities, he or she may be able to feel considerable anxiety imagining take-off for a flight that is months away. In my usage, the imagined take-off here is still "short-term," since it is imagined as an imminent concrete experience.

3. For further discussion of some of these issues, see Chapter 4 of Hogan 2011.

WORKS CITED

Akshoomoff, Natacha A., Eric Courchesne, and Jeanne Townsend. 1997. Attention coordination and anticipatory control. In *The cerebellum and cognition*, 575–98. Edited by Jeremy D. Schmahmann. San Diego, CA: Academic Press.

Barlow, Horace. 1999. Cerebral cortex. In *The MIT encyclopedia of the cognitive sciences*, 111–13. Edited by Robert A. Wilson and Frank C. Keil. Cambridge, MA: MIT Press.

Damasio, Antonio. 1994. *Descartes' error: Emotion, reason, and the human brain*. New York: Avon.

Goldin, Philippe R., Cendri A. Hutcherson, Kevin N. Ochsner, Gary H. Glover, John D. E. Gabrieli, and James J. Gross. 2005. The neural bases of amusement and sadness: A comparison of block contrast and subject-specific emotion intensity regression approaches. *NeuroImage* 27: 26–36.

Hoffman, Donald D. 1998. *Visual intelligence: How we create what we see*. New York: W. W. Norton.

Hogan, Patrick Colm. 2007. Sensorimotor projection, violations of continuity, and emotion in the experience of film. *Projections: The Journal for Movies and Mind* 1, no. 1: 41–58.

———. 2011. *What literature teaches us about emotion*. Cambridge: Cambridge University Press.

Ivry, Richard. 1997. Cerebellar timing systems. In *The cerebellum and cognition*, 555–73. Edited by Jeremy D. Schmahmann. San Diego, CA: Academic Press.

King-Casas, B., D. Tomlin, C. Anen, C. F. Camerer, S. R. Quartz, and P. R. Montague. 2005. Getting to know you: Reputation and trust in a two-person economic exchange. *Science* 308, no. 5718: 78–83.

LeDoux, Joseph. 1996. *The emotional brain*. New York: Simon and Schuster.

LeDoux, Joseph, and Elizabeth A. Phelps. 2000. Emotional networks in the brain. In *Handbook of emotions*, 157–72. Edited by Michael Lewis and Jeannette M. Haviland-Jones. 2nd ed. New York: Guilford Press.

Oatley, Keith. 1999. Emotions. In *The MIT encyclopedia of the cognitive sciences*, 273–75. Edited by Robert A. Wilson and Frank C. Keil. Cambridge, MA: MIT Press.

———. 2004. *Emotions: A brief history*. Malden, MA: Blackwell.

Panksepp, Jaak. 1998. *Affective neuroscience: The foundations of human and animal emotions*. New York: Oxford University Press.

———. 2000. Emotions as natural kinds within the mammalian brain. In *Handbook of emotions*, 137–56. Edited by Michael Lewis and Jeannette M. Haviland-Jones. 2nd ed. New York: Guilford Press.

Pulvermüller, Friedemann. 2002. *The neuroscience of language: On brain circuits of words and serial order*. Cambridge: Cambridge University Press.

Schore, Allan N. 2000. Attachment and the regulation of the right brain. *Attachment and Human Development* 2, no. 1: 23–47.

Shakespeare, William. 1987. *Hamlet*. Edited by Edward Hubler. New York: Signet.

———. 1987. *Macbeth*. Edited by Sylvan Barnet. New York: Signet.

van Leeuwen, Cees. 2002. Perception. In *A companion to cognitive science*, 265–81. Edited by William Bechtel and George Graham. Oxford: Blackwell.

CHAPTER 6

THE LITERARY NEUROSCIENCE OF KAFKA'S HYPNAGOGIC HALLUCINATIONS: HOW LITERATURE INFORMS THE NEUROSCIENTIFIC STUDY OF SELF AND ITS DISORDERS[1]

AARON L. MISHARA

I. BACKGROUND: THE NATURAL VS. HUMAN SCIENCES

Cognitive and clinical neuroscience face very real problems about the nature of the human self, how we define and study "self," and how we treat individuals when the mind, or brain, becomes so disordered that the experience of self becomes disrupted.[2] Although we are generally equipped with commonsense folk-psychological views about self and how we experience other selves, which help us get by in everyday situations, the self has turned out to be exceptionally difficult to define, operationalize, and study in neuroscience and related disciplines. Many researchers in the fields of cognitive science and neuroscience refer to the ability to recognize self in the mirror or make judgments that indirectly involve oneself as evidence of self, but this is one-sided. Much of the self-awareness literature confuses mediated self-reference of higher-order cognition with being a self. It addresses the self as object (having a self), not self as subject (being a self). By overlooking this conceptual distinction, self-reference (representational content about self or self-awareness, i.e., self as object) is confused with "being a self" (for example, Gusnard 2005). The current exclusive focus on self as object ("self-representation," rather than subject of the experience) in neuroscience has its roots in the nineteenth-century division between the natural and human sciences.[3]

The "human sciences" (*Geisteswissenschaften* [German translation of J. S. Mill's "moral sciences"]) are based on the *"understanding"* of the "meaningful connections" between historical events, whereas the *natural sciences* find causal *explanations* between postulated natural entities (Mishara 2007b). Figure 1 indicates that natural sciences generally proceed from larger, often nebulous wholes, seeking explanatory relationships between ever-smaller, strictly de-

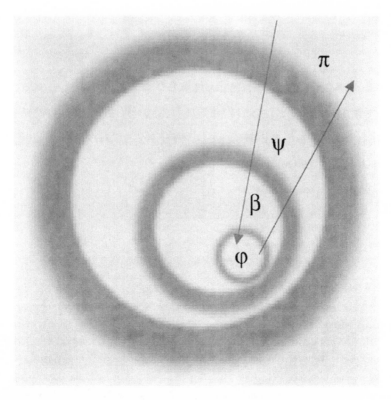

FIGURE 1. Methods of the natural human-historical sciences. Opposed
directionality between explanation (arrow pointing toward smallest circle)
and understanding (arrow pointing from smallest circle) indicate the methods
of the natural and human historical sciences, respectively. Natural sciences
proceed in terms of the "classic reductionist hierarchy" from sociology to
psychology to biology, chemistry, and physics. They generally proceed from
larger, rather nebulous wholes to seek explanatory relationships between
ever-smaller parts of these wholes. Conversely, understanding is contextual
by situating parts in ever-greater wholes, even if these totalities are ultimately
unavailable to the individual perspective but transcend or "encompass" it.
Each discipline requires an "abstraction, reduction to and idealization" (i.e.,
naming; Husserl) of the "objects" or entities of its discipline (which exclude
the objects of neighboring disciplines). Gray areas between disciplines
indicate interdisciplinary relationships that are often more fuzzy, involving
destabilizing relationships within intradisciplinary vocabulary and concepts.
φ, physis (φύσις), physical-natural sciences; β, bios (βίος), biological
sciences; ψ, psyche (ψυχή), psychological-cognitive sciences; π, polis (πόλις),
historical-cultural sciences. (Mishara 2007a, 564; figure 1) Reprinted with
permission from Wolters Kluwer.

fined parts of these wholes. Explanation (for example, causal/mechanistic, statistical/probabilistic, or functional/teleological) tries to establish relationships between subcomponent parts. Conversely, the historical-human sciences generally move "upward" from partial views to ever-larger contexts for understanding the matter at hand.[4]

Any claim to unify the natural and human sciences is burdened by seemingly insurmountable problems. These include the integration of two opposite directions of method as depicted in figure 1, the effort to make the contextual "understanding" of subjective experience somehow "objective" and also testable in the terms of natural scientific explanation—that is, in terms of cognitive and neural processes and mechanisms. However, I make the unconventional claim (requiring justification) that Kafka's literary writing provides data about the structure of the human self. That is, it documents processes that are not limited to the individual's experience of self in its historical context or the individual's "autobiographical" memory, but reflect the very structure of human self as a transformative process of self-transcendence (in symbolic dream images) with its own neurobiological underpinnings—that is, the rudiments for a discipline, "literary neuroscience." Literature documents and records cognitive and neural processes of self with an intimacy that is otherwise unavailable to neuroscience.

Such an approach is phenomenological. Founded by the mathematician turned philosopher Edmund Husserl (1859–1938), phenomenology is the rigorous, methodical description of conscious experience and how the general mental structures derived from its descriptive method may be disrupted in neuropsychiatric disorders and anomalous conscious states. In its step-wise method, phenomenology approaches literary texts as providing "data" about the general structures of consciousness and anomalous states.[5] By offering theoretically neutral descriptions of subjective experience (as far as this is humanly possible), it provides a way out of the nineteenth-century dilemma of studying human self as *either* object or subject. However, its results are provisional and may be refined by more phenomenological investigation or until tested with the experimental methods of neuroscience.[6]

II. WHY IS THE DOUBLE A GHOST? A CHILD?

Let us start with Kafka's early story "Unhappiness" (1910) to *demonstrate the structure of doubling* (that is, of the writer's self in the protagonist[7] and then a further doubling of the protagonist in the characters he encounters).[8]

In "Unhappiness," the narrator begins, with an approaching November evening, that he finds things unbearable [*unerträglich*]. He turns away from the window where the street lamps' sudden *illumination* startles him. Turning to the *interior* of his room, he finds a new goal to pursue in the depths of his own *mirror* [*im Grund des Spiegels*]. This turning away from the artificial light of the streets to the dark interior of his own room and then his mirror suggest that he is turning inward to examine the "depths" of his own self. The mirror provides no answer to his loneliness and he lets out a scream in order to hear it but no one will answer. The scream meets no resistance to reduce or stop it, even after it has already become silent (suggesting that the scream does nothing to diminish the pain which gives rise to it). As if in response, however, the door opens from the wall [*aus der Wand heraus*] and horses attached to wagons rise [*sich erheben*] in the air. At that moment a small ghost, a child, enters from a completely dark corridor where the lamps are still unlit. She is blinded by the room lit by dusk [*Dämmerung*] and covers her face. The narrator states that "in short, this visit, though I had expected it, was the one thing needful" (1983, 391).

Many of our themes are announced: loneliness, turning inward, the mirror, and the scream portending the sudden appearance of a double.[9] The narrator and his double (that is, the child-ghost) experience an oversensitivity to light (photophobia),[10] and the transformed, dreamlike, twilight state [*Dämmerungzustand*][11] of the narrator reflects Kafka's own state as a writer. Notably, the ghost is born in this moment of need, of loneliness, the searching of inner depths in a mirror, giving rise to a cry without resonance or echo, which never reaches an audience. The fact that this unusual visit was somehow "expected" by the narrator gives it a dreamlike quality. Even though the narrator reports bizarre, unusual events (the ghost, the elevated horses), he does so with the same matter-of-factness as recounting ordinary experiences during waking consciousness. As a result, these unusual turns of events are presented as expected or at least not surprising. In this respect, Kafka's narrative resembles a dream.[12]

Once the ghost enters, the (lonely) narrative transitions into a dialogue between narrator and ghost. As in many Kafka stories, the protagonist and the figure(s) he encounters are inextricably related, as if different parts of the same person. Although the narrator states that the visit was expected, he questions the ghost, asking whether she is really looking for him as so many people live in the building. However, the ghost's responses make clear that their relationship is beyond the ordinary. She states, "[N]o stranger could come nearer to you than I am already by nature" (1983, 393), thus suggesting her intimate relation to him as hallucinated double. The narrator then protests, "Your nature is mine and if I feel friendly to you by nature, then you mustn't be anything else" (1983, 393). That is, he insists that his double mirror him and not the converse.[13]

After asserting himself, the narrator goes to a night table and *lights a candle*. Since no further dialogue follows, the narrator has presumably released himself from the apparition (through lighting the candle, the previous verbal self-assertion, or their combination). He leaves and meets a neighbor on the stairs to whom he reports that he has seen a ghost. The narrator tells the neighbor (insightfully) that his real fear does not concern the ghost but "what caused the apparition" (1983, 394).

III. HOW DOES THE "BRAIN" PRODUCE HALLUCINATIONS OF A DOPPELGÄNGER?

Let us compare this story with an actual clinical case of seeing a double (what is termed "autoscopy"): [14]

After visiting the grave of her recently deceased husband, a 56-year-old, retired schoolteacher returns home. Upon opening the door, she senses that someone else is in the house occupied only by her. In the twilight-lit room, she sees that another woman is standing in front of her. As she lifts her right hand to turn on the electric light, the figure makes the same movements with her left hand so that their hands meet. She remarks that her own hand feels cold and bloodless from the contact. (Mishara 2010a; paraphrased from Lukianowicz 1958)

As in Kafka's "Unhappiness," the scene is poorly lit and occurs at dusk. It involves a mirroring of the patient's motoric body[15] in that the double anticipates or preempts the subject's intention to switch on the light.

In his diary, Kafka describes looking in a mirror. Once again, the lighting is poor. The evening light [*Abendbeleuchtung*] comes from behind and outlines a darkened face which is "unbelievably energetic, but perhaps only because it was observing me, since I was just observing myself and wanted to frighten myself" (1976, 247). The English translation is misleading. The original German states only that the mirror-face "was observing" (not that it "was observing me"), that is, that the mirror face was observing Kafka observing himself.[16] The mirror image takes on an independence from Kafka. As now a third perspective, it observes Kafka's relationship to himself—that is, a further doubling which "observes" Kafka's own split relationship with himself.[17]

In Kafka's *The Metamorphosis* (1912), Gregor Samsa (suggesting through

the ordering of the consonants and vowels Kafka's own name) finds himself—
after awakening one night from uneasy dreams—transformed into a vermi-
nous, gigantic insect. While his terrifying form [*Schreckgestalt*] clearly repels
others, it becomes useful for Gregor (1983, 131). It exempts him from the expectations that others impose on him. Having not yet seen him, his family and
the firm's chief clerk are eager to get inside his bedroom with the sole purpose of pressing him to return to his obligations to them. Inside the room,
the transformed Gregor speculates on their reaction once they see him: "he
was eager to find out what the others, after all their insistence, would say at
the sight of him. If they were horrified then the *responsibility would no longer be
his* and he could stay *quiet*. But if they took it calmly, then he had no reason
either to be upset, and could really get to the station for the eight o'clock train
if he hurried" (1983, 98; my emphases). Since the second alternative is highly
implausible, his transformation exempts him from his *responsibility* to support
the family.

Aware of its powerfully repellant effects on others, Gregor is alienated from
his own body image (as it is imagined to appear to others). Gregor's motoric
body, that is, body-schema, experienced within as agent-subject (Mishara
2004), is also compromised. First, his "numerous little legs . . . never stopped
waving in all directions . . . which he could not control in the least" (1983,
92). Second, "Weakness arising from extreme hunger, made it impossible to
move" (1983, 132). The Kafka short story "A Country Doctor" (see below)
also describes an incapacitated motoric body (not unlike the muscular paralysis [atonia] of REM sleep dreaming and the sleep paralysis of narcolepsy). The
transformed Gregor also has sensitivity to light, which he avoids (as the protagonist and his ghostly double in "Unhappiness").

Gregor stops eating and sleeping to hasten the encroaching death of his
hateful body.[18] In the end, he is just a "thing" [*Zeug*] disposed of by an elderly
charwoman. Gregor's father prevents the charwoman from explaining how
she disposed of Gregor, and the rest of the family appears indifferent. For
the others around him, Gregor becomes an object, a body stripped of human
subjectivity.

The claustrophobic conflation of the narrator's and protagonist's perspectives, or the doubling of the author as protagonist, who in turn confronts
doubles during the course of the narrative, are common features in Kafka's
stories. The protagonist is the closest double to Kafka himself and, as sur-
rogate, is the primary means by which Kafka reaches the reader. Therefore,
we will want to clarify why the protagonist's body as the narrator's double
(in what I claim to be its hidden reflexive relationship to the writing process
which creates it) is found to be unsubstantial and is eventually destroyed.[19]

The Metamorphosis begins with Gregor's transformation around Christmas and ends with Gregor's death around Easter. The timing is critical for understanding the story and we will return to its possible meaning.

IV. DOES LONELINESS INDUCE THE SOCIAL NETWORK IN THE BRAIN TO BECOME MORE ACTIVE?

The psychological researchers Epley et al. (2008) have implemented studies which suggest that people who feel lonely or lack social connection tend to attribute human characteristics to nonhuman objects—for example, machines, pets, or transcendent "objects (such as God)." They "anthropomorphize" these objects "by inventing humanlike agents in their environment to serve as potential sources of connection" (114). The researchers conclude "those who lack social connection with other humans may try to compensate by creating a sense of human connection with nonhuman agents." When they manipulated the mood of healthy subjects by showing them frightening film clips (from *Silence of the Lambs*), the fearful subjects—compared with control subjects exposed to a non-fearful film clip—tended to see faces and fear-related stimuli in ambiguous, neutral drawings.

In a similar vein, individuals isolated for long periods (for example, mountaineers, explorers, sailors, and castaways) report a variant of the doppelgänger experience, the "feeling of a presence." The "double" is felt (but not seen) to be nearby, often at a *precise distance* from the subject (see Mishara 2010a). The brain's construction of otherness is activated by emotional states of loneliness and fear (including paranoid states and possibly psychosis). That is, the brain networks that are normally required for social interaction become activated on their own during states of deprivation and fear. Loneliness and other forms of social deprivation may induce the social networks in the brain (that is, those brain networks subserving social cognition) to become more active on their own, resulting in doppelgänger experiences or hallucinations, as Kafka's child-ghost. Let us examine how this might be the case.

The reduction of social connection leads to the construction of imaginary others. The deprivation of sensory stimulation leads to hallucination. Depriving healthy individuals of sight via blindfolding for prolonged periods leads to visual hallucinations (Pascual-Leone and Hamilton 2001). If blindfolding is sustained for a day or more, both simple hallucinations (bright spots of light) and complex hallucinations (faces, landscapes, ornate objects) result.[20] Visual and other hallucinations involve activity increases in the cortical areas that give rise to them (Merabet et al. 2004). Therefore, cortical excitability may be related to the auditory and visual hallucinations reported by patients with schizophrenia. This concurs with Hoffman's (2007) hypothesis of sensory/ social "deafferentation" (that is, reduction of sensory input) in schizophrenia. Hoffman et al. (2003) found that slow-frequency, repetitive transcranial magnetic stimulation (rTMS), which decreases the excitability of the underlying cortex, reduced the incidence and severity of treatment-resistant auditory hallucinations (when applied to the temporo-parietal region). Cortical hyperexcitability would be consistent with the deficits in GABA (the major inhibitory neurotransmitter in the brain) revealed by postmortem studies in schizophrenia patients (Lewis, Hashimoto, and Volk 2005). GABA levels have been shown to reduce within minutes of light deprivation (Boroojerdi et al. 2000).

V. WHAT RELEVANCE DO THESE NEUROBIOLOGICAL STUDIES HAVE TO KAFKA'S WRITINGS?

Kafka deliberately scheduled his writing during the night, during time when he was in a sleep-deprived state. It is also known that he drew from hypnagogic imagery in his stories (Born 1988). In his *Diaries*, Kafka describes his nocturnal writing as conducted "entirely in darkness, deep in his workshop" (Kafka 1965, 518; Kurz 1980). Writing without sleep enables access to unusual thoughts and associations which otherwise would be inaccessible: "How easily everything can be said as if a great fire had been prepared for all these things in which the strangest thoughts emerge and again disappear" (Kafka 1965, 293–94; my translation). With regard to this transformed state of consciousness, he writes, "[A]ll I possess are certain powers which, at a depth almost inaccessible at normal conditions, shape themselves into literature" (1973, 270). Similarly, Kafka writes in his *Diaries*, "Again it was the power of my dreams, shining forth into wakefulness even before I fall asleep, which did not let me sleep . . . I feel shaken to the core of my being and can get out of myself whatever I desire. It is a matter of . . . mysterious powers" (cited by Corngold 2004, 23).

Kafka's "fire" suggests a creative process that provides its own illumination even in darkness. It also suggests a state of cortical excitability (and resulting hypnagogic hallucinations) following Kafka's withdrawal from sensory/social stimuli coupled with sleep deprivation. Kafka longs for "complete stillness" (*The Metamorphosis*), eager to separate himself, while writing, from his argumentative family with whom he lived for a good part of his life. The protagonist of Kafka's short story "The Hunger Artist" "withdraws deep within himself paying no attention to anyone or anything" (Kafka 1983, 268; Kurz 1980). Kafka is avoidant of unnecessary stimulation, possibly due to severe headaches (Ekbom and Ekbom 2004). However, the withdrawal from photic and social stimulation is also prerequisite for *the self-induction of hypnagogic trances*. Kafka marveled at the automaticity of his own writing. In a letter to his future betrothed, Felice Bauer (whom he persistently tried to discourage from wanting to marry him, as evidenced by this letter), Kafka writes: "I have often thought that the best mode of life for me would be to sit in the innermost room of a spacious locked cellar with my writing things and a lamp. Food would be brought and always put down . . . outside the cellar's outermost door. . . . And how I would write! From the depths I would drag it up! Without effort! For extreme concentration knows no effort" (1973, 156). Here we find solitude, the reduction of sensory stimulation in the cell's darkness, and the automaticity (effortlessness) of the writing process. According to Kafka's own reports, he experienced writing (at least in its initial phases) as automatic, effortless, and informed by hypnagogic imagery.[21] When writing is effortless, it is the product of a *trance-state* called "flow," shown to facilitate optimal mental functioning (Csikszentmihalyi 1990). Kafka writes, "All I possess are certain powers which, at a depth inaccessible under normal conditions, shape themselves into literature" (1973, 270). In a letter to Max Brod, Kafka writes that it is "not alertness but self-oblivion [that] is the precondition of writing" (1958, 385). In another letter to Felice, however, Kafka introduces the relationship between his writing and death: "What I need for my writing is seclusion, not 'like a hermit,' that would not be enough, but like the dead. Writing, in this sense, is a sleep greater than death, and just as one would not and could not tear the dead from their graves, so I must not and cannot be torn from my desk at night" (1973, 279). In his stories "Unhappiness" and "The Warden of the Tomb," Kafka's writing gives rise to ghostly doubles. This process may reflect the excitation of brain areas responsible for social experience of others and possibly hypnagogic hallucinations. But why does Kafka connect writing with death?

VI. WHY DEATH? THE UNFINISHED INNER JOURNEY, CAUGHT BETWEEN WORLDS

In Kafka's story "A Country Doctor," which unfolds like a dream, a doctor is prepared for a journey [*reisefertig*] to treat a seriously ill patient some ten miles away. His horse, however, has died *during the night* due to *overexertion*. As he stands in the courtyard, he finds himself more and more *unable to move* [*immer unbeweglicher werdend*] and the snow starts to cover him. The previous irreversible changes during the night and current immobility (both recalling *The Metamorphosis*) describe Kafka's own being transfixed by the hypnagogic imagery he records (but also shapes) while writing. The doctor then kicks at the rotting, broken door of his pigsty, which had been unused for years, in an absent-minded [*zerstreut*] manner (perhaps again reflecting Kafka's own trance state). From these small quarters, a man, crouching, emerges, *crawls out on all fours*, and asks whether he should hitch the horses. The man, a servant, is often interpreted as representing the doctor's or Kafka's primitive, instinctual side. *However, he is also somehow acquainted with the doctor's thoughts and wishes without the doctor having to express them* (Kurz 1980, 120). In a dream (or fictive narrative), all characters are to a certain extent projections of the dreamer's (or author's) own mind. Therefore, the figures as expressions of the same self should, in principle, have access to the thoughts of any other character. We see a similar feature in paranoid delusions and autoscopic hallucinations in which another (for example, the autoscopic double) has access to one's own thoughts and intentions (Mishara 2010a, forthcoming).

If the servant at first helps the doctor, he becomes impertinent and bites the face of a servant girl. The doctor warns: "You're coming with me . . . or I won't go, urgent as my journey is" (1983, 221). In response, the servant claps his hands and the doctor's carriage is carried away by the horses like a piece of wood in a strong current [*wie Holz in die Strömung*]. The doctor's ineffectiveness and ultimately passive role, which only increase as the story develops, are not unlike those of a dreamer who suffers the automaticity of the dream's events.

The doctor then encounters a second double quite different than the servant, a young male patient, who, without shirt, places his arms around the doctor's neck and addresses the doctor as "*Du*." These are unusually familiar gestures for a first meeting. The ensuing dialogue occurs like a "conversation with oneself" [*Selbstgespraech*] (Kurz 1980, 125). The youth asks the doctor to let him die, but the doctor believes there is nothing wrong with him. However, once the doctor sees his wound and its fatal seriousness, the youth, "quite blinded by the life within his wound," reverses his request: "Will you save me?" (1983, 224). The family and village elders strip the doctor of his clothes and place him next to the boy on the side of his wound. Their bed also has the meaning of a coffin (see figure 2).[22] The sharing of the bed with the youth, the symbolism of self-generation of the wound, the youth's reversal of attitude from wanting to die to wanting to live all suggest the rebirth of the self, a journey which neither the doctor nor any of Kafka's characters, who find themselves (precisely as *fictional* stand-ins for Kafka himself) on unending journeys (for example, the Hunter Graccus, the Bucket Rider), are able to complete.

Not addressed in the secondary literature, the wish for rebirth underlies

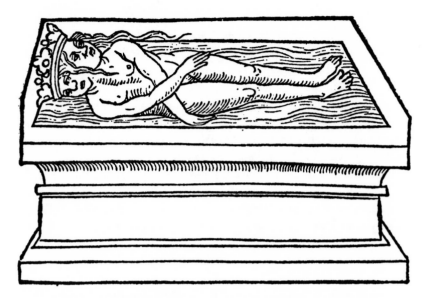

FIGURE 2. Woodcut from the alchemical work *Rosarium Philosophorum* (1550) indicating one of the stages in the alchemical process: the Tomb. This resembles the strange union between the doctor and his patient in Kafka's "A Country Doctor," which is at once dying and being reborn.

Kafka's writings as if the writing were itself a kind of rebirth of self accomplished through its hypnagogic-doubling process. Gregor's metamorphosis begins at Christmas (Christ's birth) and ends with his death around Easter (Christ's resurrection). Kafka's symbolic images of journey or rebirth indicate a threshold between worlds or mental states. To experience rebirth through writing, through the spontaneous, symbolic self-transformation of hypnagogic imagery, requires a different mental state, a trance state open to the unconscious, symbolic formation of images as an inner (transformative) "journey" of the self (for example, Jung 1969).

VII. QUEST FOR WHOLENESS: NARRATIVE AS DOUBLING SELF

The structure of the self is organized in terms of its relation to others (intersubjectivity). For Husserl (1959), intersubjectivity is possible through doubling one's experience as "body-subject" (in German, *Leib*, related to *leben*, to live). "This is so because my body is already always there in the perceptual field as body-subject" (Husserl 1959, 62; my translation). My body serves as the prototypical body-subject [*Urleib*] for how I experience others as embodied whereby I attribute to others the same inner relationship to their bodies as I do to mine. *Intersubjectivity is a doubling process*. Others are doubles of my embodied self. It is not surprising that loneliness or fear induce the social network in the brain (responsible for my experience of other minds) to actively produce imaginary doubles of the self. The cognitive neural mechanisms underlying the self as a process which spontaneously produces hypnagogic images of doubling have their basis in Husserl's theory of embodied intersubjectivity, an alternative to the prevalent theory of mind construct in cognitive psychology (Mishara, Parnas, and Naudin 1998).

The fictional narrative (as a hypnagogic-doubling process and underlying neural activity) symbolizes its own incompleteness by not being able to impart the subjective self (as it is experienced on the inside) to an audience.[23] Kafka's imagery symbolizes the structure of self as a process of self-transcendence which is condemned to remain incomplete or partial. In existential philosophical theory of self, I can only paradoxically become myself by giving up who I just was a moment ago. The "I" must let go the "me" in terms of an ongoing process of "self-transcendence." The child-ghost (in "Unhappiness") refers to the process of symbolic self-transformation through the hypnagogic image as one reborn (a child) but also one which first requires a symbolic death (the ghost).

Previously I have written that narrative enables healing (of trauma) by a process of self-transcendence (Mishara 1995). The subjective self splits into an "I" who narrates the experiences of a "me" who is in turn embedded in the unfolding scenes of the narrative. That is, the narrating "I" is both same and different than the "me" it surpasses in each narrative act. One's self—as totality in the ongoing switching but connecting between (unconscious) body schema and (conscious) body image—eludes conscious awareness but also makes the transcendence of the (painful) past possible. I have indicated elsewhere (Mishara 2007a, 2007b) that the ongoing switching between body-schema (agentic "I") and body-image (social "me") may be mapped onto underlying neural pathways.

Narrative is the ability to frame imaginary time within real time. By focusing and narrowing the audience's or even the narrator's attention to scenes in imaginary time (that is, away from the present context of embodied-sensory experiencing), narrative induces a trancelike state.[24] Narrative entrancement is common to all the arts, including performance and visual arts where language is not the primary experience. This ability is thought to have emerged pre-linguistically during the period of *Homo erectus* by means of what Donald (1991) calls "mimetic culture"—that is, the ability to tell stories through gesture and dance before language abilities evolved. Whether the details of Donald's account of cognitive evolution turn out to be correct is not critical to the current argument. Here I wish only to emphasize the human body's ability to double itself in mimetic narrative as both the current body express-ing *and* the symbolic content it refers to (for example, one's own body crawl-ing like a panther). This occurs in the trance-like context of the narrative and is a very early form of experiencing the embodied self from both internal and external viewpoints—that is, as doubled. When we speak, gesture, or write, we are simultaneously recipients and witnesses of our own communicative efforts. We hear our own voice and partially see our bodily gestures. That is, we take an external, doubled perspective on ourselves to communicate with others (see Mishara 2009). Moreover, the structure of self as symbolized in the imagery of rebirth is common to many forms of healing (for example, narra-tive approaches, shamanism, hypnosis, meditation, and mindfulness therapy) which deliberately induce an altered state of consciousness in terms of the underlying neurocircuitry of the social brain (Mishara and Schwartz 2011).

CONCLUSION

In summary, the structure of the self is vulnerable to doubling. This doubling occurs during anomalous states of consciousness (where reflection is minimal and where trance-like, dream-like single-mindedness prevails). It involves the structure of self as intersubjective. The reduction of social connection leads to the construction of imaginary other(s). However, the hypnagogic imagery also reveals the self to be self-transcendent in terms of the symbolic imagery of "rebirth." The literary data considered in this essay reflect a change of con-sciousness that has its neurobiological correlates in increased cortical excit-ability of a social network (activated during states of sensory deprivation, social deprivation, or sleep deprivation). Even when attempting to access the first-person perspective, current neuroscientific research is too restrictive in that it studies the self as object or representation. Literature informs the neuroscientific study of self with an intimacy that is otherwise unavailable to neuroscience because the structure of self (as self-transcending process—that is, as both subject and object) is captured in a literature which reflects its own creative process in hypnagogic symbols.

NOTES

1. A modified version of this essay appeared with the title "Kafka, Paranoic Doubles, and the Brain: Hypnagogic vs. Hyper-Reflexive Models of Disrupted Self in Neuropsychi-atric Disorders and Anomalous Conscious States" in *Philosophy, Ethics, and Humanities in Medicine (PEHM)* 5, no. 13; http://www.peh-med.com/content/5/1/13 (accessed April 14, 2011).

2. "Cognitive neuroscience" contains the terms "mind" and "brain," respectively. These

terms remain imprecise due to a fundamental ambiguity that we are both minds—that is, being selves (with so-called first-person experience), and brains or bodies—that is, having selves (with third-person perspective). The experienced body and implicated neural pathways are comprised by both a motoric body (proprioceptive body-schema)—the "I" (as agent), and perceptual-body (exteroceptive body-image)—the social "me," united provisionally and *fragilely in reflective conscious experience* by an interoceptive body (the "mineness" of this relationship). "Mineness" is disrupted in hallucinations of a double or doppelgänger. The verbal descriptors "I," "me," and "mine," however, are only approximations of the underlying neural processes (Mishara 2004, 2007a, 2010a).

3. The nineteenth-century dilemma is reflected in what Levine (1983) and numerous philosophers following him call the "explanatory gap" between neural processes and qualia, that is, what it is like to experience phenomenal states.

4. Understanding is contextual by situating parts in greater wholes, even if these totalities are not directly available to the individual perspective but transcend or "encompass" it (Jaspers 1955). For example, the historical-human sciences themselves stand in a historical process, which is at the same time the object (as contextual totality) of their study (Gadamer 1993).

5. Phenomenological psychiatrists and researchers (for example, Binswanger, Buytendijk, and Tellenbach) justify their use of literature as a source for phenomenological "data" by providing the structures of healthy (and abnormal) consciousness. Phenomenological research, following Husserl, calls this methodical step imaginative variation in an effort to find what is invariant about the underlying meaning structure. (For phenomenological step-wise method, see Mishara and Schwartz 1997; Uhlhaas and Mishara 2007; Mishara 2010a.) For the phenomenological study of unconscious processes, see Mishara 1990, forthcoming.

6. Recent efforts to apply phenomenological methods to describe the first-person perspective as "pre-reflectively self-aware" (a position I label "neo-phenomenology") oversimplify the problem. First, a phenomenological method reflects on experience; since reflection is retrospective to the experience it reflects on, there is no reflective access to putative immediate self-awareness without knowing whether reflection itself has transformed the experience. Second, the methods of neuroscience are only able to measure subjective processes and experiences in terms of the subject's responses (verbal, nonverbal, or neural). Even neural responses involve a "delay" in real time as measured by fMRI, PET, EEG, etc. Therefore, there is no experimental access to this putative construct that supposedly "constrains" the very methods which are unable to test it. "Neo-phenomenology" claims that any reflective grasping of self-awareness "must" have been preceded by an "immediate" pre-reflective experience. This relies on a putative "memory" of the original experience constructed in the reflection, and resembles a dog chasing its own tail (see Mishara 2007a, 2010b). Therefore, the construct can neither be established in phenomenological reflection nor falsified with scientific method, and thus is not able, as its proponents claim, to "constrain" neuroscience. Unlike Sass (a proponent of this neophenomenological approach), who claims that Kafka presents "the most vivid evocation of schizophrenic experience in all of Western literature" (cited in Mishara 2010b), I do not "explain" Kafka's writing in terms of putative but ultimately indemonstrable psychopathology. For a critique of recent "neo-phenomenological" efforts to unsuccessfully leap over the explanatory gap between human and natural science approaches to the mind-body problem, see Mishara 2007b, 2010b.

7. In Kafka's work, there are various ways that the writer's self is doubled in the pro-

tagonist. For example, the narrator's and protagonist's perspectives may collapse into one another. That is, the narrator's purview may be limited to that of the protagonist so that we experience everything from the point of the protagonist (see *The Trial* and *The Castle*). Frequently the protagonist is named some variant of Kafka's own name, such as "K" or "Josef K." The protagonist's name in Kafka's *The Metamorphosis*, Gregor Samsa, resembles Kafka's own name (*Samsa* = *Kafka*), and the Hunter Gracchus in Kafka's story with the same name also suggests the name Kafka (*Kavka* in Czech means "Jackdaw," whereas *graccio* in Italian means "Crow's caw or call"). That is, the protagonist stands in for the author as a double, but starts to take on a life of his own.

8. This second type of doubling has been emphasized in the previous literature on doubles in Kafka. The twin helpers in Kafka's *The Castle*, the narrator's stroll with his new acquaintance in "Descriptions of a Struggle" and the two "small white celluloid balls" which seem to pursue the protagonist in "Bloomfield, the Elderly Bachelor" are the most-cited examples of doubling in Kafka's work. Pertinent to the current discussion, the two balls appear at that moment when Bloomfield, in his loneliness, expresses the wish to have a "companion, someone to witness" his daily activities (see the discussion below of how social deprivation or lack of feelings of social connectedness can itself give rise to hallucinations of ghostly doubles by activating the networks in the brain subserving social cognition).

9. The mirror is locus of both self and double.

10. Curiously, the light of streetlamps and the dusk (which are not particularly intense sources of light) cause discomfort first in the narrator and then in the ghost. We do know that Kafka suffered from severe, possibly cluster headaches (Ekbom and Ekbom 2004), which may, in part, explain his tendency to withdraw from excessive stimulation.

11. The word "dusk" [*Dämmerung*] refers both to the transitional light between day and night when the ghost arrives and the narrator's (writer's) state of consciousness, a "twilight-state" (in German, *Dämmerungszustand*).

12. Dreaming has been characterized as "single-minded" (Rechtschaffen 1978). In waking consciousness, we usually are able to reflect on, compare, or recall experiences or thoughts apart from the current one we are experiencing. It is not that these processes are completely excluded during dreaming—a counterexample is lucid dreaming. It is rather that they are massively attenuated so that dreaming is "isolated" from other capacities or functions of consciousness. One finds a similar inability to transcend one's current perspective, to reflect on, monitor or consider alternative views in acute psychosis of schizophrenia. As in dreaming, one is trapped in the "now" (see Mishara 1995, 1997, 2007a).

13. For the hallucinated double in doppelgänger (autoscopic) hallucinations as stranger and intimate in neurologic disorders and anomalous conscious-states (for example, dream states) and for the struggle of who "mirrors" whom, see Mishara 2010a.

14. Autoscopy (from the ancient Greek, "seeing oneself") is a loosely related complex of experiences in which one sees or experiences a "double" as external to one's current vantage point. These hallucinations may occur in epilepsy, brain tumors, schizophrenia, depression, intoxication, dissociative experiences, and hypnagogic/hypnopompic hallucinations, and in individuals with high fantasy proneness. Literary authors often describe autoscopy (e.g., G. D'Annunzio, F. Dostoevsky, J. W. v. Goethe, E. T. A. Hoffmann, G. de Maupassant, A. de Musset, E. A. Poe, J. P. Richter, P. B. Shelley, R. L. Stevenson), many of whom experienced autoscopy themselves.

15. However, the double moves her left arm symmetrically to the patient's, as in a mir-

ror. This suggests that the perceptual body image is also involved. The two experiences (and underlying neural systems) of body, one motoric (proprioceptive), the other perceptual (exteroceptive), have been called in the neurologic literature "body-schema" (the agentic "I") and "body-image" (the social "me") (Mishara 2004, 2007a). When we look at a mirror we see only the perceptual body (the body as we see or imagine it from outside) reflected in terms of a left-right reversal: when I move my right arm, the mirror-double moves his left. As the perceptual body image, the mirror image is computed in allocentric, object-centered coordinates. If the double, however, moves the contralateral arm to me (for example, his right arm, when I move my right arm), then the double is engaging my motoric body (moving in the same egocentric, body-centered coordinate reference frame in which I move my own body, the body schema as agentic "I") and indicates a "deeper," more engaged hallucinatory involvement with the self. Interestingly, although more convincing, the motor doubles are much less lifelike than the perceptual mirror doubles and tend to be colorless, pale, transparent, cloudy, misty, or ghostlike. In contrast, the perceptual-body-image autoscopy, predominantly involving lesions to visual-occipital areas of the brain, is generally more vivid and brightly colored. However, the motoric double (often involving parietal and tempo-parietal junction areas) is experienced as more convincing than its perceptual counterpart. The view that the more motoric, body-schema autoscopy may be delusional (or dreamlike) is supported by the fact that this form of autoscopy can lead to death or suicide through fighting with or trying to free oneself from one's double (an I-I rather than the mirror-like I-me relationship of body-image autoscopy) (Mishara 2010a).

16. "[W]ar er nur beobachtend, da ich mich eben beobachtete" (Kafka 1984, 342).

17. If the motoric body is implicated, the hallucinatory double takes independence from the self and anticipates the subject's actions. One's own self is experienced as correspondingly passive, as if the double were usurping or preempting the sense of self as an empowered agent (Mishara 2010a). Unlike the mirroring in visual autoscopy which involves body image, the motoric, body-schema autoscopy is characterized by the feeling that one (ironically) becomes the mirror image of the double, who usurps the feeling of being the "real self." There may be a feeling of oneness with the hallucination, as if the two terms ("self" and "double") are "emotionally linked," share a "feeling of belonging," or complete one another.

18. "The decision he must disappear was one that he held to even more strongly than his sister, if that were possible" (1983, 135).

19. The protagonist's body is destroyed in other Kafka stories (for example, "The Hunger Artist," "In the Penal Colony," "The Bridge").

20. Experimental light deprivation temporarily induces Charles Bonnet Syndrome (the experience of complex visual hallucinations, often accompanying visual degeneration). Similarly, subjects who participated in Lilly's "isolation-tank" (sensory-deprivation) experiments (floating in darkness immersed in saltwater at body temperature) reported vivid hallucinations.

21. While Kafka was writing, the psychoanalyst Herbert Silberer (1909) conducted introspective experiments. Sleepy one afternoon, Silberer struggled to think through a philosophical problem. To his astonishment, the dream images that had appeared while he was dozing off (hypnagogic hallucinations) represented the concepts he had just been considering but now were in pictorial, visual form. Encouraged by this, he conducted introspective experiments of exerting cognitive effort while falling asleep. He concluded that the hallucination "puts forth 'automatically' . . . an adequate symbol of what is thought (or felt)

at a given instant" ([1909] 1951, 196). Of the example of falling asleep while thinking through a solution, Silberer later admits that this "forces a problem into a preconceived scheme." It is followed by the hypnagogic-symbolic image: "I am pressing a Jack-in-the-Box into the box. But every time I take my hand away it bounces out gaily on its spiral spring" (204). Silberer interprets the hypnagogic image to be "autosymbolic." Its content refers to the thought process, mental function or feeling in conscious awareness that just preceded it before falling asleep. It occurs in the "transitional," "twilight" state between sleep and waking in which hypnagogic/hypnopompic images are spontaneously produced. Critically, the autosymbolic hallucination requires that the subject is unaware at the time that his or her own mind is producing it or its symbolic meaning.

22. As in Kafka's fragment, "I Was a Visitor among the Dead." In Jung's (1969) analysis of the woodcuts in the alchemical work *Rosarium philosophorum* (1550), one of the stages in the alchemical process is depicted as two figures, King and Queen, who are joined into one figure in a tomb in a similar manner to the strange union between the doctor and his patient in "A Country Doctor" (see figure 2).

23. Kafka's story "An Imperial Message" suggests the hopelessness of the subjective self ever reaching the audience by means of the narrative text. Despite the athletic efforts of the king's messenger to deliver a message from the *dying* king to the reader ("you"), "still he is only making his way through the chambers of the innermost palace; *never will he get to the end of them.* . . . But you sit at your window when evening falls and dream it to yourself" (1983, 5; my emphases). The writer and his audience have only language to convey subjective experiences. Dreaming, however, with its common neurobiological mechanisms, transcends the division between our minds encapsulated by the physical body, but remains a private universe (*idios kosmos*) (Binswanger 1957; Mishara 1997).

24. The anthropologist Lévi-Strauss (1963) describes the shaman's practice of placing a tuft of down into his mouth, biting his own tongue, and then spitting out the bloody feather as if it were the pathological "foreign body" extracted from the patient. To cure the patient, he places the patient and the surrounding audience into a trance but, like the narrator, he must put himself into the same trance — that is, somehow believe his own "performance" — to be convincing.

WORKS CITED

Binswanger, L. 1957. *Schizophrenie*. Pfullingen, Germany: Neske.

Born, J. 1988. *"Daß zwei in mir kämpfen" und andere aufsätze zu F. Kafka*. Wuppertal: Wuppertaler Broschüren zur Allgemeinen Literaturwissenschaft.

Boroojerdi, B., L. G. Cohen, O. A. Petroff, D. L. Rothman. 2000. Mechanisms of light deprivation-induced enhancement of visual cortex excitability. *Society for Neuroscience Abstracts* 26: 821.

Corngold, S. 2004. *Lambent traces, Franz Kafka*. Princeton: Princeton University Press.

Csikszentmihalyi, M. 1990. *Flow: The psychology of optimal experience*. New York: Harper and Row.

Donald, M. 1991. *Origins of modern mind: Three stages in the evolution of culture*. Cambridge, MA: Harvard University Press.

Ekbom, T., and K. Ekbom. 2004. Did Franz Kafka suffer from cluster headache? *Cephalalgia* 24, no. 4: 309–11.

Epley, N., S. Akalis, A. Waytz, and J. T. Cacioppo. 2008. Creating social connection through inferential reproduction: Loneliness and perceived agency in gadgets, gods, and greyhounds. *Psychological Science* 19, 2: 114–20.

Gadamer H-G. 1993. *Truth and method*. 2nd ed. Translated by J. Weinsheimer and D. G. Marshall. New York: Continuum.

Gusnard, D. A. 2005. Being a self: Considerations from functional imaging. *Consciousness and Cognition* 14, no. 4: 679–97.

Hoffman, R. E. 2007. A social deafferentation hypothesis for induction of active schizophrenia. *Schizophrenia Bulletin* 33, no. 5: 1066–70.

Hoffman, R. E., K. A. Hawkins, R. Gueorguieva, N. N. Boutros, F. Rachid, K. Carroll, and J. H. Krystal. 2003. Transcranial magnetic stimulation of left temporoparietal cortex and medication-resistant auditory hallucinations. *Archives of General Psychiatry* 60, no. 1: 49–56.

Husserl, E. 1959. *Erste Philosophie, 1923/24, II, Theorie der Phaenomenologischen Reduktion*. The Hague: Martinus Nijhoff.

Jaspers, K. 1955. *Reason and existenz*. Translated by W. Earle. New York: Noonday Press.

Jung, C. G. 1969. *The psychology of the transference*. Translated by R. F. C. Hull. Princeton, NJ: Bollingen.

Kafka, Franz. 1958. *Briefe 1902–1924*. Edited by Max Brod. Frankfurt am Main: S. Fischer Verlag.

———. 1965. *Diaries: 1910–1913*. Translated by J. Kresh. New York: Schocken Books.

———. 1973. *Letters to Felice*. Translated by J. Stern and E. Duckworth. New York: Schocken Books.

———. 1976. *The Diaries: 1910–1923*. Edited by Max Brod. New York: Schocken Books.

———. 1983. *The complete stories*. Edited by N. Glatzer. New York: Schocken Books.

———. 1984. *Tagebücher 1910–1923*. Frankfurt am Main: Fischer-Taschenbuch-Verl.

Kurz, G. 1980. *Traum-schrecken, Kafkas literarische existenzanalyse*. Stuttgart: J. B. Metzlersche Verlag.

Lévi-Strauss, C. 1963. The sorcerer and his magic. In *Structural anthropology*, 167–85. New York: Basic Books.

Levine, J. 1983. Materialism and qualia: The explanatory gap. *Pacific Philosophical Quarterly* 64: 354–61.

Lewis, D. A., T. Hashimoto, and D. W. Volk. 2005. Cortical inhibitory neurons and schizophrenia. *Nature Reviews Neuroscience* 6 (April): 312–24.

Lukianowicz, N. 1958. Autoscopic phenomena. *Archives of Neurology and Psychiatry* 80: 199–220.

Merabet, L. B., D. Maguire, A. Warde, K. Alterescu, R. Stickgold, and A. Pascual-Leone. 2004. Visual hallucinations during prolonged blindfolding in sighted subjects. *Journal of Neuro-Ophthalmology* 24, no. 2: 109–13.

Mishara, A. L. 1990. Husserl and Freud: Time, memory and the unconscious. *Husserl Studies* 7, no. 1: 29–58.

———. 1995. Narrative and psychotherapy: The phenomenology of healing. *American Journal of Psychotherapy* 49, no. 2: 180–95.

———. 1997. Binswanger and phenomenology. In *Encyclopedia of phenomenology*, 62–66. Edited by L. Embree et al. Dordrecht, Netherlands: Kluwer Academic Publishers.

———. 2004. The disconnection of external and internal in the conscious experience of schizophrenia: Phenomenological, literary and neuroanatomical archaeologies of self. *Philosophica* 73: 87–126.

———. 2007a. Missing links in phenomenological clinical neuroscience: Why we are still not there yet. *Current Opinion in Psychiatry* 20, no. 6: 559–69.

———. 2007b. Is minimal self preserved in schizophrenia? A subcomponents view. *Consciousness and Cognition* 16, no. 3: 715–21.

———. 2009. Human ambivalence to body: Precondition for social cognition and its disruption in neuropsychiatric disorders. *Philosophy, Psychiatry and Psychology* 16, no. 2: 133–37.

———. 2010a. Autoscopy: Disrupted self in neuropsychiatric disorders and anomalous conscious states. In *Handbook of Phenomenology and Cognitive Science*, 591–634. Edited by S. Gallagher and D. Schmicking. Berlin: Springer.

———. 2010b. Kafka, paranoic doubles, and the brain: Hypnagogic vs. hyper-reflexive models of disrupted self in neuropsychiatric disorders and anomalous conscious states. *Philosophy, Ethics, and Humanities in Medicine (PEHM)* 5, no. 13, http://www.peh-med.com/content/5/1/13 (accessed April 14, 2011).

———. Forthcoming. The "unconscious" in paranoid delusional psychosis? Phenomenology, neuroscience, psychoanalysis. In *Founding psychoanalysis: Phenomenological theory of subjectivity and psychoanalytic experience*. Edited by D. Lohmar and J. Brudzinska. New York: Springer.

Mishara, A. L., and M. Schwartz. 1997. Psychopathology in the light of emergent trends in the philosophy of consciousness, neuropsychiatry, and phenomenology. *Current Opinion in Psychiatry* 10, no. 5: 383–89.

———. 2011. Altered states of consciousness as paradoxically healing: An embodied social neuroscience perspective. In *Altering consciousness: Multidisciplinary perspectives, volume 2: Biological and psychological perspectives*, 327–53. Edited by E. Cardeña and M. Winkelman. Santa Barbara: Praeger Press.

Mishara A. L., J. Parnas, and J. Naudin. 1998. Forging the links between phenomenology, cognitive neuroscience and psychopathology: The emergence of a new discipline. *Current Opinion in Psychiatry* 11, no. 5: 567–73.

Pascual-Leone, A., and R. Hamilton. 2001. The metamodal organization of the brain. *Progress in Brain Research* 134: 427–45.

Rechtschaffen, A. 1978. The single-mindedness and isolation of dreams. *Sleep* 1, no. 1: 97–109.

Silberer, H. [1909] 1951. Report on a method of eliciting and observing certain symbolic hallucination-phenomena. In *Organization and pathology of thought*, 195–207. Edited and translated by D. Rapaport. New York: Columbia University Press.

Uhlhaas, P. J., and A. L. Mishara. 2007. Perceptual anomalies in schizophrenia: Integrating phenomenology and cognitive neuroscience. *Schizophrenia Bulletin* 33, no. 1: 142–56.

LANGUAGE, LITERATURE, AND MIND PROCESSES

These essays relate to one of the main areas of study in cognitive literary studies, the investigation of how the linguistic features of poetry and narratives reflect and elicit mind processes. They constitute four different perspectives on the cognitive mechanisms involved in the creation and experience of verbal art. The first two studies revolve around one of the most important theories on the way we think, conceptual integration or blending (the creation of new meaning by integrating existing information). Focusing on poetic iconicity, Freeman shows us how the patterns of language that express live experiences depend on our feelings and attitudes, and argues for an inclusion of feeling, along with concept, when approaching literature through blending theory. Sinding takes the discussion to the realm of genre mixture, demonstrating how a cognitive approach based on conceptual integration can help us understand the complexity of genre transformations in their multiple dimensions and contexts. Fabb and Halle's theory of meter in poetry underscores the domain-specific processes behind counting in metrical verse, suggesting that there are connections among the mental abilities involved in literature, music, and aspects of language. Rice's essay explores the sense of experiencing a consciousness that is not our own when reading lyric poetry, pointing at the somatosensory aspects involved in our linguistic processing of motion verbs. His essay brings us back to the role of emotion in poetic art that Freeman introduced earlier in the section, while echoing the theme of the embodied mind's response to fictional narratives presented in Section III.

CHAPTER 7

BLENDING AND BEYOND: FORM AND FEELING IN POETIC ICONICITY

MARGARET H. FREEMAN

INTRODUCTION

A most important development in studies of human cognition has been the emergence of Fauconnier and Turner's (2002) Conceptual Integration Network theory, or "blending." The blending model accounts for many seemingly divergent phenomena, from talking donkeys to complex numbers. A significant achievement is the principled way in which it shows how new meaning can emerge from old information. The creation of meaning occurs through the metaphorical processes of mappings across different mental spaces. Thus cognitive metaphor becomes a crucial element in the construction of meaning. Blending is a theory still in process (as all good theories are), and a great deal of research is currently taking place to elaborate and extend blending to include art in general and literary forms in particular (Turner 2006; see his webpage).

Focus on conceptual metaphor and blending reveals cognitive processes common to both logical reasoning and imaginative creativity. This is an important step both in revealing the integral role of imaginative creativity in human cognitive processing and in providing a basis on which one might explore what makes aesthetic creativity "special." Although I explore aesthetic creativity in literature, the development of a cognitive theory for literature might apply to a theory of art in general (Langer 1953, 1967).

The questions I raise in this essay, then, deal with how blending theory is being developed to include consideration of the arts, and what is needed to enable the theory to encompass literary imagination. I argue for a special understanding of what I call "poetic iconicity," that is resultative, not causal, and not representational, as in "copy," but an aesthetic iconicity achieved through full symbolic representation in order to capture and express the relationship between form and feeling in creating a semblance of precategorial reality (Merleau-Ponty [1945] 1962, 1968). This semblance occurs through an integration of the processes of motivation, isomorphism, and imitation (or mimesis)—and the terms "motivation," "isomorphism," and "imitation" are in themselves complex and understood in somewhat different ways in current iconicity research (Iconicity website and Freeman 2007). I suggest that the opportunity for poetic iconicity arises when the isomorphic structures of the generic space that enable blending to occur depend on *metaphoric* schemas (Freeman 2011). Poetic iconicity is achieved when the conceived feeling of being emotionally engaged in the present moment of lived experience is expressed through form in creating the complex blend that is the poem as a whole (Freeman 2005).

I. BLENDING: AN OVERVIEW

One problem in blending theory is identifying the motivating principles that determine what gets selected for the various mappings across mental spaces to occur. The answer, I believe, lies in the role of feeling in formulating thought, in initiating what is generally known as "value-driven selection." Feelings arise from the interaction of two sources: sensations, from the external world through the five senses, and internally generated physiological sensations and emotions. In this way we both act upon and are acted upon by our environment as we develop mental concepts. The role of feeling in creating meaning is not accounted for in the original blending model. Nor is the notion of form, except for a very sketchy treatment of structure in the generic space.

The term "cognition" initially referred to mental conceptualization and reasoning. However, increasing evidence points to a more integral relationship among the various brain processes involving perception, memory, emotion, intuition, etc., in the way we think. As a result, the term "cognitive" has been broadened to include all aspects of brain-mind functioning, including emotion. Some critics have assumed that emotion arises from cognition, an assumption known among psychologists as appraisal theory (Ortony, Clore, and Collins 1988; Scherer, Shorr, and Johnstone 2001). More recent research, however, has acknowledged the primacy of the emotions in *forming* cognition (Damasio 1999; Frijda, Manstead, and Bem 2000). For literary texts, the challenge of determining the role of the emotions has been taken up by, among others, Gibbs (1994, 1999), Miall (2006), Robinson (2005), Tsur (1992, 1998, 2003, 2008), and van Peer (2008). This research has focused primarily on readers' emotional responses to literary works, though Robinson and Tsur also explore the emotional qualities of the text itself. There are three points of entry for feelings in a literary text: the author's initial motivation, symbolic conception within the text, and the text's affect upon the reader.[1]

Brandt and Brandt's (2005) semiotic modification of the blending model incorporates the notion of feeling in motivation, symbolic conception, and affect. The advantage of the Brandts' model is that it includes feeling as a dynamic schema at various points in the discourse situation, from the point of view of both originator and respondent. Its disadvantage lies in losing the generic space that enables structural mappings among spaces to occur. In order to account for poetic iconicity, both form and feeling need to be incorporated into the blending model.

1. BLENDING AND ICONICITY

Studies of iconicity in the arts have usually adopted one of two perspectives: iconography or iconology. Iconography refers to an intentional (not arbitrary) relation between the elements of the art medium and the images or ideas expressed through them. In music, for example, the ascending scale of the repetitions of the phrase "We are climbing Jacob's ladder" in the gospel hymn simulates the ascending movement of the climbers. Poetry can simulate both aural and visual relations—aural as in Tennyson's (1847) line "murmuring of innumerable bees," where the phonetic sounds simulate the buzzing of bees, or visual as in Herbert's ([1633] 1992) "Easter Wings," where the poem's two stanzas form the shape of wings. Iconology refers to the study of the symbolic significance of these iconographic features in order to understand the societal attitudes underlying them. For example, Mitchell (2008) explores the elements of pictorial representations of Christ's Passion in the notorious photograph of the "Hooded Man of Abu Ghraib," which "transform" the photograph "into an indelible icon of what a Christian nation accomplished in its crusade to liberate the Middle East" (86).

The term "iconism" historically referred to the metaphorical quality of the icon. Although the term is not used much anymore, it points to the integral role metaphor plays in creating an icon. As already noted, metaphor is also a crucial element in blending. Hiraga (1994, 2005) was the first to apply blending theory to the relation between metaphor and iconicity in poetic texts. Following Peirce's theory of the icon as comprising image, diagram, and metaphor, Hiraga shows how iconic mappings occur, not simply through the rudimentary representation of auditory and visual images as in onomatopoeia and graphic design, but as diagrammatic components of meaning through structural and relational analogies.[2] Grammatical metaphor, in Hiraga's theory, thus becomes the bridge that links form and meaning.[3] Building on Hiraga's work, I explore how meaning that emerges as the result of blending becomes iconic in nature, through the metaphorical fusion of the material-medial modes of feeling, form, and function (Freeman 2007, 2008, 2009, 2011).[4]

2. BLENDING: FEELING, FORM, AND ICONICITY

Recent advances in blending theory and its relation to artistic creation, as represented in *The Artful Mind* (Turner 2006), provide a more complex and sophisticated account of the roles of emotion and form in the creation of meaning.[5] Thus, Deacon (2006, 41), noting that emotion and cognition cannot be dissociated, calls for an augmentation of blending theory in order to "link it to a theory of emergent emotional states—that is, to recognize the inescapable interweaving and interdependency of the dimensions of mind we divide into cognition and emotion." He sees blending as "the basic *iconic* interpretive process that allows symbols to be projected to novel referential roles" (my emphasis). Missing in his explanatory diagrams, however, is the interrelation of emotion and form. In a parallel vein, Lakoff (2006) focuses on form, not feeling. He explores the fact that "form has inferential structure" through his "cog hypothesis" that links sensory-motor components of the brain to neural processes: "Examples of cogs are aspectual schemas, image schemas, and force-dynamic schemas" (167). These schemas, Lakoff suggests, are what "give form to art" (154). They are, in my account, motivated by feeling. They are the structural links between the sensory and the emotional that engender meaning and significance. When they are metaphoric in function, iconicity may occur.[6]

Brandt (2006) deals with aesthetic evaluation. In the situational context of an observer looking at a painting, the presentation and reference spaces of the Brandts' semiotic blending model become respectively the two-dimensional physical form of the painter's brush strokes, color, and line, and the three-dimensional "scene, the landscape, the configuration of things that moved the painter's representational hand and mind" (182). The relation between the two spaces, Brandt argues, is one of both structural mapping and emotional resonance or "passion," resulting in a tension between presentation and reference that creates "the blend that our aesthetic sensitivity captures in its desire-based schema of attentional dynamics" with the impact of emotional response (181). The success of this dynamic tension in creating the blend constitutes aesthetic evaluation for the observer. Deacon's, Lakoff's, and Brandt's explorations of the role of blending in emotional, formal, and aesthetic effects in art are suggestive in their anticipation of the fusion of these elements in aesthetic or, specifically for the literary arts, poetic iconicity.

II. BEYOND BLENDING: POETIC ICONICITY

Blending theory explains the cognitive processes by which we integrate multiple aspects of our experience to achieve human scale. This conceptual integration ability developed in humans from aesthetic experience (Dewey [1925] 1981, [1934] 1987).[7] Johnson (2007, xi) defines aesthetic experience as "the vast, submerged continents of nonconscious thought and feeling that lie at the heart of our ability to make sense of our lives." Although Johnson recognizes that an "adequate" aesthetics of cognition must reach beyond the arts, it is with the arts that any exploration of what Langer calls "the mind feeling" must begin.[8] By exploring the cognitive dimensions that create art in all its forms, we may plumb the depths of the human capability to create meaning and significance. For poetry, this exploration takes two major forms: investigation into 1) the phenomenology of our lived experience as part of the external world, and 2) how our feelings and attitudes both motivate and structure the patterns of language to iconically express those lived experiences.

Matching language to experienced reality is the goal of all poetry. Even the so-called "language poets" wrestle with this task. Words are made to work, not to communicate meaning but to express a reality that lies beyond words. Hecht (1995, 130) describes poetry as capturing "the rich complexity of actuality—the unsimplified plenitude of the objective world"; Wordsworth ([1798] 1904) calls poetry the means by which we are able to "see into the life of things." Art has the capacity to conjure up the feelings of experiencing the concrete, precategorial world before the mind conceptualizes it into more generalized abstraction, what MacLeish (1926) infers by his statement that "A poem must not mean / But be." The matching of language to the forms of experienced reality is achieved through the ways in which our feelings and attitudes both motivate and structure the forms in which the language is expressed.

A poem achieves iconicity not simply by including iconic-aesthetic (iconographic) elements, but by making them interact within a web of words and ideas to create a semblance of reality that draws the reader in through the narrative strategies of suspense, curiosity, and surprise (Sternberg 2003a, 2003b). The meaning that emerges is, as Stevens (1965, 96) observes, "the sense that we can touch and feel a solid reality which does not wholly dissolve itself into the conceptions of our own minds."[9] The creative arts thus restore us to the primordial, precategorial experience of being part of the structure of reality through the processes of the imagination in individuating the feelings that structure the forms of material expression. Just as the artist uses the elements of paint, brush, and color to create the contours and lines of a painting, so the

poet uses the elements of sound, rhythm, and other linguistic features to create the rhythmic patterns, repetitions, and arrangements of a poem.

Artists and poets capture lived experience through the sensations and emotions that constitute feeling. As Coleridge (1817) notes, the poet "diffuses a
tone and spirit of unity, that blends, and (as it were) *fuses*, each to each, by that
synthetic and magical power, to which we have exclusively appropriated the
name of imagination." This human capacity to synthesize through fusion or
blending enables the poet to create through language a semblance, or icon,
of reality—not the reality that arises from our conceptualized representations
of the world, but the reality of our being part of Merleau-Ponty's (1968) "in-
visible" world, the immediate, always-fleeting present that forever escapes our
objectivizing gaze.

This, then, is what I mean by poetic iconicity. It is the ontological actu-
alization of being in the timeless moment of the perpetual present, achieved
through the cognitive processes of metaphorically blending the material-
medial modes of feeling, form, and function.

III. POETIC ICONICITY AT WORK

How the structural forms of metaphor are realized as feeling in linguistic
expression through blending the material-medial modes can be explored
through poetic analysis. Emily Dickinson's poetry characteristically makes
this iconic connection through a metaphoric blend that creates identity
among self, poem, and nature. Consider, for example, the following poem:

1   *I dwell in Possibility -*
2   *A fairer House than Prose -*
3   *More numerous of Windows -*
4   *Superior - for Doors -*

5   *Of Chambers as the Cedars -*
6   *Impregnable of eye -*
7   *And for an everlasting*
8   *Roof*
9   *The Gambrels [Gables] of the Sky -*

10 *Of Visitors - the fairest -*
11 *For Occupation - This -*
12 *The spreading wide my*
13 *narrow Hands*
14 *To gather Paradise -*
     H 106 Fascicle 22.11 F466/J657[10]

The poem's structural schema depends on a comparison between "Possi-bility" and "Prose," based on the metaphor of a physical house, defined by windows, doors, chambers, and roof. But what is the house a metaphor for? Had Dickinson written "I dwell in poetry, not prose," the comparison would be obvious. But in writing "Possibility," Dickinson invokes a different kind of comparison, plumbing the inferential meanings of the words, so that "Prose" may be understood to refer to the matter-of-fact, taken for granted, every-day commonplace events of experience, and "Possibility" to the potential that exists in reaching beyond the prosaic into the transcendental reaches of the creative imagination. In this sense, a poet dwells in possibility. The argu-ment of the poem is not simply that poetry is preferable to prose because it is better, but that "Poetry" creates a relation between us and the world that is not possible by limiting ourselves to "Prose." That relation is the achievement of *poetic iconicity*, as the house of possibility becomes the poem itself in all its iconographic manifestations in creating the semblance of a poetic, not pro-saic, self-world. In the following analysis I show how the blending of meta-phoric schemas structures the relation between the material-medial modes to create such poetic iconicity.

The prosodic features of a poem carry its emotional weight. That is, feeling becomes formulated when the motivations that inspired the poet are mani-fested through the selection of prosodic and linguistic features that result in the poem's poetic structure. An examination of that structure leads to the discovery of the metaphorical schemas (image, aspectual, force dynamic) that trigger the blending of the material-medial modes. In Dickinson's poem, these metaphorical schemas convey the positively valenced feeling of expansion (as opposed to contraction) that accompanies movement outward in order to gather in. The force-dynamic schema is comparative, realized through fictive motion in contrasting the seen and the unseen, inner and outer, less and more within a CONTAINER image schema.[11]

On the macro level, the poem's three stanzas set up the possibility of the CONTAINER schema: an outer frame of two enclosing an inner one. This frame is grounded by the opening words that contain the only main verb in the poem, "dwell," together with the preposition "in," and by the closing lines that refer to the subject persona's actions of spreading (out) and gathering (in). Several features support the idea of movement IN and OUT as schemas for this frame. First, each stanza repeats the pattern of the prepositions "of" and "for," all of which describe the constitution *of* and the purpose *for* the "house" *in* which the speaker dwells: stanza 1 has "of Windows" and "for Doors"; stanza 2 has "Of Chambers" and "for [a] Roof"; stanza 3 has "Of Visitors" and "For Occupation." The constituting *of* prepositional phrases all indicate a certain inwardness, the purposive "for" prepositional phrases a certain outwardness. Thus windows reflect the image of being inside looking out; chambers are described as being inside and unseen from without; visitors are seen as they come in. On the other hand, from inside, doors lead one outside; the roof is described as the outermost reaches of the sky; occupation is described as "spreading wide." The order of these prepositions thus reflects a progressive, recycling movement from IN (constitutive-seeing) to OUT (participatory-moving), a movement that culminates in the final climactic moment of spreading out to gather in.

Second, external features of nature in the middle stanza are introduced by an analogy between "Chambers" hidden inside houses and the dense "Cedars" outdoors blocking the eyes from seeing through them. The linguistic shift from simile to metaphor changes analogy to identity as the protective covering of a house roof becomes the "Gambrels [Gables] of the Sky -" so that the "fairer House" becomes external nature.

The schema of *moving outward* is reinforced by the schemas of LESS/MORE and MORE IS GREATER, both with respect to quantity ("more numerous of Windows") and quality ("Superior - for Doors - "), which also invoke the metaphorical schema of MORE IS UP. Moving up and out is what the poem does in the inner stanza as it expands the CONTAINER schema by moving the image of the house outdoors at the same time as it shifts perspective from looking out (of windows in stanza 1) to not being able to look in ("Impregnable of eye - "), and moving the image upward to the "Gambrels [Gables] of the Sky - ." This seemingly paradoxical movement outward inside the unseen recesses of "Chambers" and upward to the covering roof of the sky establishes the underlying metaphorical schema that governs the poem as a whole, the blending of the interior self with external nature. We cannot stand outside nature looking in if we are part of nature, no more than we can stand outside ourselves to look in at our interior self. As Dickinson says at the beginning of another poem: "Growth of Man - like Growth of Nature - / Gravitates within -" (F790/J750).

Perception (seeing) has to be connected to participation (moving) in order for the poet to grasp and contain this felt reality. The connection is created through the opening up that "Possibility" provides. This opening up is achieved through the way the metaphorical schemas described above blend the poem's material images with the medium of its prosodic forms, the crucial elements of a poem's emotional affects. Some of these affects, reflected in the poem's sound patterns, metrical stress placements, rhyme schemes, and line breaks, are described below.

1. THE METRICAL MOVE FROM LESS TO MORE

Although the poem ostensibly conforms to the hymn pattern of common meter, only half of the six eight-position lines realize all eight positions, and these occur in each of the three stanzas (lines 1, 7–8, 12–13). Of these three eight-position lines, line 1 has only two major stresses that reinforce the iambic pattern, both in the first half of the line, so that the line opens out to unrealized potentiality on the word "Póssibìlity -" (with Dickinson's open-ended marking indicated here by a hyphen further extending idea and feeling).[12] The other two lines increase both the number of realized major stresses from line 1 and the line count by placing "Roof" and "narrow Hands" on separate lines. Only two lines in the entire poem are regular both in the number and placement of stresses. It is not accidental that these lines occur after and before the framing first and last lines: the second line, "A fairer House than Prose -," refers to "Possibility"; and the penultimate lines, "The spreading wide my / narrow Hands," describe what "Possibility" enables the speaker to do. These lines contrast with each other in at least two ways that indicate movement from less to more: the number of positions in the line, from six to eight, and the arrangement of the lines, multiplying one into two.

The line breaks foreground the weak stress positions at line end, a characteristic that is also true of the other three eight-position lines that are missing their final syllable (lines 3, 5, 10). These lines also occur in each of the three stanzas, all contain the constituting prepositional *of* phrases—"of windows," "of chambers," "of visitors"—, and all end on the seventh, weak position so that the final strong position is occupied by a stress rest (that is, unrealized by a linguistic morpheme), prosodically inviting the idea of openness to potentiality that was introduced by "Possibility" in the opening line of the poem.

The effect of displacing metrical position across two lines in the last two stanzas creates double emphasis, both on the words before and after the line breaks, namely "everlasting / Roof" and "spreading wide my / narrow Hands," which also reinforce the MORE IS GREATER, MORE IS UP, and MORE IS MOVING OUT schemas, as well as the schema of an expanding CONTAINER, in conceiving of the sky as a roof and the narrow self spreading wide.

2. THE PHONETIC MOVE FROM
CONTRACTION TO EXPANSION

On the micro level, sound patterning simulates the metaphorical schemas. The three words that begin with the capitalized letter "P" are "Possibility," "Prose," and "Paradise," all occurring at line end, with "Possibility" and "Paradise" beginning and ending the poem. "Prose," which comes between them, and what is being compared with them, is monosyllabic as against the polysyllabic, less rather than more. The polysyllabic words also differ from the monosyllabic by opening up to a vowel after the [p] onset. The vowels move in quality, from the open back position in "P*O*ss" to front rounded position in "Pr*O*se" to open central in "P*A*r," a movement from open to less open to even greater opening at the end, a progression that indicates the need to move out, then in, in order to achieve a greater movement out, a progression that the three stanzas as a whole create. It is like the force-dynamic action of exerting some energy (stanza 1), then withdrawing somewhat into one's inner resources (stanza 2) to enable the exertion of even greater energy (stanza 3). The r that closes off the p from the following vowel in "P*R*ose" is moved away from the p by the vowel in "P*A*radise," and that is not all. All three words contain [s], though contrasting: it is voiced in "Pro*Z*e," another opposition to the unvoiced "s" in both "Po*SS*ibility and Paradi*S*e," and moves from the first syllable in "Possibility" to the last in "Paradise," thus creating in the increasing distance between [p] and [s] an even further extension and opening up of sound as the poem concludes.

The demarcation of the second stanza as being "inside" the outer two is marked both by the material images of "Chambers" and "Roof" that enclose and cover, and by a formalized change in the patterning of closed and open sounds. The unvoiced sound [p] occurs three times in the first and last stanzas and only once in the inner stanza. In contrast, its voiced counterpart [b] occurs once in the first stanza (in "Possibility") and three times in the inner stanza, in "Chambers," "Impregnable," and "Gambrels [Gables]." The voiced consonant [m] also occurs in these three words (though not in the variant "Gables"). The consonants [p], [b], and [m] are the only three in the English sound system that are formed with both lips together, a closing as opposed to an opening up. The choice of the word "impregnable" seems fortuitous in bringing together the unvoiced and voiced sounds [p], [b], and [m] in a word that implies the existence of what is hidden, unseen. Its association with the open sound [ai] in the phrase "impregnable of eye" marks the move from closed to open. This stanza is also the only one to realize perfect rhyme in the six-position lines of the poem, on "eye" and "Sky," which are the only two words at line end, along with "my" in the last stanza and "possibility" in the first, that end in open vowels. The short [i] of "Possibilit*Y*" thus opens up, in the inner stanza, to the most open sound in English phonetics—the diphthongized [ai]—as the images of the poem move outdoors to the "Cedars" and the "Sky." The schemas of this stanza pair off in complex patterns: "Chambers": "Cedars"; "Impregnable": "eye"; "Roof": "Sky." The effect is to create a blend of house, self, and nature.

The final stanza creates a climactic movement of form, as it brings together the patterns of the preceding stanzas. The comparative "fairer" in the first stanza becomes the superlative "fairest" in the last, a move from MORE to MOST. The capitalized "- This -," set off both by its position at line end and the markings that separate it from the rest of the sentence, suggests a deictic reference to the poem itself as well as referring anaphorically to the "Possibility" of line 1 and cataphorically to the final lines of the poem. The closed rounded "PrOse" in the first stanza moves to the open-ended vowels of [ae] and [ai]: "The spreading w*I*de m*Y* / n*A*rrow H*A*nds / To g*A*ther P*A*rad*I*se." The [ai], denoting both the "I" persona of the poem and the widest sound in English, surrounds and thus contains the [ae], which is the most open, giving the feel of an expanding CONTAINER schema. The emotive force of these prosodic and sound forms culminates in the greatest move of all, from indoors to outdoors, with the heavens of the "everlasting" sky to the gathering in of Paradise itself.

Paradise, Dickinson notes elsewhere, is the "Eden of God" (L234, Johnson 1965), and Eden is frequently her description for Nature: "Eden is that old fashioned House / We dwell in every day" (F1734/J1657). If "Prose" is the matter-of-fact, everyday life of the household, where "Occupation" consists in laying fires, setting clocks, dusting and sweeping, churning and baking, "Possibility" becomes the freedom of the garden, with bees, birds, and butterflies its fairest "Visitors," and "Paradise" the flowers the speaker gathers. However, this metaphorical schema goes further. The constitutive images of the house of possibility are "More numerous," "Impregnable of eye," and "the fairest." The purposive images are "Superior," "everlasting," and "Paradise." In each case, the movement IN to OUT from *of* to *for* increases the comparison with "Prose" to invoke images that transcend the everyday natural world. In Romantic terms, it is a movement from nature to Nature. The pun on the word "occupation," with its dual meaning of residing in a place (constitutive) and being engaged in activity (purposive), becomes the central focus or, in Chinese terms, the "eye" of the poem, capturing both the *of* that is constitutive and the *for* that is purposive, as the self is identified with Nature through poetic realization in the deixis of "- This -."

This "Nature" is the unseen reality of the self-world, hidden from us by the processes of human cognition that create a conceptual barrier between us and the primordial, precategorial world, Paul Eluard's *autremonde*, that John Burnside (2005, 60) describes as

that nonfactual truth of being: the missed world, and by extension, the *missed self* who sees and imagines and is fully alive outside the bounds of socially-engineered expectations—not by some rational process (or not as the term is usually understood) but by a kind of radical illumination, a re-attunement to the continuum of objects and weather and other lives that we inhabit.

Poetry, as all art, thus connects us to that "in-visible" world that is present as an underlying reality to our "socially-engineered expectations." In fusing the constitutive, the IN (seeing) and the purposive, the OUT (moving), Dickinson's poem presents the poem's persona as becoming one with Nature. By fusing the world of nature, the consciousness of the self, and the writing of poetry in a metaphoric blend, Dickinson makes them iconic of each other and her poetry an icon of (her) reality.

CONCLUSION

In the compressions of its complex blendings, poetry offers both challenge and opportunity for exploring in more depth the way the human mind engages in cognitive integration, cognitive in both concept and feeling. As Dickinson's poem—and its extension in the way her poetics reveals the connection between self and nature—shows, integration is not simply conceptual but cognitive, a matter of meaning, feeling, and form. If blending is to fully account for literary creativity, the role of feeling in motivating the blending of the material-medial modes needs not only to be recognized but modeled.

What makes art special is not the cognitive processes that enable us to make sense of our world and our lives, but how they are exploited in order to put us in touch with the conditions of our emotional and sensuous experiences as participants in the world we share. No less than studies in the natural and the social sciences, studies in the arts are crucial if we wish to understand and map human cognition. Aesthetic evaluation enables us to determine the extent to which a given work of art successfully simulates those conditions in being iconic of reality. Aesthetics may thus be understood both in its philosophical sense of exploring the conditions of our sensuous and emotional experience *and* in its artistic sense of appreciating the nature of art in all its forms.

As cognitive researchers increasingly turn their attention to understanding how our emotional being is both a primary and necessary part of our rational being, the importance and significance of the integration of emotion and reason in the aesthetic dimension of the arts becomes more relevant to the perennial question, not only of what makes us human, but, being human, of what makes us the way we are.

NOTES

1. The emotion conceived by the author may not be the same as the emotion the reader experiences. I am not frustrated or angry at Casaubon's treatment of Dorothea in George Eliot's *Middlemarch*, though Will Ladislaw is. Recognizing *his* emotion, I rather empathize with him (Freeman 2009; see also Carroll 2010).

2. The term "image" is used in its philosophical sense as a conceptualization in the mind arising from any of the five senses. By "image," Peirce means the mental representation of sense perception that is abstracted from the singular and individual impressions of physical experience; by "diagram," he means the forms of relations that enable the mental representation of an image.

3. The dualistic notion of form and meaning (or content) as separate entities comes from their reification. That is, neither form nor meaning are entities. Both are dynamic processes: "form" produces the material realization of kinetic or dynamic relations that serve to differentiate the precategorial experience of the physical world; "meaning" results from the cognitive processes that draw significance from the differentiations caused by formal operations on undifferentiated or formless matter. Reification obscures the fluidity of form-meaning kineses. It occurs through the need for cognitive economy that results in naming. This cognitive economy has both advantages and disadvantages. Naming can aid in memorization and concept formation; through this very same process, however, it can block alternate ways of seeing. In an attempt to avoid the philosophical problems associated with terms such as "form," "content," "image," "diagram," "meaning," and so on, I adopt in this essay the term "material-medial mode" to indicate that in language the distinction between them cannot be characterized by simple division into substantial (content-related) and functional (structural) terminology (see note 4).

4. Following Wellek and Warren's (1956, 129) discussion of the problems associated with the form-meaning distinction, Tsur (2008, 639) proposes "a theoretical framework that proposes to do away with the form-content distinction." All contents, he says, including such elements as meaning, sound representation, imagery, and so on, are "materials" ("norms" in Wellek and Warren's terminology). "Structures," he says, "are the various combination of these norms." These combinations may be related to Fauconnier and Turner's "vital relations"—that is, such operations as categorization, comparison, identity, change, and so on. Since these structures mediate among norms or materials, I call them "medial modes."

5. Cognitive linguists have primarily focused on the language of emotion and metaphors for emotion but not so much on the cognitive processes involved (Geeraerts and Cuyckens 2007). A notable exception is Getz and Lubart's "Emotional Resonance Model" (2000). Mark Johnson's (2007) work calls for the need to reevaluate the role of aesthetics and emotion in human understanding.

6. Metaphorical schemas may be necessary but not sufficient conditions for iconicity. Whether iconicity can occur without metaphorical schemas as I am describing them still needs to be tested. Also involved is the perceiver's or reader's role in recognizing iconic emergence in making sense of the virtual blend (Brandt and Brandt 2005). Christina Ljungberg (personal correspondence), noting that for Peirce a sign must stand for something to somebody, comments that metaphoricity is "a form of iconic parallelism between the viewer/reader and the sender of the message which must 'excite in the mind of the receiver familiar images, pictures, reminiscences of sights, sounds, feelings, tastes, smells, or other sensations, now quite detached from the original circumstance' (C P 3.433)—which the sender assumes

are more or less the same but of course are not always, which is what makes communication asymmetrical and dialogic and a prototypical example of the generation of new meaning."

7. "Aesthetic" comes from the Greek *ἀισθε-*, "to feel, apprehend by the senses" (*OED*). In the eighteenth century, Baumgarten applied the term to "criticism of taste" considered as a science or philosophy; Kant insisted that the term be restricted, following the distinction between *αἰσθητά* and *νοητά*, to science dealing with sensuous perception. The quarrel between Baumgarten and Kant can be resolved by defining the arts as the sciences of sensuous (affective) experience (Gross 2002). Just as rational hypotheses in the natural sciences may be proven wrong, so affective representations in the arts may fail to capture the "truth" of lived experience. Thus evaluation plays an integral part in both.

8. Langer (1967, 243–44) notes: "No matter how complex, profound and fecund a work of art—or even the whole realm of art—may be, it is incomparably simpler than life. So the theory of art is really a prolegomena to the much greater undertaking of constructing a concept of mind adequate to the living actuality."

9. It is beyond the scope of this essay to explore the philosophical difficulties inherent in the term "reality." Wallace Stevens's quote captures Merleau-Ponty's phenomenological notion of precategorial experience that balances between subjective solipsism and objective mind-independent reality by recognizing that we are part, not mere observers, of the external, physical world (Freeman 2007).

10. Numbers attached to Dickinson's poems refer to the (F) Franklin (1998) and (J) Johnson (1955) editions. Quotes from letters are identified by the letter L (Johnson 1965). The manuscript (marked H) is archived at the Houghton Library, Harvard University. Line breaks follow the manuscript copy.

Reprinted by permission of the publishers and the Trustees of Amherst College from *The Poems of Emily Dickinson*, variorum ed., edited by Ralph W. Franklin, Cambridge, MA: The Belknap Press of Harvard University Press, copyright 1998 by the President and Fellows of Harvard College, copyright 1951, 1955, 1979, 1983 by the President and Fellows of Harvard College.

11. "Fictive motion" is Talmy's (2000a, 2000b) term for conceptual as opposed to physical movement. In the poem, Dickinson blends fictive and physical motion, so that the poem transcends its own containment to become an icon of the self-world. Conceptual schemas and metaphors are rendered in small capital letters in the cognitive literature to distinguish them from linguistic forms.

12. The word "Possibility" extends over five metrical positions so that three of its syllables fall on strong stress positions. As a lexeme with morphemic suffixes, it contains only one major stress. Although this stress would normally fall on the antepenultimate syllable, it shifts to the first syllable as a result of the pressure to accent *Pós-*, both because of its placement on a strong stress position and its alliteration with *Próse*. Because "everlasting" is a compound word, the fact that its original two major stresses (*éver* and *lásting*) fall on metrically strong positions reinforces the tendency to maintain their stress in spite of the tendency in conversational pronunciation to weaken the second stress (cf. Halle and Keyser 1971).

WORKS CITED

Brandt, Line, and Per Aage Brandt. 2005. Making sense of a blend: A cognitive-semiotic approach to metaphor. *Annual Review of Cognitive Linguistics* 3: 216–49.

Brandt, Per Aage. 2006. Form and meaning in art. In *The artful mind: Cognitive science and the riddle of human creativity*. Edited by Mark Turner, 171–88. Oxford: Oxford University Press.

Burnside, John. 2005. Travelling into the quotidian: Some notes on Allison Funk's "Heartland" poems. *Poetry Review* 95, no. 2: 59–70.

Carroll, Noël. 2010. On some affective relations between audiences and the characters in popular fictions. In *Art in three dimensions*. New York: Oxford University Press.

Coleridge, Samuel Taylor. 1817. *Biographia literaria*, chap. 14. Project Gutenberg. http://www.gutenberg.org/dirs/etext04/bioli10.txt (accessed April 14, 2011).

Damasio, Antonio. 1999. *The feeling of what happens: Body and emotion in the making of consciousness*. New York: Harcourt Brace.

Deacon, Terrence. 2006. The aesthetic faculty. In *The artful mind: Cognitive science and the riddle of human creativity*, 21–53. Edited by Mark Turner. Oxford: Oxford University Press.

Dewey, J. [1925] 1981. *Experience and nature. John Dewey: The later works, 1925–1953*, vol. 1. Edited by Jo Ann Boydston. Carbondale: Southern University Illinois Press.

———. [1934] 1987. *Art as experience. John Dewey: The later works, 1925–1953*, vol. 10. Edited by Jo Ann Boydston. Carbondale: Southern University Illinois Press.

Fauconnier, Gilles, and Mark Turner. 2002. *The way we think: Conceptual blending and the mind's hidden complexities*. New York: Basic Books.

Franklin, R. W., ed. 1998. *The poems of Emily Dickinson*, variorum ed. 3 vols. Cambridge, MA: The Belknap Press of Harvard University Press.

Freeman, Margaret H. 2005. The poem as complex blend: Conceptual mappings of metaphor in Sylvia Plath's "The Applicant." *Language and Literature* 14, no. 1: 25–44.

———. 2007. Poetic iconicity. In *Cognition in language: Volume in honour of Professor Elżbieta Tabakowska*, 472–501. Edited by Władisław Chłopicki, Andrzej Pawelec, and Agnieska Pojoska. Kraków: Tertium.

———. 2008. Revisiting/revisioning the icon through metaphor. *Poetics Today* 29, no. 2: 353–70.

———. 2009. Minding: Feeling, form, and meaning in the creation of poetic iconicity. In *Cognitive poetics: Goals, gains & gaps*, 169–96. Edited by Geert Brône and Jeroen Vandaele. Berlin: Mouton de Gruyter.

———. 2011. The role of metaphor in poetic iconicity. In *Beyond cognitive metaphor theory: Perspectives on literary metaphor*, 158–75. Edited by Monika Fludernik. London: Routledge.

Frijda, Nico H., Antony S. R. Manstead, and Sacha Bem, eds. 2000. *Emotions and beliefs: How feelings influence thoughts*. Cambridge: Cambridge University Press.

Geeraerts, Dirk, and Hubert Cuyckens, eds. 2007. *The Oxford handbook of cognitive linguistics*. Oxford: Oxford University Press.

Getz, Isaac, and Todd I. Lubart. 2000. An emotional-experiential perspective on creative symbolic-metaphorical processes. *Consciousness and Emotion* 1, no. 2: 89–118.

Gibbs, Raymond W. Jr. 1994. *The Poetics of mind: Figurative thought, language, and understanding*. Cambridge: Cambridge University Press.

———. 1999. *Intentions in the experience of meaning*. Cambridge: Cambridge University Press.

Gross, Steffen W. 2002. The neglected programme of aesthetics. *The British Journal of Aesthetics* 42, no. 4: 403–14.

Halle, Morris, and Samuel Jay Keyser. 1971. *English stress: Its form, its growth, and its role in verse*. New York: Harper and Row.

Hecht, Anthony. 1995. *On the laws of the poetic art*. Princeton, NJ: Princeton University Press.

Herbert, George. [1633] 1992. *The temple*. In *George Herbert: The complete English poems*. Edited by John Tobin. New York: Viking Penguin.

Hiraga, Masako. 1994. Diagrams and metaphors: Iconic aspects of language. *Journal of Pragmatics* 22, no. 1: 5–21.

———. 2005. *Metaphor and iconicity: A cognitive approach to analysing texts*. Basingstoke: Palgrave Macmillan.

Iconicity. Iconicity in language and literature. Olga Fischer and Christina Ljunberg. http://iconicity.ch/ (accessed Nov. 8, 2011).

Johnson, Mark. 2007. *The meaning of the body: Aesthetics of human understanding*. Chicago: University of Chicago Press.

Johnson, Thomas H., ed. 1955. *The poems of Emily Dickinson: Including variant readings critically compared with all known manuscripts*. Cambridge, MA: The Belknap Press of Harvard University Press.

———. 1965. *The letters of Emily Dickinson*. Cambridge, MA: The Belknap Press of Harvard University Press.

Lakoff, George. 2006. The neuroscience of form in art. In *The artful mind: Cognitive science and the riddle of human creativity*, 153–70. Edited by Mark Turner. Oxford: Oxford University Press.

Langer, Susanne K. 1953. *Feeling and form: A theory of art*. New York: Scribner.

———. 1967. *Mind: An essay on human feeling*. Baltimore: Johns Hopkins Press.

MacLeish, Archibald. 1926. *Streets in the moon*. Boston: Houghton Mifflin.

Merleau-Ponty, Maurice. [1945] 1962. *Phenomenology of perception*. Translated by Charles Smith. London: Routledge and Keagan Paul.

———. 1968. *The visible and the invisible*. Edited by Claude Lefort. Translated by Alphonso Lingis. Evanston: Northwestern University Press.

Miall, David S. 2006. *Literary reading: Empirical and theoretical studies*. New York: Peter Lang.

Mitchell, W. J. T. 2008. The fog of Abu Ghraib: Errol Morris and the "bad apples." *Harper's* (May): 81–86.

Ortony, Andrew, Gerald Clore, and Allen Collins. 1988. *Cognitive structure of emotions*. Cambridge: Cambridge University Press.

Robinson, Jenefer. 2005. *Deeper than reason: Emotion and its role in literature, music, and art*. Oxford: Oxford University Press.

Scherer, K. R., A. Shorr, and T. Johnstone, eds. 2001. *Appraisal processes in emotion: Theory, methods, research*. Oxford: Oxford University Press.

Sternberg, Meir. 2003a. Universals of narrative and their cognitivist fortunes (I). *Poetics Today* 24, no. 2: 297–395.

———. 2003b. Universals of narrative and their cognitivist fortunes (II). *Poetics Today* 24, no. 3: 517–638.

Stevens, Wallace. 1965. *The necessary angel: Essays on reality and the imagination*. New York: Vintage Books.

Talmy, Leonard. 2000a. *Concept structuring systems. Toward a cognitive semantics*, vol. 1. Cambridge, MA: MIT Press.

Talmy, Leonard. 2000b. *Typology and process in concept structuring. Toward a cognitive semantics*, vol. 2. Cambridge, MA: MIT Press.

Tennyson, Alfred Lord. 1847. Come down, O maid. In *The Princess: A Medley*. London: E. Moxen.

Tsur, Reuven. 1992. *Toward a theory of cognitive poetics*. Amsterdam: North Holland.

———. 1998. *Poetic rhythm: Structure and performance*. Berne: Peter Lang.

———. 2003. *On the shore of nothingness: A study in cognitive poetics*. Exeter, UK: Imprint Academic.

———. 2008. *Toward a theory of cognitive poetics*. 2nd expanded and updated ed. Brighton: Sussex Academic Press.

Turner, Mark. 2006. Blending and conceptual integration. http://markturner.org/blending .html (accessed April 14, 2011).

———, ed. 2006. *The artful mind: Cognitive science and the riddle of human creativity*. Oxford: Oxford University Press.

Van Peer, Willie, ed. 2008. *Linguistic studies in literary evaluation*. Amsterdam: John Benjamins.

Wellek, René, and Austin Warren. 1956. *Theory of literature*. New Haven: Yale University Press.

Wordsworth, William. [1798] 1904. Lines composed a few miles above Tintern Abbey: On revisiting the banks of the Wye during a tour, July 13, 1798. In *Wordsworth: Poetical works*, 163–65. Edited by Thomas Hutchinson and Ernest De Selincourt. Oxford: Oxford University Press.

CHAPTER 8

"A SERMON IN THE MIDST OF A SMUTTY TALE": BLENDING IN GENRES OF SPEECH, WRITING, AND LITERATURE

MICHAEL SINDING

INTRODUCTION

Some suggest that genre mixture may particularly mark the postmodern era (Luke 1994), but like observations apply to the Renaissance (Colie 1973) and the eighteenth century (Olshin 1971, 522; Hunter 1971, 631–32). Modernism inherited the Romantic opposition to essentialist and prescriptive views of genre (Duff 2000, 3–6); medieval genres evolved through shifts and mixtures (Jauss 1982); and classical genres were far less "pure" in practice than in theory (Farrell 2003). Indeed, we encounter genre mixture in everyday life, in the recent phenomena of e-mail, text messaging, etc. Somehow we grasp and get along with both the relative stability of genres, and their flexibility and regular mixture. While it is "an issue over which duels were once fought and blood once spilled" (Duff 2000, 6), Hayden White sees "mixture, hybridity, epicenity, promiscuity," and consequently an anti-essentialist historical approach as the rule now in genre studies (2003, 602). As genre mixture can define literary creativity, change, and history, and point up extraliterary contexts of texts, I take up Ralph Cohen's suggestion, to reexamine "generic combinations" with a view to "a generic reconstitution of literary study" (2003, xvi). I hope to complement historical approaches by treating genre mixture in terms of conceptual blending theory. This has the advantage of avoiding the disavowal of theory White cautions against, while helping cognitive criticism get more historical and cultural context in its diet. I propose a general model for genres, analyze a case of extraliterary-in-literary blending and its ramifications, and reflect on what genre principles are revealed.

Mikhail Bakhtin was especially fascinated with the novel's "wide and substantial use" of many extraliterary genres, including "letters, diaries, confessions," philosophical tracts, political manifestos, and more: "These phenomena are precisely what characterize the novel as a developing genre. After all, the boundaries between fiction and nonfiction, between literature and nonliterature and so forth are not laid up in heaven" (1981, 33). He developed a view of how this works: simple ("primary") genres of everyday life are assimilated into complex ("secondary") ones: "These primary genres are altered and assume a special character when they enter into complex ones. They . . . retain their form and their everyday significance only on the plane of the novel's content. They enter into actual reality only via the novel as a whole, that is, as a literary-artistic event and not as everyday life. The novel as a whole is an utterance just as rejoinders in everyday dialogue or private letters are (they do have a common nature), but unlike these the novel is a secondary (complex) utterance" (1986, 61).

Let us suppose that Bakhtin is talking, without knowing it, about conceptual blending. Like Bakhtin's genre dynamics, it too is an ordinary cognitive operation, and applies across the full gamut of dimensions here: domain of experience, communication media, scale, and aesthetic and social status (from the short rejoinder of everyday speech to the multivolume epic). Blending theory analyzes how simple, schematically structured input "mental spaces" interconnect and interact to create complex imaginative constructs. Blends begin with mappings across input spaces: selected input elements are mapped into a "blend space" (*composition*), while shared input structure is mapped into a "generic space." Then blend structure may be "filled in" from background knowledge (*completion*), and situations or processes in the blend may be simulated or "run" (*elaboration*). (For details, see Fauconnier and Turner 2002, and Turner's website.)

I. THE GENRE GENERIC SPACE

I begin by defining the "common nature" Bakhtin mentions as the "shared structure" common to input spaces that allows blending across genre boundaries to begin—the "genre generic space," so to speak. Because genres are highly complex and their members highly variable, they frustrate treatment in terms of the "classical" view of categories as definitions. They are far more amenable to cognitive category theory, and much is gained when we regard genres as schemas.[1] To do genres justice, we must consider them as "multidimensional schemas" (Steen 2002), or complex models—constellations of features at multiple levels.[2] I propose the following tentative model for genres of all kinds:

- *Sociocognitive Action Frame*: occasion, communicative purpose, social action context (including other genres)

- *Rhetorical Situation Frame*: setting, speaker, audience, medium
- *Discourse Structure Frame*:

> Extraliterary: sequence of discourse elements and relations (moves and steps), including form, speech act type, style, etc.

> Literary (Fiction): narrative (fictional rhetorical situation, story-world with settings, characters, actions), narration (order of narration, form, style, etc.)

Prototypically, each frame is embedded in the previous one, but they are separable, and this helps them to blend. The parameters of each frame are related in certain ways. In the sociocognitive action frame, the action is performed to achieve a purpose on an occasion, within a certain rhetorical situation. In the rhetorical situation frame, the speaker communicates to the audience via a certain medium in a certain setting, using a certain discourse structure. In the discourse structure frame, the discourse proceeds through a certain order, according to a certain form and style. The model gives us a set of parameters integrated from the micro level of linguistic patterning up to the macro and meta levels of participants and settings and the contexts of action and situation in which they participate.

Specific schemas have mandatory, default, and optional "settings" for their elements, which provide both flexibility and structure. Not all genres have all parameters specified, and both within and without literature some genres are "more formal" or fully specified (for example, the sonnet, the tax return) than others (for example, the novel, the essay). Genres may also have various primary (or essential) criteria: the encomium must be a certain speech act type (praise); the drama requires a certain rhetorical situation (the stage). I suspect that a certain level of structural detail is necessary for a genre to attain enough coherence to be recognized as a genre, and flexibility on some parameters will tend to be compensated for by fuller specification of others. So for example, the sonnet is easily recognizable by its stanzaic structure, regardless of topic (though it does have typical topics), whereas the novel has a much looser formal structure, and its subgenres are often characterized by topic (romance, mystery, etc.).

II. ADJACENT TOPICS, FIELDS, THEORIES

It is worth noticing that Bakhtin is one of very few links between extraliterary and literary genre research. Extraliterary genres are studied in rhetoric, applied linguistics, and discourse analysis. Carolyn Miller set the course here with her 1984 article "Genre as Social Action." That title captures the approach; more precisely, genres are "typified rhetorical actions based in recurrent situations" (1984, 158). Hence "communicative purpose" is the "privileged criterion" defining genre (Swales 1990, 58). Analysis typically links a highly standardized discourse structure of "moves" and "steps" to action in a social and institutional context (for example, "workplace," "academic," and "legal" genres) (Freedman and Medway 1994; Coe, Lingard, and Teslenko 2002). Literary studies often ignore the action frame, characterizing genres mainly in terms of discourse structure (that is, interrelated types of story, character, form, style: patterns of both story-world and narration) and "tradition"—although this may include fictional action and situation frames. The rare efforts to connect these theories turn up special problems: most importantly, literary genres do not clearly accomplish any communicative purpose in this sense. Partly because of that, I call this aspect "sociocognitive" (following Berkenkotter and Huckin 1993).[3] I hope a study of genre blending across boundaries will suggest new ways to bring these theories together, and also, by pushing the boundaries of genre categorization, discover something about the relative stability and variability of genre features and functions.

III. THE EXAMPLE

In 1760, Laurence Sterne became famous. He had published the first volumes of his great, rambling, satirical antinovel *Tristram Shandy*, which included the full text of a sermon he had preached ten years earlier, and a pitch for a collection of his sermons, which were published later in the year. Both novel and collection were enormously successful. Consider the history of versions of "The Abuses of Conscience Considered." It was first preached at York Minster Cathedral as the annual assize sermon on July 29, 1750. By request of the audience, it was published as a six-penny pamphlet on August 7, 1750. In December 1759 and January 1760, *Tristram Shandy* was published, and the sermon was incorporated into Chapter 17 of Volume 2. In 1766 it was incorporated as the final sermon (number twelve) of Volume 4 of Sterne's *The Sermons of Mr. Yorick, by Laurence Sterne* (Volume 1 was published on May 22, 1760).

Even to try to sketch how the sermon is interpolated in *Tristram Shandy* is to give an idea of the waywardness of narrative in the book. Trim, a young corporal and servant to retired Captain "Uncle Toby" Shandy, discovers the sermon's text accidentally in the pages of a military book Toby has sent him to retrieve, so that Toby can make a point in a discussion. Trim, Toby, Toby's brother Walter (father of Tristram), and Dr. Slop (the "man-midwife") are gathered in the parlor of Walter's house, Shandy Hall, awaiting the birth of Tristram. Trim reads the sermon to the group while they wait. His posture and voice, and the frequently interrupting reactions (physical, mental, verbal) of all present, are described in excruciating and ludicrous detail. When the sermon is over, Walter identifies the author as Parson Yorick, parts of whose story precede and follow the reading. Then the narrator (Tristram) announces "[t]hat in case this character of parson *Yorick*, and this sample of his sermons is liked," his family is "now in the possession of . . . as many as will make a handsome volume, at the world's service" (1978, 167).

IV. GENRE BLENDING IN COMPOSITION

To look at Sterne's genre blending, we need models for specific genres, beginning with the sermon:

COGNITIVE MODEL: SERMON

Sociocognitive Action Frame:

    Occasion: regular religious service, or special occasion

    Communicative Purpose: interpret scripture, apply meaning to lives of audience, exhort them to suitable attitude and behavior (possibly including ideology, politics)

    Action Context: call, invocation, hymns, affirmations, readings, prayers, dedication, benediction; with associated postures, such as standing, kneeling, sitting, bowing, etc.

Rhetorical Situation Frame:

    Setting: church; priest in pulpit before seated congregation

    Speaker: priest

    Audience: congregation

    Medium: spoken voice, using script or notes, posture and gesture

Discourse Structure Frame: Moves and Steps

    1. *Text*: scriptural verse; historical and textual context; interpretation

    2. *Development*: outlined headings; argument by reason and scripture; refutation of objections

    3. *Application*: emotional appeal to drive home points

    Form: approximately fifteen to thirty minutes long, relatively simple and clear style of language and delivery

Various readers may see differences in detail, and there are denominational and historical variations in this pattern. The point is that very many people know what sermons are, more or less, and schemas like this one represent that knowledge.[4]

Sterne and his culture knew this schema very well, largely from direct experience of a recurrent rhetorical situation. He preached often, and his talent won him prestigious invitations. There were treatises on all aspects of preaching, and very many examples in print. The interconnection among all frames and parts is more conscious for experts. Sterne's contemporary George Secker links purpose, situation, and style as follows: "Let your Sentences, and the Parts of them, be short, where you can. And place your Words so, especially in the longer, that your Meaning may be evident all the Way. For if [the audience] take it not immediately, they have no Time to consider of it, as they might in reading a Book: and if they are perplexed in the Beginning of a Period, they will never attempt going on with you to the End" (qtd. in Downey 1969, 110). Variations in one frame have ramifications for others: the Methodist focus on conversion experience led to much more passionate sermons than those of Sterne's Latitudinarian sect, which (not to exaggerate unduly) viewed religion as a kind of rational self-interest. Similarly, Sterne's sermons reflect his preference for sympathetic feeling over logic chopping. He dispenses with scholarly exegesis and formal divisions. He sometimes opens with an attention-grabbing challenge to his scriptural text—one famously declares "*That*, I deny" (see New, Davies, and Day 1984, 170; New 1996, vii–viii, xix). The text serves as a springboard to imaginative ethical reflection, via essayistic discussion and dramatic storytelling. They are quite short, and end abruptly.

I take it that the sermon *as preached* in 1750 embodied this schema pretty fully. But again, variant sociocognitive and rhetorical specifications shape specifications of discourse. The sermon "comments upon the inadequacy of human laws and the obligations to obey the higher, unwritten laws of reason and religion" (Cash 1975, 234). In the context of the "assizes"—the sessions of the "spiritual courts" to which Sterne belonged—it challenges the occasion, the audience of judges, legalistic attitudes, and Sterne's own institutional role. We also know Sterne modified what he borrowed from Swift, to suit the audience. We might speculate about *how* he delivered it: we know of his dramatic style, impersonations of characters, etc.; he might have improvised a peroration. Still, there is no difficulty fitting these details into the contours of the schema.[5]

The *pamphlet* sermon would also be easily recognized, but it bears on other genre dynamics and structure. Sterne adds a genre of "dedication" to fit the new situation: it tells of the original occasion from which the sermon is torn, and says that "the members of the Grand Jury . . . unanimously requested [it] be sent to the press" (234). This highlights the *diachronic* aspect of genre: it is a link in a chain of responses to situations. Processing this new medium requires knowledge of the original situation. But sociocognitive and rhetorical aspects (including functions) are also modified: it is sold in a bookshop, customers decide to buy it or not, and they peruse it at leisure, including perhaps rereading (as Secker saw), but there is no spoken delivery to augment its text. These shifts in the genre's *rhetorical* nature reflect larger shifts in history, culture, and technology. Downey (1969, 3) observes that this was "the first time in the history of preaching" that written and read sermons "gained ascendancy over" the spoken "direct appeal to the audience." This shift is an aspect of the genre context so far-reaching as to be a "form of life."

Turning to *Tristram Shandy*, to see how the sermon blends in, we need a novel model (again, approximate not exhaustive):

COGNITIVE MODEL: NOVEL

Sociocognitive Action Frame:
  Occasion:
    Production: individual initiative, artistic ambition, "to be fed/famous," etc.
    Reception: individual enjoyment, study, etc.
    Communicative Purpose: imaginative, entertaining, reflective, ideological, etc.
  Action Context:
    Production: reading, planning, writing, publishing; income, fame, etc.
    Reception: SHORT-TERM: buying, reading, responding (feeling, reflecting, discussing, reviewing, communicating with author, imitating, etc.); LONG-TERM: studying, teaching, library distribution/lending, editing, annotating, etc.
Rhetorical Situation Frame:
  Setting: decision of writer and reader; often private
  Speaker: individual writer
  Audience: readers, many kinds, any number (across space and time)
  Medium: printed book
Discourse Structure Frame:
  Fictional Narrative: story-world (settings, characters, action); plot subgenres (life story, love story, journey, philosophical quest, etc.)
  Narration: conventions depend on subgenre—for example, comic/tragic; realistic/stylized; fictional genre and narrator (memoir, journal, treatise, letters, etc.) or self-conscious fiction and narrator; form and style (plain, parodic, etc.)

This too would have been quite familiar to Sterne's audience. His parody of almost every part of the rhetoric and discourse frames here depends on his audience knowing the schema well.[6]

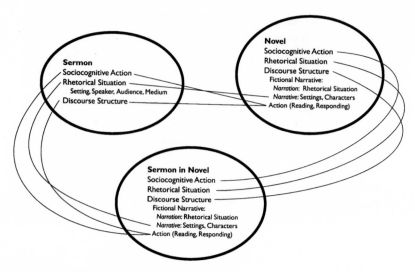

FIGURE 1. Genre Blend: Sermon in Novel 1

Next we indicate how Sterne connected elements of sermon and novel and projected them into his blend (see Figure 1). (For the sake of clarity, I leave out the generic space and show only categories of structure.)

The following schema specifies the blended space alone—that is, what happens in and around the sermon-reading scene:

GENRE BLEND: SERMON IN NOVEL 2

Blended Discourse Structure Frame: Sermon-reading Scene

Occasion (church service role): Awaiting Tristram's birth, and Dr. Slop's medical bag; discoursing; Yorick's sermon accidentally found in book; Walter: "nothing better to do"

Characters: Walter Shandy (father), Toby Shandy (uncle), Trim (Toby's valet), Dr. Slop

Rhetorical Situation:

   Setting (church role): Shandy Hall parlor: Trim standing, audience in chairs

   Speaker (priest role): Trim, then Walter

   Audience (congregation role): Walter, Toby, Dr. Slop, Trim

   Medium (script, voice, gesture role): same (read from script)

Narrative Actions:

   Trim's reading = Sterne's sermon quoted (slightly modified)

   Audience (including speaker) interrupts often to discuss text and delivery

Dr. Slop sleeps and wakes

Walter finishes when Trim emotionally overwhelmed

Narration:

Narrator describes in detail Trim's stance, gestures, intonation, and audience responses—verbal, emotional, physical

Epilogue on Yorick and the sermon (linked to earlier and later Yorick story)

Narrator advertises sermon collection

In this case, blending processes of "completion" and "elaboration" operate in the "novel" discourse: it is the fictional narrative that is "filled in" and "run." (The sermon is slightly modified to fit the fictional situation better.)[7] In short, Trim takes on the "preacher" role, and the other men are the congregation audience. What is most notable is that Trim himself is not only the preacher but also part of the audience, and everyone, Trim included, interrupts him to comment on text and performance. So unlike in the original, text is repeated. As well, the narrator participates by describing the scene in minute detail.

We may summarize the principles of the interrelation of *framing* and *emergent structure* that are revealed by the example:

1. Overall, the blend inherits the action and situation of the novel. The *sermon's* action and situation are projected into the *novel's* discourse structure frame. That is, in the blend, Sterne's actual novelistic action and situation frame the fictional rhetorical situation of Tristram writing his life story (mock autobiography), which *frames* the story-world, which both *frames* and *fills in* the sermon's sociocognitive action and rhetorical situation.

2. Because of this frame inheritance the *framed* genre (the sermon) *shares* the situation, and *contributes* to both the story-world action and the sociocognitive action of the *framing* genre (the novel). This modifies the situation of the sermon, by giving it a new audience (early reviewers remarked on this), and presents its action and situation in a new light— foregrounding and defamiliarizing it, we might say.

3. The blend expands the action potential of the *framing* genre: the author can comment on the framed genre, implicitly and explicitly—including advertising his own sermons.

I suspect these conclusions may apply much more widely to inserted extra-literary genres.

This supports Bakhtin's view that the appropriate response is to the whole text, according to the interpretive principles of its framing genre, and not to inserted genres directly. Most modern critics have responded accordingly, interpreting the novelistic meaning deriving from the juxtaposition of genres. Studies consider how Trim-as-preacher relates to the eighteenth-century "dialectic of art and nature," hence to techniques of drama, painting, statuary, and music (Price 1964), and to traditions of the Holy Fool (Petrakis 1972), and liturgical parody (Gilman 1974); how "audience" reactions illustrate a debate over the relation between rhetoric and response (Hunter 1971); how the sermon text is a norm for satire (New 1969), or a paradigm of failed rhetoric (Hunter 1971); how the sermon text embodies Locke's philosophy, and/or Christian values (Cash 1964; New 1969); and parallel events elsewhere in the novel, of interruption (Hunter 1971) or of accident (Brown 1984), of interpolated stories and genres (Rosenblum 1978), and of "readers reading" scenes (Brown 1984); and more.

The blend analysis shows some constraints on interpretation, but does not specify readings. Critics differ over which genre suffers the satirical weight of the scene most heavily (whether sermon satirizes story-world or vice versa), evaluating the relative authority of novel and sermon (which is norm, which deviation). All such commentary is based in one way or another on the relation between framing and framed genres—the sermon as discourse, as situation, or as action in the story-world—and many critics are spurred to reflect on the relation of text to context (Hunter 1971; Brown 1984). Of course, none of these responses, or "uses" of the genre, are possible with the other versions of the sermon. Many of Sterne's inserted genres are straightforwardly, ironically "reaccentuated," as Bakhtin (1986, 91–93) says. But the sermon's reaccentuation is more complex, partly due to its relations with other genres (with novelistic affinities), and partly due to *how* it is inserted—into the story-world, not just the narration.

However, some differing early responses reveal what we could call their tolerance for genre variation and mixture. Rather than go into blend details, I'll note some major factors involved in these judgments. One reviewer waxed sarcastic: *"Tristy's* a clergyman of the church of *England* . . . he makes such a joke of religion!—What do you think of his introducing a sermon in the midst of a smutty tale, and making the preacher curse and swear by way of parenthesis?—('D--n them all, quoth *Trim.*' There's divinity for you)" (qtd. in Ross 2001, 224). Here the sermon genre as such, due to the moral importance of its action frame, is degraded by any other context. The ostensible "preacher" mustn't curse, even when he is a fictional character, not the sermon author, and of a different occupation. But this seems a minority view.

The *sermon collection*, though, was widely attacked for going under the name of "Mr. Yorick," the jester-parson from *Tristram Shandy*. This, even though Sterne added a "second title-page" with his own name, to "ease the minds of those who see a jest, and the danger which lurks under it, where no jest was meant" (qtd. in Ross 2001, 230).[8] Only one critic was pleased to see "this son of Comus descending from the chair of mirth and frolick, to inspire sentiments of piety, and read lectures in morality, to that very audience whose hearts he has captivated with good-natured wit, and facetious humour" (qtd. in Cash 1986, 43). Many complained that "Yorick" "was a *Jester*" in "an obscene Romance.—But are the solemn dictates of religion fit to be conveyed from the mouths of Buffoons and ludicrous Romancers? Would any man believe that a Preacher was in earnest, who should mount the pulpit in a *Harlequin's coat?*" (qtd. in Petrakis 1972, 431n4). Or again, "must the exordium to a sermon, be a smutty tale?" (qtd. in Cash 1986, 44).

Both reviewers see the issue as the *roles* the speaker takes. But the admirer sees a *switch* of roles such that one *assists* the other (you catch the audience with wit, then sermonize), whereas the detractor sees a *blend* of roles such that one *mocks* the other (the sermon's a joke). Here we're bumping up against some limits of category-variation tolerance. There's still disagreement, but many cannot accept Sterne's kind of genre blending because of how it unsettles social roles, and by implication, the institutions and beliefs that underpin them. Genre boundaries are not laid up in heaven, but some seem, in places, to share jurisdictions with it.

V. GENRE BLENDING GLOBALLY

If we remain within this scene, we get this view of literary genre integration as primarily reframing extraliterary genres by projecting them into fictional situations, thus prompting their various literary contextualizations. When we move out to the larger book, Sterne's "dramatick" audacity brings to our attention two further principles.

First, overlaps among genres help us understand genre distinctions, hence genre systems, and also genre blending, as those overlaps constitute potential shared structure. Given sufficient overlap, we can regard or frame one genre as another entirely. Sterne's sermons are regarded as rebelling against the genre's roots in classical oratory (Downey 1969, 154), and are often seen as dramatic (for example, Petrakis 1972), and (less often) as satiric (New 1969) and essayistic (Downey 1969, 127, 137). Indeed, some sermons reflect on their own generic affiliations.[9] Using our model, we might generalize that sermons are similar to essays in their discourse structure, similar to drama in discourse and situation, similar to satire in discourse and action, and similar to oratory in discourse, situation, and action. The distinctions among these genres become clear when their models are fully specified, but their commonalities ease the sermon's integration into the novel, and support inferences relating it to other scenes, characters, and themes. Complementarily, Sterne's deep interest in the nature and effects of rhetorical styles motivates his making his novelistic world hospitable to spontaneous orations (some so sermonic that characters borrow them from Sterne).[10] So, in their responses to Bobby's death, Sterne satirizes Walter's head-first essayistic oratory (borrowed from Burton's *Anatomy of Melancholy*) (5.3–4), and celebrates Trim's heart-first dramatic oratory (5.6–10). The genre-system and whole-book perspectives could help us construe a more detailed generic space and genre blend for this scene and others.

This brings us to the second principle. Gilman (1974) points out that one of the parodic sermon's main developments was to make the preacher a character. The point can be generalized: character and narrative modeling and transformation are major structural principles of genres and genre blending. In the story-world, the sermon needs an author, and although he is absent from the scene, Parson Yorick is a key character in *Tristram Shandy* and later work, and probably the most important emergent structure of our genre blend.[11] It is significant that Tristram advertises the *character* of Yorick along with the sermons.

Let us consider Yorick's relation to genre, and to *Tristram Shandy*. Actions and roles imply and constitute one another, and extraliterary genres imply both. Literary genres are often defined by action scripts (some based outside literature) that afford an overall story structure (for example, tragedy and mystery). Roles can spawn literary character types (for example, tragic hero or detective). These do not fully define genres, but as they can bind together schematized traits, emotions, behavior, speech, and themes, so they specify more than do actions the emotional tone and style of genres. And as they are more unified than actions, they are more portable into other generic contexts. Literary and extraliterary actions and roles can *modulate* a text's genre (as subplot or minor character). "Characters, like frames, are basic cognitive cultural instruments" (Fauconnier and Turner 2002, 250), and although characters transport across frames and vice versa, some characters "seem to be attached to their frames. . . . Sherlock Holmes brings his detective frame with him and causes a frame-blend just by appearing: If Sherlock Holmes comes to your dinner party, someone is going to get killed" (252).

Yorick's extraliterary "parson" role ties him to the sermon genre, but he is schematized in literary ways by blending with character types. As a Holy Fool he is part of a long tradition, with global generic implications due to attitude and tone (comedy and satire). As a Don Quixote type (1.10–12) (also a Holy Fool exemplar), he participates in the newer, more specific genre of the comic novel (Walter and Toby are also Quixote-like, in different ways [1.19, 2.3]). His defining actions have little to do with his role; indeed, his apparent unsuitability for it shows his greater importance for theme than for plot. He fulfills his vocation in a "higher" sense, as he embodies an ideal of "levity" that both fails and transcends the social demands of "gravity." Like Sherlock Holmes, the Holy Fool, and Don Quixote, Yorick contains the seeds of certain kinds of events and moods.

Principles of literary creativity and change are bound up with this loosely interdependent script-role relation. Genre critics, regardless of their more particular theoretical commitments, seem unavoidably to discuss literary history in terms of transformations or substitutions of roles and action structures (see Duff 2000). Cognitive criticism has much to contribute in characterizing these operations across literary and extraliterary genres.

CONCLUSION

Blending theory both clarifies and complicates how in uses and transformations of genre the "literary world in which we live . . . impinges upon the social, political, and religious world" (Cohen 2003, xvi). An array of new problems, from the fine-grained to the global, becomes visible as we move to broader synchronic and diachronic views. Genre blending opens out into many dimensions: genre evolution, genre systems, and the deep sociocognitive footing of genre in culture and human life.

Perhaps this is the pattern of new approaches: the light shed by bringing cognitive theory into the neighborhood of literary studies also reveals new questions to struggle with. As one theory meets another, each expands and adjusts. I notice a tentative but growing interest in cognitive research as a post-poststructuralist resource. To take one prominent example from genre theory, John Frow has drawn cognitive perspectives into a largely Foucauldian view (2006, 2007). Cognitive criticism is significant in being rich and flexible enough to matter for many areas on both sides of the interdiscipline, and not just as decoration. If I may reframe Yorick's sermon once more, we should remember Trim, whose stance hits the "true persuasive angle of incidence"—and Tristram, who then remarks, "does it not shew us, by the way,— how the arts and sciences mutually befriend one another?" (2.17, 140–41).

NOTES

AUTHOR'S NOTE: I thank the Social Sciences and Humanities Research Council of Canada and the Alexander von Humboldt Foundation for their generous support of this research.

1. Cognitive category theory explains the unclassical facts about "prototype effects"— gradience within categories and at their boundaries—by rejecting the "definitional" view of categories in favor of other representational structures, such as exemplars, prototypes, and

schemas. See Sinding (2002), Steen (1999, 2002), Swales (1990), Mancing (2000), Chandler (1997). Types of blends are characterized according to the relative contributions of input-space frames, and in order to highlight text-context interactions in genre blending, I use "frame" to mean the structure of a mental space (Fauconnier and Turner 2002, 102–4), and not to contrast situation-schemas (frames) with event-schemas (scripts).

2. My model differs from Steen's. It has been influenced by Hernadi's (1972) advocacy of a "polycentric" genre theory, Jauss's polycentric studies (1982), Fowler's concept of the functional interrelations of features (1989) in the generic repertoire (1982), by studies of extraliterary genres (Miller 1984; Swales 1990; Freedman and Medway 1994; Coe, Lingard, and Teslenko 2002), and by studies of the interplay of literary and extraliterary genres (Traugott and Pratt 1980; Bakhtin 1986; Todorov 1990; Devitt 2000; Frow 2006).

3. I accept Traugott and Pratt's assessment of literature's plurality of purpose: "What sort of communication do people undertake to accomplish in novels, poems, and short stories? Some have argued that the communicative act involved in literature is simply that of projecting oneself into an imaginary world; others have said the communicative purpose is to produce pleasure and approval in the audience; still others have said it is to produce shared understanding and evaluations of problematic aspects of existence. And there is always Horace's dictum that literature is to teach and delight. In reality, we are not likely to find a single description of literary communication that will do for all works and all genres. Instead, we must think of the literary context as one that admits a wide range of communicative action" (1980, 258–59). Bakhtin (1986), Swales (1990), and Devitt (2000) also see literary genres as plurally purposive.

4. My schema is informed by Downey (1969), Gilman (1974), Traugott and Pratt (1980, 242), and New (1996, especially his Preface and Introduction).

5. New, Davies, and Day annotate "Abuses" in *Tristram* thoroughly (1984, 166–90). They discuss previous scholarship; sources in sermons by Swift and others, including one of Sterne's own (assuming it was written first); parallels in many other sources; and contexts for both the sermon and the scene. New annotates it in its collection context (1996, 58–59, 283–98), describing its relations to other sermons by Sterne and others, the Bible, and the thought and writing generally of Sterne and his contemporaries. Hammond (1970) details how Sterne's sermons borrow extensively from others. Downey (1978) dismantles Hammond's broader hypotheses about the sermons' composition. Plagiarism in sermons was accepted, even encouraged (Downey 1969, 123), which may be why Sterne saw their function as *reminding*: preaching is "a theological flap upon the heart, as the dunning for a promise is a political flap upon the memory:—both the one and the other is useless where men have *wit enough* to be honest" (qtd. in Downey 1969, 137).

6. Keymer (2002) is an excellent recent study of *Tristram*'s intertextual relations with specific novels, and with the prototypical features of the novel genre at the time.

7. New et al. (1984, 946–51) updates New (1979), listing the substantive variants between the 1750 pamphlet, the *Tristram Shandy* text, and the 1766 *Sermons* collection.

8. Elements of the collection indicate adaptations of the sermons to the new generic context. The first volume had a second title page with Sterne's real name (as mentioned); a preface; a list of 661 subscribers (many eminent); and an engraving of Sterne. An "Advertisement" precedes "Abuses," noting its popularity in *Tristram Shandy*, and justifying its reprinting as better reflecting the original. We might also say that the context of the collection reframes the Shandy Hall sermon as a "sample" or "puff."

9. For example, Sterne mentions elements of satire (raillery, wit, sarcasm, scorn, scoff-

ing, mocking) (1996, 175–76, 184–85, 197), drama and narrative (186 ff.), parable (186, 191), conversation (194), and pictures (187). He reflects on sermons in *Tristram Shandy* through Yorick (4.25–26, 6.11).

10. Sterne cribbed from his sermons for other speeches in *Tristram Shandy*: Walter's address to Toby (4.7–8), and Tristram's to the reader (4.17), both on the mind's ability to bear the vexations of life. Petrakis compares Trim's funeral sermon on Bobby with Sterne's "Job's Account of the Shortness and Troubles of Life, Considered" (1972, 444–45).

11. Yorick is the protagonist of *A Sentimental Journey*, and was a well-known Sterne alter ego (to his friends, and even in the *Journal to Eliza*). Each manifestation differs somewhat. Sterne's pre-Yorick satires, the *Rabelaisian Fragment* and *A Political Romance*, also revolve around preachers and ecclesiastical roles. The former has a priest imagining an "art of sermon-writing" (Kerukopaedia).

WORKS CITED

Bakhtin, M. M. 1981. *The dialogic imagination: Four essays*. Edited by Michael Holquist. Translated by Caryl Emerson and Michael Holquist. University of Texas Press Slavic series 1. Austin: University of Texas Press.

———. 1986. *Speech genres and other late essays*. Edited by Caryl Emerson and Michael Holquist. Translated by Vern W. McGee. University of Texas Press Slavic series 8. Austin: University of Texas Press.

Berkenkotter, Carol, and Thomas N. Huckin. 1993. Rethinking genre from a sociocognitive perspective. *Written Communication* 10, no. 4: 475–509.

Brown, Homer Obed. 1984. Tristram to the Hebrews: Some notes on the institution of a canonic text. *Modern Language Notes* 99, no. 4: 727–47.

Cash, Arthur H. 1964. The sermon in *Tristram Shandy*. *English Literary History* 31, no. 4: 395–417.

———. 1975. *Laurence Sterne: The early and middle years*. London: Methuen.

———. 1986. *Laurence Sterne: The later years*. London: Methuen.

Chandler, Daniel. 1997. An introduction to genre theory. Media and Communications Studies Site, University of Wales, Aberystwyth, http://www.aber.ac.uk/media/Documents/intgenre (accessed April 15, 2011).

Coe, Richard, Lorelei Lingard, and Tatiana Teslenko, eds. 2002. *The rhetoric and ideology of genre: Strategies for stability and change*. Cresskill, NJ: Hampton Press.

Cohen, Ralph. 2003. Introduction: Notes toward a generic reconstitution of literary study. Theorizing genres II. *New Literary History* 34, no. 3: v–xvi.

Colie, Rosalie. 1973. *The resources of kind: Genre-theory in the renaissance*. Edited by Barbara K. Lewalski. Berkeley: University of California Press.

Devitt, Amy J. 2000. Integrating rhetorical and literary theories of genre. *College English* 62, no. 6: 696–718.

Downey, James. 1969. *The eighteenth-century pulpit: A study of the sermons of Butler, Berkeley, Secker, Sterne, Whitefield and Wesley*. Oxford: Oxford University Press.

———. 1978. The Sermons of Mr. Yorick: A reassessment of Hammond. *English Studies in Canada* 4: 193–211.

Duff, David, ed. 2000. *Modern genre theory*. Essex: Pearson Education.

Farrell, Joseph. 2003. Classical genre in theory and practice. Theorizing genres II. *New Literary History* 34, no. 3: 383–408.

Fauconnier, Gilles, and Mark Turner. 2002. *The way we think: Conceptual blending and the mind's hidden complexities*. New York: Basic Books.

Fowler, Alastair. 1982. *Kinds of literature: An introduction to the theory of genres and modes*. Oxford: Clarendon.

———. 1989. The future of genre theory: Functions and constructional types. In *The future of literary theory*, 291–303. Edited by Ralph Cohen. New York: Routledge, Chapman and Hall.

Freedman, Aviva, and Peter Medway, eds. 1994. *Genre and the new rhetoric*. London: Taylor and Francis.

Frow, John. 2006. *Genre. The new critical idiom*. London: Routledge.

———. 2007. "Reproducibles, rubrics, and everything you need": Genre theory today. Special issue, *Publications of the Modern Language Association* 122, no. 5: 1626–34.

Gilman, Sander L. 1974. *The parodic sermon in European perspective: Aspects of liturgical parody from the Middle Ages to the twentieth century*. Wiesbaden: Franz Steiner Verlag GMBH.

Hammond, Lansing Van der Heyden. 1970. *Laurence Sterne's "Sermons of Mr. Yorick."* Yale studies in English 108. Hamden, CT: Archon Books. (Orig. pub. by Yale University Press, 1948)

Hernadi, Paul. 1972. *Beyond genre*. Ithaca, NY: Cornell University Press.

Hunter, J. Paul. 1971. Response as reformation: *Tristram Shandy* and the art of interruption. Reprinted in *Tristram Shandy*, 623–40. Edited by Howard Anderson. New York: Norton, 1980.

Jauss, Hans Robert. 1982. *Toward an aesthetic of reception*. Translated by Timothy Bahti. Minneapolis: University of Minnesota Press.

Keymer, Thomas. 2002. *Sterne, the moderns, and the novel*. Oxford: Oxford University Press.

Luke, Allan. 1994. Series editor's preface. *Genre and the new rhetoric*, vii–xi. Edited by Aviva Freedman and Peter Medway. London: Taylor and Francis.

Mancing, Howard. 2000. Prototypes of genre in Cervantes' *Novelas ejemplares*. *Cervantes: Bulletin of the Cervantes Society of America* 20, no. 2: 127–50.

Miller, Carolyn R. 1984. Genre as social action. *Quarterly Journal of Speech* 70: 151–67.

New, Melvyn. 1969. Swift and Sterne: Sermons and satire. *Modern Language Quarterly* 30, no. 2: 198–211.

———. 1979. Sterne as editor: The "abuses of conscience" sermon. *Studies in Eighteenth-century Culture* 8: 243–51.

———, ed. 1996. *The sermons of Laurence Sterne: The notes*. Vol. 5 of the Florida edition of the works of Laurence Sterne. Gainesville: University Press of Florida.

New, Melvyn, Richard A. Davies, W. G. Day, eds. 1984. *The life and opinions of Tristram Shandy, gentleman: The notes*. Vol. 3 of the Florida edition of the works of Laurence Sterne. Gainesville: University Press of Florida.

Olshin, Toby A. 1971. Genre and *Tristram Shandy*: The novel of quickness. Reprinted in *Tristram Shandy*, 521–32. Edited by Howard Anderson. New York: Norton, 1980.

Petrakis, Byron. 1972. Jester in the pulpit: Sterne and pulpit eloquence. *Philological Quarterly* 51: 430–47.

Price, Martin. 1964. Sterne: Art and nature. Reprint of "The art of the natural" in *Tristram Shandy*, 562–70. Edited by Howard Anderson. New York: Norton, 1980.

Rosenblum, Michael. 1978. The sermon, the king of Bohemia, and the art of interpolation in *Tristram Shandy*. *Studies in Philology* 75: 472–91.

Ross, Ian Campbell. 2001. *Laurence Sterne: A life*. Oxford: Oxford University Press.

Sinding, Michael. 2002. After definitions: Genre, categories and cognitive science. *Genre* 35, no. 2: 181–220.

Steen, Gerard. 1999. Genres of discourse and the definition of literature. *Discourse Processes* 28, no. 2: 109–20.

———. 2002. Metaphor in Bob Dylan's "Hurricane": Genre, language, and style. In *Cognitive stylistics: Language and cognition in text analysis*, 183–209. Edited by Elena Semino and Jonathan Culpeper. Amsterdam: John Benjamins.

Sterne, Laurence. 1978. *The life and opinions of Tristram Shandy, gentleman: The text*. Edited by Melvyn New and Joan New. Vols. 1–2 of the Florida edition of the works of Laurence Sterne. Gainesville: University Press of Florida.

———. 1980. *Tristram Shandy: An authoritative text, the author on the novel, criticism*. Edited by Howard Anderson. Norton Critical Editions. New York: Norton.

———. 1996. *The sermons of Laurence Sterne*. Edited by Melvyn New. Vol. 4 of the Florida edition of the works of Laurence Sterne. Gainesville: University Press of Florida.

Swales, John M. 1990. *Genre analysis: English in academic and research settings*. Cambridge: Cambridge University Press.

Todorov, Tzvetan. 1990. *Genres in discourse*. Translated by Catherine Porter. Cambridge: Cambridge University Press.

Traugott, Elizabeth Closs, and Mary Louise Pratt. 1980. *Linguistics for students of literature*. San Diego: Harcourt Brace Jovanovich.

Turner, Mark. Blending and conceptual integration. http://markturner.org/blending.html (accessed April 15, 2011).

White, Hayden. 2003. Anomalies of genre: The utility of theory and history for the study of literary genres. *New Literary History* 34, no. 3: 597–615.

CHAPTER 9

COUNTING IN METRICAL VERSE

NIGEL FABB AND MORRIS HALLE

INTRODUCTION

In this essay we approach the study of "cognition and literature" by examining a problem presented by metrical verse. When a poet composes a metrical line, or an audience judges that line to be metrical, they must be counting syllables, but how is that counting performed? This is a problem of particular interest, given that poets can compose lines of a particular number of syllables while being innumerate in other ways; thus metrical counting does not obviously draw on other kinds of counting ability. Though some regularity of rhythm is often a characteristic of metrical verse, it is always the case that in metrical verse the number of syllables in the line is controlled: for example, an iambic pentameter line normatively has ten syllables (sometimes eleven), a French alexandrine (*alexandrin*) line has twelve syllables (with additional syllables permitted under specific circumstances), and so on. We will present reasons to think that the poet or audience is not counting syllables by exploiting some general cognitive ability to count any kind of element, but instead by specialized mechanisms. Specifically, we propose that syllables are counted by a cognitive process which instantiates a simple formal procedure that we will be describing in detail. We focus almost entirely on the formal procedure itself, without referring to the cognitive implementation of this formal procedure (about which we—like all other researchers in this area—have no direct evidence). The best evidence that there is a cognitive implementation is that the formal procedure works, in spite of the fact that at this time we have very little direct evidence for what might be the neurological bases of these metrical abilities. We suggest at the end of the essay, however, that the same formal procedures might operate in other domains that may involve specialized kinds of cognition, such as language and music, and hence that linguistic, metrical, and musical cognition might share some component parts.

I. METRICAL VERSE

The crucial distinction between verse and prose is that all verse is composed of lines, but there are no lines in prose. Jeremy Bentham's remark that "prose is when all the lines except the last go on to the end, poetry is when some of them fall short of it" is thus a sober statement of the facts, rather than the joke for which it has been taken. A widely practiced form of verse in all ages and languages is metrical verse, a form of verse, which, as we shall see, is based on grouping the syllables that make up each line. This grouping is reflected in the traditional terminology of poetic metrics, where syllables are grouped into feet, feet into metra, etc. It is this hierarchical grouping of syllables that is at the heart of metrical verse of every known kind. In many cases, the hierarchical grouping of syllables is reflected in some regularity of rhythm in the line: in English iambic pentameter, the ten syllables are grouped into pairs, with a tendency for the second member of each pair to be stressed. It is particularly worth noting that this kind of regularity of rhythm in language is found only in verse: the division of the text into lines is a prerequisite for the organization of the rhythm, and we argue that this is because the division of the text into lines allows special groupings of syllables, and that this in turn is the basis for the rhythmic organization of syllables.

Lines lacking this hierarchy of syllable groupings are not metrical verse. One well-known type of non-metrical verse is that encountered in the Old Testament, where the lines are instead subject to syntactic parallelism. Perhaps the best known non-metrical verse is free verse, the type of verse widely favored by poets writing since the beginning of the twentieth century. We have nothing to say here about these non-metrical kinds of verse.

The hierarchy of metrical units of the verse line is the result of a simple formal procedure, which we now describe step by step. (The procedure is illustrated extensively in Fabb and Halle 2008; we reflect on its implications for literature and cognition at the end of this chapter.) In order to model this procedure, we will be employing simple symbols (asterisk, left parenthesis, and right parenthesis) and complex symbols (grids). The formal procedure, consisting of a set of rules that add simple symbols and thereby build complex symbols, is intended as a model of the computations performed by cognition as part of the mental process by which verse is scanned. In the first step, a mark (we write this as an asterisk) is projected from each syllable of the line, and the sequence of projected units is labeled gridline 0. This procedure takes each line in (1a) and forms from them the representation in (1b).

(1)
a.
Airly Beacon, Airly Beacon,
Oh the weary haunt for me,
b.
Airly Beacon, Airly Beacon,

| * * * * * * * | *gridline 0* |

Oh the weary haunt for me,

| * * * * * * | *gridline 0* |

In order to group the asterisks in the sequence, we employ here ordinary parentheses, to which we impute the grouping property as specified in (2).

(2)
A left parenthesis groups the asterisks on its right, a right parenthesis groups the asterisks on its left.

We illustrate how the grouping works with an invented sequence of asterisks and parentheses:

(3)
* * *) * * (*

As a consequence of (2), the sequence of asterisks in (3) includes two groups, of which one is made up of the three asterisks at the left end of the sequence and the other of the single asterisk at the right end of the sequence. The two asterisks in the middle of the sequence (3) belong to neither group: they are ungrouped.

We have said above that in a metrical line asterisks are projected from each syllable, and as illustrated in (1) we have taken this literally and have projected a single asterisk from each of the syllables in the lines that we have quoted from a poem by Charles Kingsley. This observation leads naturally to the question of where, within the model, the parentheses in (3) come from. Our answer is that there are special metrical rules that group these asterisks by inserting parentheses into asterisk sequences. Our rules, and the simple and complex symbols they operate with, are models of how we think the mind might operate in scanning a line of verse: we assume a computational model of the mind, in which computations are performed over symbols.

The central rule of parenthesis insertion is a special iterative rule, which, once it comes into play, has the effect of inserting a parenthesis starting at one edge of the sequence and continuing to insert the same parenthesis at regular intervals until it reaches the opposite edge of the asterisk sequence. Such a rule, as we formulate it, is a hypothesis about a mental procedure and the operations of and limits on that procedure. Our parenthesis-insertion rule has a limited number of degrees of freedom. These are described in (4); we restate them more formally later in the chapter as (32).

(4)

Iterative parenthesis-insertion rule (template). The rule is formed by fixing five parameters, and then applies consistently for a specific gridline. According to this rule:

a. One of two kinds of parentheses may be inserted: either a right parenthesis) or a left parenthesis (.
b. The parenthesis selected in (4a) can be inserted either from left to right or from right to left.
c. The parenthesis is inserted at intervals of either two or three asterisks.
d. The insertion begins either flush at the edge of the asterisk sequence, so that if insertion proceeds from left to right (see (4b)) it starts at the left edge of the sequence, but if the insertion proceeds from right to left, it starts at the right edge. There is in addition also the option to begin insertion after skipping the first or even the first two asterisks in the sequence (i.e., the leftmost or two leftmost, or rightmost or two rightmost asterisks depending on the direction of insertion).
e. One element in each of the groups resulting from parenthesis insertion is designated as head and projected to the next higher gridline. Here again there is a binary choice to be made: the head is either the left- or the rightmost element in the group.

Option (4d) presents a choice between three alternatives; the other four options involve binary choices. In making the five choices in (4), and thereby determining the iterative rule which defines one gridline, there is a selection of one grouping from among 2x2x2x2x3 = 48 alternatives.

We illustrate in (5) the effect of applying one setting ("a standard trochaic setting") of the iterative parenthesis insertion rule to the two (trochaic) lines in (1).

(5)
Airly Beacon, Airly Beacon,
(* *(* * (* *(* *(*gridline 0*
*   *   *   *   *gridline 1*

Oh the weary haunt for me,
(* *(* *(*   * (*   *gridline 0*
*   *   *   *   *gridline 1*

To obtain the groupings in (5) we inserted left parentheses (4a) from left to right (4b) at binary intervals (4c) starting flush at the left line edge (4d) and generating groups that are left-headed (4e). This is one of the forty-eight possible iterative rules, as defined by (4). Note that the second line has an incomplete rightmost group; though incomplete, this is still a group as defined by rule (2).

The groupings in (5) have yet another property, which is of fundamental importance in English verse: they determine where in the line syllables bearing the word stress must or may be located. As is well known, in syllabo-tonic verse, the location of word stresses is largely restricted to certain positions, which are two or three syllables apart (giving the groupings called iambic, trochaic, anapestic, and dactylic feet). This is related to the metrical grid by the statement in (6), which we call a "condition," a statement that holds of the grid once completed. Condition (6) exploits the fact that groups are binary or ternary and right- or left-headed.

(6)
The syllables bearing the stress in polysyllabic words must appear always in head positions of the gridline 0 groups.

This condition has the consequence that the lines in (7) may not have their asterisks (projecting from syllables) grouped by the same iterative rule as those in (5). If we apply the same rule as was used in (5), we get the result shown in (8), where all five polysyllables violate the condition in (6).

(7)
Hence loathèd melancholy
Of Cerberus and blackest midnight born

(8)

Hence loathèd melancholy

```
( *    *  (*   *(*  *(*        gridline 0
   *        *     *     *        gridline 1
```

Of Cerberus and blackest midnight born

```
(*   * (* *(*     * (*   * (*    *(        gridline 0
  *     *   *        *       *               gridline 1
```

The iterative rule which must instead be used to group the asterisks in conformity with (6) has its effects illustrated in (9). It inserts right parentheses (4a) from right to left (4b) at binary intervals (4c). In the first of the two lines, parenthesis insertion starts one asterisk in at the right edge, but in the second line, insertion starts at the edge (4d). The groups generated are right-headed (4e).

(9)

Hence loathèd melancholy

```
) *    *)  *    *)*   *)*        gridline 0
    *        *     *              gridline 1
```

Of Cerberus and blackest midnight born

```
)*   *) * *)*     *) *    *) *     *)    gridline 0
   *    *        *       *        *      gridline 1
```

Note that the grouping of syllables (as left-headed pairs in (5) and as right-headed pairs in (9)) has a role in explaining the rhythm but is not a direct expression of the actual rhythm of the line. As a representation, the metrical grouping is uniformly binary and right-headed in (9) because it is produced by the same rule iteratively inserting parentheses from right to left and projecting the rightmost asterisks. But in reading the line aloud, the rhythm need not be uniformly "binary right-headed." In fact, a plausible performance of these lines would give the lines two and four stressed syllables respectively ("melancholy" would have only its first syllable prominent, and similarly "Cerberus"). Thus the metrical grid does not directly resemble the spoken rhythm, but is distinct from it.

The approach described here is in part a formalization of a traditional way of thinking about these meters, which puts syllables into binary or ternary groups called "feet" and then counts feet. So the groups in (5) are trochees, and there are four in each line (trochaic tetrameter). By contrast, the groups in (9) are iambs and there are three and five in the lines (iambic trimeter and pentameter).

II. GROUPING AS COUNTING

Lines of metrical verse are of a certain length. This is captured in the traditional terms such as "trochaic tetrameter," which describes the line as consisting of four trochees; because the trochee is a pair of syllables, the line has eight syllables. There is some permitted variation in length, also captured by traditional terminology. So, for example, the final trochee can fall short or "be catalectic," so that a trochaic tetrameter catalectic is three full trochees and a short trochee, to give seven syllables (as in the second line of (5)). Or there can be an extra syllable, called "extrametrical," as in the first line of (9), where the iambic trimeter line would normally have three full iambs, giving six syllables, but there is an extra syllable, giving seven syllables.

These facts are readily captured in our formalism. Construction of the metrical grid that represents the meter begins by projecting an asterisk from each syllable in the line. We label the sequence of projected asterisks "gridline 0." Next, an iterative rule applies and groups the asterisks into pairs or triplets. The rule also projects the right- or leftmost asterisk in each group (called the head) onto the next gridline, which we label "gridline 1." The asterisks on gridline 1 are grouped into pairs or triplets, and the heads of the (new) groups are projected onto gridline 2. Application of additional rules generates additional gridlines. It is to be noted, however, that the number of asterisks decreases on each successive gridline, and that we soon reach the topmost line of the grid, which (in poetry) must project but a single asterisk. (The fact that the topmost line must consist of just one asterisk is the key factor in restricting the number of syllables in the line.) We illustrate this in detail with the construction of a grid for the lines of (1a). The rules are (10) and (11). Each of the rules in (11) is an iterative rule, based on the general template for such rules given in (4); as it happens, each of the three gridlines 0, 1 and 2 makes use of the same rule, but this is not a general requirement.

(10)
Project each syllable as an asterisk on gridline 0.

(11)
a. gridline 0: starting just at the L(eft) edge, insert a left parenthesis, form binary groups, heads L.
   An incomplete group is permitted.

b. gridline 1: starting just at the L edge, insert a left parenthesis, form binary groups, heads L.
c. gridline 2: starting just at the L edge, insert a left parenthesis, form binary groups, heads L.

When applied to each of the lines in (1a), rule (10) produces the result in (12).

(12)

All alone on Airly Beacon,
* ** * * * **   *gridline 0*
Oh the weary haunt for me,
*   * * *   *   *   *gridline 0*

We now demonstrate the operation of the rule (11a). The rule inserts a left parenthesis, and keeps repeating this operation until there are no further places where a parenthesis can be inserted. The first parenthesis is inserted at the left edge, as in (13).

(13)

 All alone on Airly Beacon,
(* ** * * * *   *gridline 0*
 Oh the weary haunt for me,
(*   * * *   *   *   *gridline 0*

Now the rule repeats, inserting another left parenthesis. It skips two asterisks before doing so (this is what "form binary groups" means).

(14)

 All alone on Airly Beacon,
(* *(* * * * *   *gridline 0*
 Oh the weary haunt for me,
(*   * (* * *   *   *   *gridline 0*

The rule keeps repeating until the first gridline has the structure in (15). Note that the final group for the second line is incomplete (because the rule has run out of asterisks: a fifth parenthesis cannot be inserted because there is not a pair of asterisks at the end to skip). This is still a group, by definition (2), which admits groups that are incomplete. This corresponds to what traditional metrics calls a "catalectic foot." Since this iterative rule inserts parentheses from left to right, the incomplete group produced by this rule must always be at the right edge.

(15)
All alone on Airly Beacon,
(* *(* * (* * (* *(*gridline 0*
Oh the weary haunt for me,
(*   * (* * (*   * (*   *gridline 0*

The final stage of the rule (11a) requires heads to be L (left). This means that in each of the four groups (as defined by (2)), the leftmost asterisk is identified as the head of the group and so projects to the next gridline as shown in (16).

(16)
All alone on Airly Beacon,
(* *(* * (* * (* *(*gridline 0*
*   *   *   *   *gridline 1*
Oh the weary haunt for me,
(*   * (* * (*   * (*   *gridline 0*
*   *   *   *   *gridline 1*

Gridline 1 asterisks now serve two functions. They are the elements by which the gridline 0 groups are "counted," because these gridline 2 elements are themselves grouped; and the gridline 1 asterisks are also the elements which are taken into account by (6) in checking the rhythm of the line.

At this point, rule (11b) applies (iteratively) to the asterisks on gridline 1, projecting asterisks onto gridline 2. These asterisks are subject to rule (11c), which results in the single asterisk that constitutes gridline 3. The grid generated here is shown in (17).

(17)
All alone on Airly Beacon,
(* *(* * (* * (* *(*gridline 0*
(*   *   (*   *(*gridline 1*
(*   *(*gridline 2*
 *   *gridline 3*

Oh the weary haunt for me,

```
(*   * (* * (*    *  (*       gridline 0
(*      *  (*        *(       gridline 1
(*          *(               gridline 2
 *                           gridline 3
```

The rules (11) generate the bracketed grids in (17) from the eight-syllable first line and the seven-syllable second line. A grid is well formed if it has one asterisk on its final gridline (here, gridline 3). Because of this, the rules (11)—the rules for English trochaic tetrameter—will generate a well-formed grid only from an initial sequence of either eight or seven asterisks.

If there are six asterisks to be grouped, the rules (11) generate the grid in (18). This grid is not permitted by the rules because gridline 1 ends on an incomplete group, something that is possible for metrical rules in principle, but is not explicitly permitted by the rules for this meter. A six-syllable line is thus not a possible variant of trochaic tetrameter, but instead must be scanned by a different rule set.

(18)
```
(*      *(*    *  (*    *(       gridline 0
(*       *    (*                 gridline 1
(*              *(               gridline 2
 *                              gridline 3
```

If there are nine asterisks, the rules (11) will generate the grid in (19). This has incomplete groups on gridlines 0, 1 and 2 (of which the latter two are not explicitly permitted). But, fatally, the grid has two asterisks on the final gridline, and this is forbidden in all metrical grids: a metrical grid must have one and only one asterisk on the final gridline.

(19)
```
(*     *(*   * (*   * (*   *(*       gridline 0
(*      *    (*    *    (*           gridline 1
(*           *          (*           gridline 2
 *                      *            gridline 3
```

Because the initial line of asterisks is transformed into a grid by iterative rules on every gridline, and because the final gridline must contain one asterisk, the iterative rules thus achieve the result of ensuring that the lines in a poem have no more than a given number of syllables. Note that even though the rules for trochaic tetrameter generate a grid from a line of eight asterisks, the rules never make explicit that there are eight asterisks (syllables) in the line: the number "eight" never appears in a metrical rule. In fact, metrical rules know only the numbers 1, 2 and 3 (in the sense that they form groups of one, two, or three asterisks). It is the combination of iterative rules (and the constraint that the final gridline contain one asterisk) which determine that this set of iterative rules—those for trochaic tetrameter—generate a well-formed grid from a line of specifically seven or eight syllables, and not six or nine.

Lines that are in a given meter can nevertheless vary in length. The types of variations noted above have all been discussed in traditional metrics, and all receive an explanation also in our theory. One type of variation occurs when the line is one syllable short or two syllables short at one or the other end. If syllables are missing (or a single syllable is missing) at the beginning, the line is called acephalous; if missing at the end of the line, the line is called catalectic. In our terms, the line is metrical if a well-formed grid can be formed from it by the iterative rules, and the condition of being well formed is not affected if the last group on a gridline is incomplete (so long as the rules for the meter specify this as a potential variation). A second type of variation occurs when the line is a syllable or two longer at one or the other end. If the extra syllable is at the beginning, the line is said to have anacrusis; if located at the end, the line is said to have an extrametrical syllable. We explain this by permitting our parenthesis-insertion rule to skip one or two asterisks before the first parenthesis is inserted, thus leaving an asterisk ungrouped; thus an extra syllable is permitted because it does not affect the number of groups. Our iterative rules progress from one side of the line to the other. If they progress from left to right, as in trochaic lines, then the initial syllable may be extra (anacrusis) and the final syllable missing (catalexis); if they progress from right to left, as in iambic lines, then the final syllable may be extra (extrametrical) and the initial syllable missing (acephalous). In iambic and trochaic lines, a single syllable may be omitted at one end (because an incomplete group still exists, containing one asterisk), while in anapestic and dactylic lines, one or two syllables may be omitted at one end, because this still leaves an incomplete group. In this way, our rules explain why metrical lines can vary in the number of syllables in distinct ways in different meters.

There is another kind of variation, found when some syllables are not counted for metrical purposes, a phenomenon sometimes called "resolution" in traditional metrics (and well known to the practitioners of metrical verse in many traditions). This can be seen in the following line from *Paradise Lost*, where the second syllable of "evil" is not counted for metrical purposes in its first use (but it is counted in its second use).

(20)
Created evil, for evil only good.
** *   * * * * * *

We explain this by permitting occasional exceptions to rule (10). It is likely that these exceptions reflect the influence of the Romance metrical tradition on the practice of English poets. In Romance languages, word-final vowels are systematically omitted from the count if they are followed by a vowel that begins the next word, a phenomenon often referred to as synaloepha. This metrical rule is an example of a cognitive process that goes beyond those involved in the ordinary use of language. This distancing of metrical cognition from the ordinary cognition of language is paralleled by a similar distancing of metrical cognition from the ordinary perception of music, which is briefly discussed below. (Fabb 2009, 2010a, 2010b further discusses ways in which poetic language can be seen as organized by principles different from those that characterize ordinary language.)

We conclude this section by reflecting on the fact that we have numbered the gridlines (here, the four gridlines are labeled gridline 0 to gridline 3, but in other work we have argued for gridline 4, and we have not formulated a principle restricting the overall number). Is this another form of counting? In fact it is not: the numbering of the gridlines reflects only the fact that they are generated by rules which follow in a particular sequence. Conditions may refer to a particular gridline (for example, condition (6) refers to gridline 1) but this is a label for the gridline unrelated to sequence, and the use of a number as part of the label is not crucial; we could equally have labeled the gridlines "red, orange, yellow, blue," etc.

III. ANOTHER EXAMPLE: FRENCH *ALEXANDRIN*

To further illustrate our approach, we now discuss the set of rules and conditions which comprise a different meter, the French-meter alexandrine (discussed in detail in Fabb and Halle 2008). A line by Jacques Davy in this "twelve-syllable" meter is given in (21).

(21) Quand au dernier sommeil la Vierge eut clos les yeux,

The first rule is (10), which is subject here to the special proviso that prevents a word-final syllable from projecting to gridline 0 if it has as its nucleus a schwa vowel (*e-caduc*), as does the final vowel of "*vierge*," and immediately precedes another vowel, in this case "e-." Thus, in (21) there are actually thirteen syllables in the line; the final syllable of *"vierge"* does not project, giving twelve asterisks on gridline o, as shown in (22).

(22)

Quand au dernier sommeil la Vierge eut clos les yeux,

   *   *   *   *   *   *   *   *   *   *   *   0

Now the iterative rules in (23) generate the grid in (24). The rules form binary groups on gridline o, ternary groups on gridline 1, and binary groups on gridline 2. There are no incomplete groups, and no options, so the grid can only be generated from a line of twelve asterisks (2x3x2).

(23)

a. gridline o: starting just at the R edge, insert a right parenthesis, form binary groups, heads R.

b. gridline 1: starting just at the R edge, insert a right parenthesis, form ternary groups, heads R.

c. gridline 2: starting at the L edge, insert a left parenthesis, form binary groups, heads L.

(24)

Quand au dernier sommeil la Vierge eut clos les yeux,

```
)*   *)  *  *) *   *) *  *)  *   *) * *)      0
     )*      *       *)    *     *   *)       1
                     (*              *(       2
                     *                        3
```

This fixes the length of the line at twelve asterisks (projecting from twelve syllables). The rules cannot generate a well-formed grid from any other number of initial asterisks. The condition holding in this meter is stated in (25).

(25)

Syllables projecting to gridline 2 must bear word stress and must be followed by a word boundary (caesura).

This condition ensures that the sixth and twelfth syllables are both the final (metrically visible) syllables in their words — that is, syllables which are word-final and are also stressed.

The metrical rules generate a grid by assigning parentheses iteratively on every gridline. This enables the rules to fix the length of the line. The grid also provides a structure to which a condition such as English (6) or French (25) can refer. Note that different aspects of the grid are relevant in different meters. In English, the relevant question to ask about a syllable is whether it projects to gridline 1. In French, the relevant question is whether it projects to gridline 2. One of the consequences of this difference is that in French the condition does not really define a "rhythm": only one line-internal syllable (the sixth) is controlled. Nevertheless, the basic metrical rules for French are very similar to the superficially different "rhythmic" English meters.

In Fabb and Halle (2008), we show that our method of accounting for metricality covers a large variety of different kinds of metrical verse, perhaps the widest variety yet covered by a single theory. This is because, unlike all other theories, we see metricality fundamentally as a mode of controlling the number of syllables in the line: both the line as an entity, and the fact that it consists of a certain number of syllables, are the salient facts which we think a theory must explain. The variety of other phenomena, including rhythm, which are associated with counting, are derived in our theory largely by adding conditions on the output of the grid-generating rules.

IV. THE GRID IN OTHER DOMAINS

We have suggested that metrical verse is scanned by a set of rules which are instantiated in cognition (in a manner still to be determined). The scansion proceeds by applying a set of rules to each line, and thereby generating a bracketed grid from each line. The rules both govern the rhythm or other phonological aspects of the line, and also fix the number of syllables in the line. The fact that the iterative rules fix the number of syllables comes from two general characteristics of metrical grids in verse: there are iterative rules on every gridline, and there must be one asterisk on the final gridline. We will now argue that iterative rules generate grids in two other domains: in language (the assignment of stress in words) and in music (the organization of regular rhythms in music). However, as we will see, in neither case do the iterative rules fix the length of the input.

1. PAIRS AND TRIPLETS IN THE ASSIGNMENT OF STRESS IN WORDS

We begin with the assignment of stress in words, in an account based on Idsardi (1992; see also Halle and Idsardi 1995). Idsardi introduced the technical innovation that asterisks are grouped by a single unmatched parenthesis, and he applied this insight to an explanation of the patterns of word stress in many different languages. We briefly illustrate this approach by considering the stress patterns of a subset of words in the American Indian language Creek (Haas 1977). The words in question can be of various lengths, and in each word a single syllable carries stress (the others are unstressed). The syllable that carries stress is the final even-numbered syllable. For example, in a four-syllable word, the fourth syllable is stressed; in a five-syllable word, the fourth syllable is again stressed; in a six-syllable word, the sixth syllable is stressed, and so on.

The explanation of this is as follows. There is a "stress assignment module" (a part of the language faculty) that takes a word consisting of a sequence of syllables, and assigns stress to one or more of the syllables (possibly different degrees of stress). The rules that make up this module for Creek consist of the projection rule (10), the parenthesis-insertion rules in (26), plus the stress-assignment rule (27). Note that while rule (26a) is iterative, rule (26b) is not. In constructing the grids that assign stress to words in a language, iterative rules need not apply on every gridline: there may be gridlines to which only non-iterative rules apply. We discuss some consequences of this fact below.

(26)
  a. gridline 0: starting just at the L edge, insert a right parenthesis, form binary groups, heads R.
  b. gridline 1: starting just at the R edge, insert a right parenthesis, heads R.

(27)
Assign stress to the syllable projecting to gridline 2.

We illustrate with one seven-syllable word; given the grid in (28), the penultimate syllable is assigned stress, to give *itiwanayipíta* with stress on the penultimate syllable, "pi."

(28)
  itiwanayipita
```
)* *)* *)* *)*   0
   *   *   *)    1
           *     2
```

The iterative rule on gridline 0 is such that the rightmost group always has an even-numbered syllable as its head; any final odd-numbered syllable will be ungrouped, as here. The gridline 1 rule then picks out just the head of the rightmost group for projection to gridline 2. Note that the grid for the word has a periodic "iambic" type of structure, but that the word does not have a periodic iambic type of stress pattern; instead the grid serves the function of picking out the final even-numbered syllable. As in poetic meter, the grid does not directly represent the rhythm of the word.

The iterative parenthesis-insertion and asterisk-projection rules that assign stress to the syllables of a word are of the same kind as the rules that determine the metricality of a line. There are two important differences. First, the stress rules actually alter the structure of the word (they assign stress), while the metrical rules just act as a filter on the production of metrical lines without actually altering linguistic structure. But more significantly for our purposes, the word-stress module does not count (and hence does not fix) the total number of syllables in a word. Words can be of any length. Examination of the rules for Creek tell us why this is: gridline 1 lacks an iterative rule. A single parenthesis is inserted at the right edge, and (by (2)) this defines all of the preceding asterisks as in a single group, which projects its head to gridline 2. It is the requirement for iterative rules on every gridline that results in the metrical rules fixing the length of the line. This again shows that (poetic) metrical cognition and linguistic cognition share some aspects but are not the same.

2. PAIRS AND TRIPLETS IN MUSIC

Lerdahl and Jackendoff (1983) show that in the metrical organization of music, beats are grouped into pairs or triplets, which in turn are grouped into pairs or triplets, and so on, to ever higher levels of structure. They model metrical structure in music as a grid (consisting just of asterisks, no parentheses). They constrain the structure of the grid by a set of filters ("metrical well-formedness rules"). As we argue in Fabb and Halle (2008, 36–39) and Fabb and Halle (2011), Lerdahl and Jackendoff's metrical well-formedness rules can be derived by generating the grid as a parenthesized grid by the usual iterative rules. For example, the rules in (29) would generate a grid in 6/8 time from a series of beats (each projecting as an asterisk), as shown in (30).

(29)
a. gridline 0: starting just at the L edge, insert a left parenthesis, form ternary groups, heads L.
b. gridline 1: starting just at the L edge, insert a left parenthesis, form binary groups, heads L.

(30)

```
b    b  b  b  b  b    b  b  b  b  b  b  ...
(*   *  * (*  *  *   (*  *  * (*  *  *    0
(*      *           (*        *           1
*                   *                     2
```

It seems that this aspect of musical structure is derived by the same iterative rule system, and the same symbolic elements (asterisks, parentheses, grids) as are used in metrical verse (and the assignment of stress in words).

There are several differences between the grid in music and the grid in poetry. First, the grid in music is used to assign strength of beat, and can be used to determine a range of different strengths. This is rather similar to the function of the grid in the assignment of stress in words, but it is quite unlike the function of the grid in metrical poetry, which does not assign stress at all, but rather takes already-assigned stress into account in assessing the metricality of the line. (In other words, rhythm in music is determined by the grid, while in poetry it is understood as a condition on the relation between the grid and the line.) Second, and more significantly for our purposes, the grid is not used to fix the overall length of a rhythmic sequence, for there is no counterpart in music to the line in poetry. This is because in music there is no requirement that the last gridline (here gridline 2) contain only one asterisk. This difference between metrical poetry and the metrical aspects of music is manifested as an interesting fact about poetry, which we noted early in this essay. Wherever there is a regular rhythm in a verbal text, the text is always broken up into lines of fixed length (i.e., regular rhythm entails verse): there is no regularly rhythmic prose. Music is the equivalent of what would be regularly rhythmic prose, in the sense that the regular rhythmic organization does not depend on dividing the musical sequence into subsections (lines).

3. WHAT METRICAL VERSE, WORD-STRESS RULES, AND METRICAL MUSIC HAVE IN COMMON

All three domains—metrical verse, word-stress rules, and metrical music—project their own proprietary material (syllables or musical beats) as asterisks (by rule (31), a version of (2)).

(31)
Project each syllable (or beat) as an asterisk on gridline 0.

In all three domains, asterisks are put into groups, defined as in (2).

(2)
A left parenthesis groups the asterisks on its right; a right parenthesis groups the asterisks on its left. Asterisks that are neither to the right of a left parenthesis, nor to the left of a right parenthesis, are ungrouped.

On each gridline, parentheses are inserted, and the groups so formed project one asterisk each to the next gridline; so the grid is generated. The most important type of rule is an iterative rule (and in metrical poetry, there must be iterative rules on every gridline). The possible iterative rules are defined by setting parameters from a basic rule template as stated in (32), a restatement of (4).

(32)
a. Nature of parenthesis inserted (L/R).
b. Edge of the sequence (L/R) at which insertion begins.
c. Interval between consecutive insertions (2/3).
d. Insertion starts just at the edge of the gridline, one asterisk in, or two asterisks in.
e. Head location in group (L/R).

We propose that the rules and the simple symbols (asterisk, left parenthesis, and right parenthesis) and complex symbols (grids) represent the operations of cognition, though in ways not yet understood.

V. CONCLUSION: COUNTING AND IMPLICATIONS FOR "LITERATURE AND COGNITION"

Metrical verse is a type of literary form that involves the counting of syllables. In this chapter we have argued that counting is a side effect of the application of a set of rules to each line. The line, consisting of a sequence of syllables, is first projected as a sequence of asterisks. Then the asterisks are put into pairs or triplets by a rule that iteratively inserts parentheses, thus forming groups, from each of which another asterisk is projected to the next gridline. The combined requirement that there are iterative rules on every gridline and that the grid have a single asterisk on its final gridline means that the iterative rules for a specific meter can generate a well-formed grid only from a line that does not exceed a maximum length: in this way, the syllables in the line are "counted."

There are other ways of counting syllables, but none of these ways of counting syllables explains the specific characteristics of metrical counting: the specific variabilities in number, or the relation between counting and rhythm (or other characteristics such as French caesura). For example, syllables can be counted by assigning number words to them. One reason for thinking that number-word assignment is implausible as a general explanation is that it cannot explain the ability to compose metrical verse shown by poets who are not numerate, or metrical traditions in a language where the number vocabulary is quite limited, such as Dyirbal, which has eleven-syllable meter but no word for "eleven" (Dixon and Koch 1996; Fabb 1997, 115). As an aside we note that, in rare cases, line length in poems is however controlled by counting the syllables by assigning number words—that is, without grouping them into pairs or triplets. In Fabb and Halle (2008) we show that this is the case for some of the Psalms, including Psalms 23, 24, and 137. However, in general, general methods of counting cannot be possible. Consider the possibility (sometimes floated) that finger counting is a way of measuring the length of the line (see Fabb 2002, 48–51 for discussion). But if this were really the basis for counting syllables, we might expect to find five and ten syllables as typical lengths for lines, and might not expect to find meters longer than ten syllables (because they would be difficult to count on the fingers). We note that the line length in the Homeric hexameter varies between thirteen and seventeen syllables, numbers which make no sense in terms of fingers and thumbs—but which we can explain in terms of a grid (Fabb and Halle 2008, 169–73).

Butterworth (1999) discusses the various kinds of mathematical ability from a cognitive perspective, involving the use of number words, or finger (and body) counting. It is possible that there is a psychological faculty (or module) specialized for the counting of things in general (see also Carruthers 2006, 99). However, the implications of the present chapter are that syllables are counted in metrical verse by a special mechanism that is not necessarily part of the general psychological faculty for counting. Instead, this mechanism—the use of iterative rules to generate a bracketed grid—is specific to certain domains, and shared between literature, music, and aspects of language. Little is yet known about the cognitive structures that constitute our mental abilities to use language or compose metrical verse or music. However, the discussions here suggest that there are connections between the mental abilities involved in all three of these. We regard the proposals made in this essay as a first step toward setting the parameters that some future cognitive science will need to explain.

NOTE

AUTHOR'S NOTE: Thanks to Stefano Versace and Gary Thoms for comments on this essay.

WORKS CITED

Butterworth, B. 1999. *The mathematical brain*. London: Macmillan.

Carruthers, P. 2006. *The architecture of the mind*. Oxford: Oxford University Press.

Dixon, R. M. W., and G. Koch. 1996. *Dyirbal song poetry: The oral literature of an Australian rainforest people*. St Lucia: University of Queensland Press.

Fabb, N. 1997. *Linguistics and literature: Language in the verbal arts of the world*. Oxford: Blackwell.

———. 2002. *Language and literary structure: The linguistic analysis of form in verse and narrative*. Cambridge: Cambridge University Press.

———. 2009. Why is verse poetry? *Poetry Nation Review* no. 189: 52–57.

———. 2010a. Is literary language a development of ordinary language? *Lingua* 120, no. 5: 1219–32.

———. 2010b. The non-linguistic in poetic-language: A generative approach. *Journal of Literary Theory* 4, no. 1: 1–18.

Fabb, N., and M. Halle. 2008. *Meter in poetry: A new theory*. Cambridge: Cambridge University Press.

———. 2011. Grouping in the stressing of words, in metrical verse, and in music. In *Language and music as cognitive systems*. Edited by Patrick Rebuschat, Martin Rohrmeier, John Hawkins, and Ian Cross. Oxford: Oxford University Press.

Haas, M. R. 1977. Tonal accent in Creek. In *Studies in stress and accent*, 195–208. Edited by Larry Hyman. Southern California occasional papers in linguistics, 4. Los Angeles: University of Southern California.

Halle, M., and W. Idsardi. 1995. General properties of stress and metrical structure. In *The handbook of phonological theory*, 403–43. Edited by J. Goldsmith. Oxford: Blackwell.

Idsardi, W. J. 1992. The computation of prosody. PhD diss., MIT.

Lerdahl, Fred, and Ray Jackendoff. 1983. *A generative theory of tonal music*. Cambridge, MA: MIT Press.

CHAPTER 10

FICTIVE MOTION AND PERSPECTIVAL CONSTRUAL IN THE LYRIC[1]

CLAIBORNE RICE

A COGNITIVE SCIENCE APPROACH to poetry will ask first what a reader's response to a text is, and second what kind of cognitive architecture is necessary to create such a response from that text. As Hogan (2003) describes, cognitive architecture is understood as having three separate components: structures, processes, and contents. Structure refers to "the general organizational principles of the mind" (30), such as the distinction between long-term and short-term or working memory. Content usually refers to representations or symbols that have specific locations in structures, and processes are structurally constrained operations that are performed on contents. For example, our mental storehouse of words, the lexicon, is a substructure of our long-term memory system that provides structural links between individual words, such that the activation of one word primes, or prepares, many other words for access. The meanings of each word, in this view, are representational contents, and formulating a sentence for pronunciation would be a process that at some point involves accessing the lexicon to retrieve the phonemic profile for the appropriate words.

Establishing what responses to literature cognitive approaches should attend to is no trivial matter, and empirical procedures have become more adept at identifying such literary responses (Miall 2006). This essay, however, will focus on a response frequently attested to by readers of lyric poetry, the sense they often have of experiencing a consciousness that is not their own. I will use the term "voice poetry" to denote the kind of poem that aims to produce this effect in the standard first-person, free verse, lyric form that is familiar to readers of the largest American poetry magazines, like *Poetry* or *American Poetry Review*, or in large-circulation magazines like the *New Yorker* or *Atlantic Monthly*. This is the kind of poem preferred by Helen Vendler, former poetry editor for the *New Yorker*, who states that the reading of a poem should cause one "to be transformed into the poem's . . . speaker" (2002). The poem "ma[kes] us want to enter the lyric script" (1997, 18) even to the extent of "losing our own identity" (1983, 246). Similarly, the Romanticist Anne Williams has said that a lyric poem "induces the reader to know, from within, the virtual experience of a more or less particularized consciousness" (1984, 15). Billy Collins is a good example of a popular contemporary poet who attempts to write poems that create such a lyric consciousness. As a former US poet laureate (2001–2003), Collins has been acclaimed as one of the country's leading poets, and has the book sales to show for it (Merrin 2002, 202). Describing the kind of poetry he prefers, Collins has said that "[w]hen we read a poem, we enter the consciousness of another" (2001). In order to make this happen, Collins says, the poem must conform to certain expectations regarding how information has to "be shaped and contoured to be intelligible" (2001). In addition, he says, the poem's language must slow readers down so that they can begin to sense the richness of linguistic response that readers usually neglect in favor of searching for meaning.

If we accept Collins's description of the usual response to properly shaped voice poetry, then what is the cognitive architecture that can generate such a response from reading the poetic text? Of the few elaborated theories of how consciousness arises, neuroscientist Antonio Damasio's "somatic marker hypothesis" (1994) is unique in describing a means by which subjectivity arises within consciousness (240–44). Because the subjective perspective is so obviously important to any theory of lyric, Damasio's approach provides a basis for beginning to understand how a lyric text can prompt one to construct a mental representation that can be recognized as consciousness-like yet that is not one's own self. According to Damasio, three particular states of consciousness are associated with three particular conditions of the subject of consciousness, what we normally identify as our "self." The *proto-self*, of which we are not conscious, is the "interconnected and temporarily coherent collection of neural patterns which represent the state of the organism" (1999, 144). The *core self*, a "subtle, fleeting feeling of knowing" (1999, 196), arises with core consciousness, which is "continuously and consistently reconstructed" moment by moment as our organism registers the changes of state introduced by experiencing any object that affects us (1994, 238–40; see Table 1 below). Finally, the *autobiographical self* that we recognize as our stable and permanent self, capable of long-term planning, is associated with extended consciousness, the effect of a large long-term memory both for sequential events and for those events recalled as experiences of a knower (1999, 197). Table 1 summarizes the characteristics of the self that are linked with the three different states of consciousness.

Damasio has studied stroke victims who have suffered left-side paralysis

Table 1. Three types of consciousness and self
(adapted from Damasio 1994, 1999, 2010; Bucci 2002)

State of Consciousness	State of Self
Nonconscious	Proto-Self An interconnected and temporarily coherent collection of neural patterns which represent the state of the organism, moment by moment
Core Consciousness Created in pulses as objects perturb the organism, and the organism generates an account of how the organism's own state is affected by the processing of an object, it focuses attention on an object and increases object salience	Core Self A second-order nonverbal account that occurs when an object modifies the proto-self, this can be triggered by any internal or external object; because provoking objects are continually available, core self is continuously available, thus it appears continuous in time
Extended Consciousness The capacity to be aware of a large compass of entities and events: ability to generate a sense of individual perspective, ownership, and agency linked to autobiographical self	Autobiographical Self A self based on autobiographical memory constituted by implicit memories of multiple instances of individual experience of the past and of the anticipated future; it does not require language

caused by damage to the right hemisphere of their brains. If a particular part of the right hemisphere is damaged, the patients will suffer from anosognosia—they will be unable to acknowledge or recognize their infirmities. The patients may be unable to walk or lift their left arms, but will deny that they are sick at all or that they cannot move their limbs. He believes that what has been damaged is the area responsible for a group of cognitive functions that he calls the "somatosensory map."[2] It comprehensively describes the current body state, integrating the ongoing feedback both from our organism's external senses of touch, temperature, and pain, and our internal senses of joint position, visceral state, and pain (1994, 65). The somatosensory map plays a special role in the production of consciousness. As an organism experiences an object, the object perturbs the current state of the organism. A moment later, "the brain creates a description of the perturbation of the state of the organism," which leads to the generation of "an image of the process of perturbation." This image of the "self perturbed" can then be nominated as the focus of attention, serving as a perturbing object and starting the cycle again (241). Object images reconstructed from memory or prompted by language are "less vivid than those prompted by the exterior" (108) but they are images nonetheless, and as such can be the basis for the creation of core consciousness. Literary experiences take their place within the panorama of feelings and experiences that the organism evaluates on an ongoing basis. Core consciousness provides the transient feeling of self-awareness that lies behind the array of established memories that are the content of our autobiographical self.

Emotions and feelings are tied to the cycle of consciousness because they are part of the organism's self-monitoring system. Background emotions (closely tied to core consciousness) are indices of momentary parameters of inner organism states, such as fatigue, energy, wellness, sickness, relaxation, harmony, and discord. What we normally recognize as having an emotion is a well-orchestrated, observable change in body state in response to a perturbing object, for the purpose of preparing and executing attract/repel behavior.

Damasio also distinguishes between primary and secondary emotions. Primary emotions are "early," "innate," "preorganized," and "Jamesian," involving the limbic system, amygdala, and anterior cingulate (1994, 133–34). Secondary emotions are acquired associations between categories of objects/situations and primary emotions; they involve the prefrontal and somatosensory cortices. Finally, a feeling is always a feeling of an emotion: the internal state of an organism is undergoing changes in response to an object, and the ongoing changes are re-represented as associated with the object (158–64).

This interlinking of the organism's collected somatic accommodations is exactly the mechanism behind the "somatic marker" as Damasio describes it. The image of the current organism state can be filed in memory and recalled if necessary. Somatosensory images become attached to particular memories and, his research shows, often serve to aid decision making. Somatic states mark the outcome of a situation as positive or negative by activating a generally positive or negative body state that accompanies what he calls the "as-if" body loop, the ability of the somatosensory map to model a procedure as if it were happening to the body (using the so-called "mirror neurons"; 2010, 102–3). Strong negative responses generate explicit imagery related to outcome and raise these images to consciousness, or they could "inhibit regulatory neural circuits located in the brain core, which mediate appetitive, or approach, behaviors," reducing the chance of a potentially negative decision, the functional equivalent of "intuition" (1994, 187).

To summarize, in Damasio's theory emotion, feeling, and consciousness are strongly body-involved. The apparent self emerges as the feeling of a feeling—that is, as a feeling is nominated for focal attention, "the answer to a question never asked." Self is inferred from the linkages between the images that stimulate bodily responses and the body that executes the responses, thus is a self always associated with a perspective (2010, 198). One's sense of action is inferred from the fact that certain images are tightly associated with certain options for motor response.

Damasio's reliance on humans' general inferential capabilities is important here, because inference implies categorization, which opens the door for similar but not identical things to be taken as tokens of the same type. For example, alliterative patterns in poetry can draw attention during reading because they amount to unanticipated patterned feedback from anticipated and executed bodily actions. That is, in reading silently or aloud, one sets about to execute sequences of muscular actions and anticipates certain somatic responses that characterize accurate rendering of the phonological codes, "memories of the future" as Damasio refers to these kinds of anticipated responses (1999, 203). Alliterative patterns that arise in free verse garner attention because one's habitually anticipated responses do not include experiencing patterns of repeated sounds. In other words, in normal speech one is consciously attending to meaning while the speech apparatus operates without conscious monitoring. If alliterative patterns happen in normal speech they usually do not attract attention because they are not relevant to meaning. But if a focus on meaning does not immediately reward primary attention, alternative patterns in the speech can become nominated for attention. Because alliterative patterns are sensory, they can function as convergent somatic evidence that gives rise to the inference of self. In general, because images are being produced in the as-if body loop in response to words, one can be vaguely aware that the self being inferred is not one's own. Readers know that they are reading a poem and not walking through a field of daffodils. Yet the minor somatic feedback of alliterative patterns can nonetheless serve as a substitute somatic response sufficient for inferring that a body is acting and reacting in response to environmental stimuli.

This cognitive architecture Damasio describes for the somatic marker provides the basis for understanding how reading poetry can stimulate the sense of experiencing a consciousness. In this context, the processing of verbs of motion can be understood as contributing to the overall effect of experiencing a virtual self observing and acting in an imagined world. When we process motion verbs, we engage many of the same neural and cognitive resources that we use when actually executing the motions in question or when observing those motions being executed by others (Wallentin et al. 2005; summary in Wheeler and Bergen 2010). Neural activation occurs also when action verbs are used with inanimate subjects in "fictive motion" contexts, when they describe static scenes in a way that traditionally would be considered metaphoric because something inanimate is represented as animate.

The fence follows the coastline.
The fence is next to the coastline.

Although both sentences describe the same situation, the first utilizes a verb that normally takes an animate subject. Processing fictive motion sentences can interfere with abstract reasoning, just as cognitively processing real motion can. In a series of experiments, Lera Boroditsky and her associates deployed a common English ambiguity to see if people would respond differently to the ambiguity if they were either involved in a particular action or if they simply processed a linguistic description that utilized action verbs. English has two conflicting conventional metaphors for talking about time:

Ego Moving: "We are rapidly approaching our first anniversary." (The ego is moving forward toward the future, which stays still.)
Time Moving: "The deadline is quickly approaching us, so we'd better get to work." (The ego stays still, and the event approaches the ego from the future.)

English speakers will mix these metaphors freely without noticing any discord—as in, "The deadline is approaching, but luckily we are getting ahead of schedule." Boroditsky and Ramscar (2002) presented one group of subjects with a statement, then asked for a response: Next Wednesday's meeting has been moved forward two days. What day is the meeting now that it has been rescheduled? In a neutral context, the answers of English speakers will generally split between Friday (the ego-moving answer) and Monday (the time-moving answer), and individual speakers will often be very committed as to the correctness of their interpretations. Two other groups of speakers, however, were primed with an activity. One group was seated in a chair with wheels, like an office chair, and asked to diagram a plan for how they would propel themselves across the room. Another group was seated in a fixed location, then asked to diagram a plan for how to propel an empty, wheeled chair toward themselves. After engaging in the priming activity, speakers responded to the ambiguous question with a bias of about 67 percent in favor of the activity in which they had engaged, answering Friday (ego-moving) if they were in the mobile chair or Monday (time-moving) if they were supposed to think about drawing the chair toward themselves. The experimenters extended their investigation to people who had been waiting in lines, at the airport or the cafeteria, and confirmed that the answer bias remained for people who had recently been in motion themselves, having just flown in, for example, or who had made it nearly to the front of the cafeteria line. The bias also existed, but was slightly weaker, for people who had not been in motion but had perhaps been thinking about it, such as those waiting to catch a plane.

Later experiments with the same ambiguous question have demonstrated that processing fictive motion sentences also produces the same bias created by both real and imagined motion (Matlock, Ramscar, and Boroditsky 2003). It has also been shown that fictive motion involves mental simulation of motion that is immediately integrated with eye movement and visual processing (Matlock 2004; Richardson and Matlock 2007), and that fictive motion sentences yield no less activation in the left posterior middle temporal region than sentences with subjects to which action can be applied. The same area is implicated in processing images of motion and implied motion (Wallentin et al. 2005).

The importance of motion verbs for poetry, in the context of Damasio's somatic marker architecture, is that nerves and muscles are activated when readers process action verbs just as if action were being observed or as if the readers themselves were preparing to act. Actions executed in imagination create somatosensory feedback from the relevant motor responses, providing, even if in only a diminished way, links between images that stimulate somatic responses and the body that executes those responses, the basis for inferring a self. Rhythmic and alliterative patterns can then provide convergent evidence for an inferred, virtual consciousness.

In the semantics of cognitive linguistics, fictive motion is considered a "construal" operation associated with dynamic attention (Croft and Cruse 2004, 53–54). Language is a tool that helps a speaker organize the many aspects of an event so that the hearer can imaginatively reconstruct that event. Much of this organization is accomplished by oppositions embedded in the language from which the speaker chooses the desired conceptualization. The importance of conceptualization is easy to see when a language provides alternative means of referring to equivalent truth-conditional situations. For example, the two sentences below can describe the same house, but take different elements as their focus:

The chimney is above the window.
The window is below the chimney.

The selection of one element of the house for focal attention is a construal operation. In fictive motion sentences, the action of the verb is construed dynamically rather than statically, with the result being that more attention is given to the path than in a static representation. Matlock (2004) discovered that subjects read a fictive motion passage more slowly if primed to imagine that the path described is uneven or bumpy than if they imagine the path to be smooth. Richardson and Matlock (2007) found in an eye-tracking study that subjects look longer at a path and scan it with more fixation points if they expect it to be difficult as opposed to easy, but only if the path is indicated by fictive motion. These results suggest that the reader's somatic involvement is greater with fictive motion verbs than with static or non-motion verbs in the same context.

For Billy Collins, a poem must shape and contour information in order to be intelligible. In the poem "Looking West," from his book *Picnic, Lightning* (1998), the somatic effects of the motion verbs are both heightened and pro-longed by the addition of several prepositional phrases to each clause. Also, all six stanzas of the poem are together punctuated as a single sentence, so substantial clause boundaries must be inferred by the reader, an additional cognitive load that will direct attention to the potential argument structures of each verb.

> *Just beyond the flower garden at the end of the lawn*
> *the curvature of the earth begins,*
>
> *sloping down from there*
> *over the length of the country*
>
> *and the smooth surface of the Pacific*
> *before it continues across the convex rice fields of Asia*
>
> *and, rising, inclines over Europe*
> *and the bulging, boat-dotted waters of the Atlantic,*
>
> *finally reaching the other side of the house*
> *where it comes up behind a yellow grove of forsythia*
>
> *near a dilapidated picnic table,*
> *then passes unerringly under the spot*
>
> *where I am standing, hands in my pockets,*
> *feet planted firmly on the ground.*

The verbs of "Looking West" are muted in terms of action at the poem's outset. The easy rhythm established by the prepositional phrases helps sustain the sense of forward motion incited by just the few verbs. "Begins," "sloping," and "continues" do not seem metaphorical because they are conventionally used to talk about lines or planes. The smoothness of the terrain over the

Pacific and the "rice fields of Asia" conditions a slightly faster reading pace, consonant with the downhill path. We are not surprised, then, that as the journey reaches the bottom of the globe and begins to ascend the other side, the implication of more energy being expended will call for an image of rougher terrain. As in Matlock's (2004) experiments, conceptualizing the bumpy terrain described as the "bulging, boat-dotted waters of the Atlantic" slows readers down, as does pronouncing the line's ponderous alliteration (ending one word then beginning the next word with homologous consonants, as in "boat-dotted," also slows readers a great deal). The alliteration here is also iconic, in that the bumpy pronunciation mimics the bulging waves or the boats that interrupt the smoothness of the waters. Predictably, the journey of a circle must end where it began. The final verbs in the poem, "standing" and "planted," do not imply motion in context, and so bring any subjective sense of forward motion to an end. This is a pleasant little journey Collins has taken us on, reminiscent perhaps of T. S. Eliot's statement about poetry in *Little Gidding* that "the end of all our exploring / Will be to arrive where we started / And know the place for the first time" (lines 242–44).

This poem manifests all the characteristics of a voice lyric calculated to create the sense on the reader's part that he or she is experiencing—living, actually—the depicted actions. Of highest importance is creating a unified perspectival construal, even if that construal is fantastic. Indeed, Collins might argue that the construal of a fantastic voyage is enabled by the stability of the embedded perspective; too many distracting elements might put readers off of the poem altogether. The framing at the beginning of the poem is important to set the visual scene in some sort of delimited, contained context (as a test of how this works, invert the first two lines and see if the first couple of stanzas have the same effect). Once the scene is set, a stable construal perspective is provided. Objects are described as being in appropriate places relative to the viewer, and when the forward movement begins ("the curvature of the earth begins, / sloping down") the objects viewed are coherent with the established position of viewing (even though the trip is utterly fantastic, we can recruit analogues if necessary, such as an airplane flight or spinning a globe). Notice how construal can shift in response to lexical cues. For many English speakers, the phrase "the curvature of the earth" suggests a horizontal image, with the horizon at its highest point centrally and curving down toward the extremes. Once the verb "begins" is added, however, the path away from the viewer, across the lawn, and over the flower garden becomes more salient, so that the construal shifts to a line perpendicular to the horizon (and the line break after the verb is helpful in allowing a moment to shift construal). The fictive motion also contributes to this slippage of construal by allowing some vagueness into the interpretation of the prepositions, that is amplified by verbs later in the poem. Both "over" and "across" have competing senses by which the path of motion they imply can be either contiguous to the surface they traverse or above it without contact. The "curvature of the earth," as a characteristic of a surface, should select the contiguous senses for those prepositions, but the feeling of motion and the perspective of a swift journey allow us easily to shift construal to a linear path above the surface. Later in the poem, as the path, "rising, inclines over Europe," the default construal seems to be that of non-contiguity—the reader is in the air high above the continent, able perhaps to take in the continent and then the Atlantic Ocean in successive imaginative glances.

The sonic elements of the poem support the formation of a virtual consciousness, as described above. When the body is in motion, information from both the visual and vestibular systems causes the extra-ocular eye muscles to adjust for forward and sideways motion so that a distant object can remain in focus (Mather 2006, 71). Because neurons in the vestibular nuclei are activated by visual information as well as by vestibular signals, the sensations of body motion derived from visual and vestibular signals are indistinguishable. The reader of "Looking West" is clearly not in motion but only imagining motion, so the appropriate vestibular feedback is missing. According to Damasio's somatic marker hypothesis, however, unanticipated patterns of somatic disturbances should attract attention. In voice poetry, patterns of alliteration can serve as a sort of somatic disinformation, substituting as somatic feedback that gives the brain just enough patterned response to categorize the responses as resulting from self-initiated action, triggering in turn the inference that a self is directing that action. Notice that this discovery of the self is thematized by the poetic conceit. Once the poetic machine is set in motion, the imaginative journey has an inevitable destination, the discovery of one's self, represented by the first-person pronoun, which had been there all along, "feet planted firmly on the ground." The regular iambic rhythm of the final line underscores the sense of inevitability as well as closure—a technique Collins is overly fond of. Even this last confident emotional element contributes to the sense of a unified, embodied perspective because emotions are part of what we normally expect to experience as selves.

In contrast with the stable perspective constructed by Collins, Lyn Hejinian, as a Language poet, prefers to avoid constructing such accessible, stable perspectives in her poetry. She has been an outspoken opponent of "voice" poetry, which Ron Silliman has called "the optical illusion of reality in capitalist thought" (1984, 125). Speaking of the unified subject, Hejinian calls the "unitary, expressive self, the 'I' of the lyric poem" that seems to be the production goal of voice lyrics like Collins's, a "simpleminded model of subjectivity and authority" (2000, 329). One of her poetic goals, then, is to create a more ethical lyric by dismantling the unified subject. "Poetry refuses," she says, "either through appropriation ('you are like me'), or empathy ('I am like you'), to deny or repress the otherness of others" (2000, 332). Breaking down the unified lyric subject can be accomplished to some degree by simply failing to do those things that the voice lyric requires: Avoid the first person singular pronoun, or mix it with other ungrounded personal pronouns; avoid end-rhyme and alliteration and other sonic patterning, or use it only in very limited local instances; and rather than providing sequences of phrases which construct perspectives that allow for easy, coherent construal, juxtapose phrases that require construals that are not sequentially coherent. This to some degree describes well her long work *My Life*, but does not suffice for many of the shorter poems. In some of Hejinian's early work collected in *The Cold of Poetry* we see many lyrics that do not so much break down the unified self (as if it were something that already existed), but that might be described as providing sparser cues to assist the reader in building up a perceiving subject. The construal of scenes is not incoherent as much as it is simply hard won. Take for example "The Captive of the Eye," the first of fourteen stanzas of "Punctual" (in *The Cold of Poetry*, 81–82):

at eye level, eye
level sky, water, shelf
event—but not yet foreground

blunt or wide
it drops open
dropping open view

but bends
as bend
the bend predicts

and there's reecho
recorded, pinpointed

a life might be something (or someone's)
of dots

so doubled—not thus—so very doubled
and very much combined
bound

and in scenic accidents

as at a window I had to go on
that is, to elaborate

to mow (though it's funny to say so)
or mop at the small sun

and in the steps that all visitors take
my figure sticks
the anchor sways—

in tatters of disorder
order waves

"Punctual" bears the strong mark of Gertrude Stein, whose rhythms of repetition one can see here, for example in the repetition first of the participle then of the intensifier of "so doubled—not thus—so very doubled / and very much combined," and of the motion verbs "drops . . . dropping" and "bend" used in three successive lines, as a verb then as a noun. "The captive of the eye," like the whole poem "Punctual," concerns itself with landscape, investigating the interaction between viewer and landscape in painting and by implication between reader and poem as well. "A landscape is a moment of time / that has gotten in position," Hejinian says in "The Guard" (*The Cold of Poetry*, 11). The landscape painting is structured so that one might examine it and become captivated by its representations. In this understanding, the receding vistas in a landscape painting function doubly—they capture the eye by constructing a perspective for the viewer, and they symbolize the captivating nature of representational iconicity.

Readers not familiar with Hejinian's poetics might be surprised to discover that "The Captive of the Eye" narrates its speaker into existence much the way that "Looking West" does. The important difference is that the role of discovery is more salient for Hejinian than it is for Collins. Collins's trope of a circular voyage is suffused with the sense of inevitability, while the surprise of discovering a viewing self is more palpable with Hejinian. The poem utilizes the motion verbs at exactly the point at which the viewer becomes drawn into the landscape, "it drops open." The two stanzas constructed around "drops" and "bends" suggest forward motion as if a viewer is following a viewing pathway, but the somatic effect is strengthened almost wholly by lexical repetition. One gets motion processing with images of motion, motion words, and sentences that allow literal or fictive motion interpretations (Wallentin et al. 2005). To a certain degree, one can achieve the cognitive effects of motion processing without fulfilling even the frame requirements of the motion verb. Here, "it drops open," but we don't know what "it" represents—if we choose to decide what in the given scene could drop open, the scarcity of cues guarantees it will vary with individual readers. "Bends" is provided even less frame material, so that there is no suggestion of the theme (the item that is undergoing the change in shape; see Stockwell 2002). The shift of the word from verb to noun suggests that the motion perceived as a dynamic process can be gradually traded away for a construal in which the scene is perceived as a discrete unit rather than as a process (Croft and Cruse 2004, 53). While the chaining of prepositional phrases suited Collins's dominating trope of extending a path, and also prolonged the motion processing instigated by the lexical verbs, Hejinian's tight lexical repetition of the verbs achieves a very similar prolongation of motion processing while emphasizing the trope of doubling that pervades the poem.

Yet as with Collins's poem, the processing of motion verbs, even with a syntax that provides only a small part of the information that one expects to accompany a particular motion verb, evokes the sense of a self that subtends the body that acts. Again like Collins's, the poem narrates the coming into being of this virtual consciousness, done here with the tropes of doubling, first as a "reecho," then more surely detected as a "pinpoint" or "dot," as a silent "double," then as a full first-person pronoun, and finally as a stick figure (or "a figure that sticks"). What Hejinian seems to have discovered about poetry is that language is embodied, and that using language cannot fail to implicate the body. Since the body is the ground of consciousness, the lyric effect of the virtual consciousness is more stubborn, more insistent than voice poetry might want to admit. The human salvages meaning, even coherence, from what appears to us, trapped within our expectations of normative perceptual integrity, to be tattered remnants of the tangible world.

> *my figure sticks*
> *the anchor sways—*
>
> *in tatters of disorder*
> *order waves*

CONCLUSION

Cognitive poetics seeks to describe the cognitive architecture that accounts for responses to poetic texts, recognizing that as a genre poetry differs widely across linguistic and other cultural traditions. While many characteristics of poetry as a genre of linguistic discourse may be accounted for as evolving from specific cultural practices, it remains true that individual responses to poetry can be identified and described, either through the empirical method-ologies of psychology or the testimony of individual readers such as critics and reviewers. Rather than enunciating a normative theory of aesthetic quality, cognitive poetics seeks to describe the wide variety of stable poetic practices. In this essay I have identified examples of two different styles of lyric poetry that are claimed by their advocates to have different aims and supporting ide-ologies. The two poems appear to be quite different in their deployment of syntax and construction of point of view, yet both poems leverage the normal linguistic processing of motion verbs to create the dawning sense of a self ob-serving. The cognitive architecture that supports this process is the same one described by Damasio as supporting his "somatic marker hypothesis" (1994, 1999, 2010). For Damasio, having a body implies having a perspective, and our felt sense of self arises as the inference of agency when the body's planned ac-tions result in anticipated bodily responses (1994, 238–40). Even if some of the anticipated responses do not occur, because a reader of poetry is merely sitting in a chair rather than flying around the world, linguistic patterns like rhyme or alliteration can serve as a mild form of convergent evidence that the body is experiencing the narrated events. Collins's poetics provides a stable pathway for the appearance of this virtual consciousness by constructing a sequence of construals that invite a coherent, if unusual, perspective from moment to moment. Hejinian, on the other hand, does not provide such coherence, but gives the reader considerable leeway to construe one or several perspectives from the spare lexical prompts. Yet the repetition of the motion verbs insists on the inferential appearance of an experiencing subject. Thus both poems share an element of surprise at the result, but Hejinian's process of discovery seems more genuine because less contrived. Further examination of Hejinian's poetry using cognitive poetics would be enlightening for Damasio's theory because Hejinian's poetry emphasizes that "self-consciousness / is discon-tinuous" (*The Cold of Poetry*, 176). Damasio, however, presupposes a unity of the experiencing subject based on the stability of the body's self-regulating mechanisms and the familiarity one develops with one's body over time (1999, 141–45). One goal of using cognitive science to account for poetic practice is to discover what insights of the poets regarding how language works might in turn be helpful in developing a more accurate scientific understanding of language and cognition.

NOTES

1. "Looking West" from Billy Collins, *Picnic, Lightning* (Pittsburgh: University of Pittsburgh Press, 1998); reprinted by permission of the University of Pittsburgh Press. "The Captive of the Eye" from Lyn Hejinian, *The Cold of Poetry* (Los Angeles: Sun & Moon Press, 1994); reprinted with permission from the author.

2. Since 1994 a great deal of work has been done on the structures and roles of somatosensory maps. Damasio (2010) integrates much of this new research into his theory of self-consciousness. A good, popular introduction to body maps and the issues surrounding them is Blakeslee and Blakeslee (2007).

WORKS CITED

Blakeslee, Sandra, and Matthew Blakeslee. 2007. *The body has a mind of its own*. New York: Random House.

Boroditsky, Lera, and Michael Ramscar. 2002. The roles of body and mind in abstract thought. *Psychological Science* 13, no. 2: 185–88.

Bucci, Wilma. 2002. The referential process, consciousness, and the sense of self. *Psychoanalytic Inquiry* 22, no. 5: 766–93.

Collins, Billy. 1998. *Picnic, lightning*. Pittsburgh: University of Pittsburgh Press.

Collins, Billy. 2001. The companionship of a poem. *Chronicle of Higher Education*, November 13. http://chronicle.com/weekly/v48/i13/13b00501.htm (accessed April 15, 2011).

Croft, William, and D. A. Cruse. 2004. *Cognitive linguistics*. Cambridge: Cambridge University Press.

Damasio, Antonio R. 1994. *Descartes' error*. New York: Avon.

———. 1999. *The feeling of what happens*. New York: Harcourt.

———. 2010. *Self comes to mind: Constructing the conscious brain*. New York: Pantheon.

Hejinian, Lyn. 1994. *The cold of poetry*. Los Angeles: Sun & Moon Press.

———. 2000. *The language of inquiry*. Berkeley: University of California Press.

Hogan, Patrick Colm. 2003. *Cognitive science, literature, and the arts: A guide for humanists*. London: Routledge.

Mather, George. 2006. *Foundations of perception*. London: Psychology Press.

Matlock, Teenie. 2004. Fictive motion as cognitive simulation. *Memory & Cognition* 32: 1389–1400.

Matlock, Teenie, Michael Ramscar, and Lera Boroditsky. 2003. The experiential basis of meaning. In *Proceedings of the twenty-fifth annual conference of the Cognitive Science Society*. Mahwah, NJ: Lawrence Erlbaum, 792–97.

Merrin, Jeredith. 2002. Art over easy. *Southern Review* 38: 202–14.

Miall, David. 2006. *Literary reading: Empirical and theoretical studies*. New York: Peter Lang.

Richardson, Daniel C., and Teenie Matlock. 2007. The integration of figurative language and static depictions: An eye movement study of fictive motion. *Cognition* 102: 129–38.

Silliman, Ron. 1984. Disappearance of the word, appearance of the world. In *The L=A=N=G=U=A=G=E Book*, 121–32. Edited by Bruce Andrews and Charles Bernstein. Carbondale: Southern Illinois University Press.

Stockwell, Peter. 2002. *Cognitive poetics: An introduction*. London: Routledge.

Vendler, Helen. 1983. *The odes of John Keats*. Cambridge, MA: Belknap.

———. 1997. *The art of Shakespeare's sonnets*. Cambridge, MA: Belknap.

————. 2002. *Poems, poets, poetry*, 2nd ed. Boston: Bedford.

Wallentin, M., T. E. Lund, L. Østergaard, S. Østergaard, and A. Roepstorff. 2005. Motion verb sentences activate left posterior middle temporal cortex despite static context. *NeuroReport* 16, no. 6: 649–52.

Wheeler, Kathryn, and Benjamin Bergen. 2010. Meaning in the palm of your hand. In *Empirical and experimental methods in conceptual structure, discourse, and language*. Edited by Sally Rice and John Newman. Stanford: CSLI. http://www2.hawaii.edu/~bergen/papers/WheelerBergenCHAPTER.pdf (accessed December 12, 2007).

Williams, Anne. 1984. *Prophetic strain*. Chicago: University of Chicago Press.

LITERATURE AND HUMAN DEVELOPMENT

This last section opens the volume to cultural and historicist perspectives on the role of literature in human education and development, by including two essays that investigate the didactic implications of literary creation and literary response in specific sociohistorical contexts. Sullivan's essay calls attention to how Romantic poets such as Anna Barbauld and William Wordsworth draw on Hartley's 1749 theory of mind to create "cognitive experiments" aimed at shaping the minds of readers through the embodied experiencing of poetry. Focusing on J. M. Barrie's *Peter and Wendy* (1911), Sacks explores the role of narratives as make-believe play that provides readers with an alternative life scenario where they can safely test behavior and prepare for the adult social world, while also challenging established ideology. This section allows us to further reflect on the impact of literature on self and society, preparing us for the discussion that Oatley, Mar, and Djikic introduce in the volume's postscript.

CHAPTER 11

EDUCATION BY POETRY: HARTLEY'S THEORY OF MIND AS A CONTEXT FOR UNDERSTANDING EARLY ROMANTIC POETIC STRATEGIES

BRAD SULLIVAN

> *[I]n Cicero and Augustine there is a shift between the words "move" (movere) and "bend" (flectere) to name the ultimate function of rhetoric. This shift corresponds to a distinction between act and attitude (attitude being an incipient act, a leaning or inclination). Thus the notion of persuasion to* attitude *would permit the application of rhetorical terms to purely* poetic *structures; the study of lyrical devices might be classed under the head of rhetoric, when these devices are considered for their power to induce or communicate states of mind to readers, even though the kinds of assent evoked have no overt, practical outcome.*
>
> (BURKE 1962, 50)

MORSE PECKHAM, in his influential essay "Toward a Theory of Romanticism," argued that Romanticism was best understood as a "revolution in the European mind" which created a paradigm shift from "static mechanism" to "dynamic organicism." For him, the new worldview that began emerging in the late eighteenth century centered on "change, imperfection, growth, diversity, the creative imagination," and "the unconscious" (Peckham 1970, 14). Truth, he writes, could no longer be seen as preexistent; new values and meanings were to be reached only symbolically. As a result, artists had to generate their own vision of truth and then perhaps enlist readers in that vision. In Peckham's view, those who found no cosmic order to communicate became "Negative Romantics" like Byron; those who *did* find cosmic order became "Positive Romantics" like Wordsworth. Both kinds of Romantic author found themselves increasingly alienated from an audience bound to the old order of things. Peckham's theory holds true for the final trajectory of Romanticism toward "art for art's sake," but it does not closely examine the rhetorical challenges—and *commitments*—of early Romantic poets.

Lucy Newlyn argues in *Reading, Writing, and Romanticism: The Anxiety of Reception* (2000) that Barbauld, Wordsworth, and Coleridge were anxious not just about their own reputation, but about the difficulties of reaching an increasingly diverse audience. Regina Hewitt (1990) suggests that such anxiety was grounded in what she calls "the empirical dilemma": if all our knowledge emerges from personal experience, and different people living different kinds of lives have substantially different kinds of experiences, what kind of shared knowledge can we rely on? As a scholar interested in rhetoric and cognition, I see that anxiety as emerging from the difficulties—the cognitive work—of intuiting the expectations, assumptions, and existing knowledge of readers "at a distance" and creating strategies by which to engage those readers effectively. Whether to sell books or to develop a shared ground for understanding each other, early Romantic poets felt the need to create an experiential "bridge" upon which they could meet their readers. And they doubted and worried at times as they worked.

The early Wordsworth, author of *Lyrical Ballads* (1798) and the evolving "Preface" (1800–1805), was hopeful, socially engaged, and eager to develop and share new ways of understanding the world with his readers. John Nabholtz (1986) argues persuasively that the "Preface" should be seen primarily as an effort to create a well-disposed audience. Early on, Wordsworth had much in common with an important poet and woman of letters who preceded him, and to whom he sent a presentation copy of the *Lyrical Ballads*: Anna Aikin Barbauld. Daniel White (1999) illustrates nicely how strongly communitarian and audience-aware Barbauld's writing really was. Because her audience was constituted in part by what White calls the "joineriana" of dissenting culture, Barbauld did not feel as great a need to *create* an audience as Wordsworth. Samuel Taylor Coleridge, on the other hand, reached a high level of audience anxiety very early in his career. Peckham grants him the intellectual advantage over his peers for recognizing the fundamental alienation of the author as early as "Rime of the Ancient Mariner"; Coleridge early in his life was clearly more preoccupied with isolated visionary experience, disturbances of the unconscious mind, and the difficulty of reaching readers. But while all three of these authors were more or less anxious about how to reach their audiences, that anxiety was not yet despair or defeatism in the early nineteenth century. All of them set out to reach and influence their audience, each believed that it was possible and desirable to do so, and each wrote poems that were structured to do real cognitive work.

In the epigraph to this essay, Kenneth Burke suggests how poems can do such cognitive work. They can generate attention, shift attitudes, and create or re-create "states of mind." They do so by way of what Wordsworth called "pleasure"—the engagement of author and reader in the dance of meaning.

In my book *Wordsworth and the Composition of Knowledge* (2000), I began to make the case that "feeling" and "pleasure" were complicated and important concepts in early Romanticism. "Feeling," in the formulation of early Romantic poets, was a hinge word that connected sensation and emotional response. "Pleasure," of course, was a hinge word that connected sensual and intellectual states. As such, both of these terms connected physiology and psychology—body states and frames of mind. We are familiar with such connections as they have been articulated in our own times by thinkers such as Antonio Damasio (1994, 1999); the Romantic poets were familiar with a text that sketched out some similar connections: David Hartley's *Observations on Man: His Frame, His Duty, and His Expectations* (1749).

In *Literature, Education, and Romanticism: Reading as Social Practice, 1780–1832* (1994), Alan Richardson stresses "the period's 'deep interest in the early growth of consciousness' as exemplified by the Wedgwood circle—Barbauld, Priestley, Beddoes, Day, Richard Edgeworth, and, by extension, Coleridge and Wordsworth" (62). This "circle" would have been familiar with Hartley's *Observations on Man* (which was reprinted at the insistence of Priestley in 1791) and the work of other contemporary theorists of mind who engaged and debated with Hartley's "associationist" views (Dugald Stewart, for example, who published his *Elements of the Philosophy of the Human Mind* in 1792). Wordsworth and Coleridge, who named his son after Hartley, were surely grappling with the central theories of the *Observations* in the 1790s. Barbauld would have been exposed to Hartley continually in her interactions at Warrington Academy. Priestley, her friend and mentor, was one of Hartley's most vociferous supporters throughout his life.

A vast tangle of commentary has been written on the role Hartley plays in Wordsworth's thought. Many scholars have set out to prove or disprove Wordsworth's indebtedness to Hartley. Their debates have tended to begin and end with Cartesian dichotomies—attempting to place Wordsworth clearly as either a "sensationalist" or a "transcendental" poet, or trying to rationalize the admixture of these two modes in Wordsworth's work by attributing his ideas to Hartley's influence on the one hand and Coleridge's on the other. Like John Hayden, who provides a valuable overview of these debates in his "Wordsworth, Hartley, and the Revisionists" (1984), I am not as concerned with questions of direct influence as I am with understanding the creative ways in which Wordsworth (and Barbauld) drew on available models and extended and developed them in their own writings.

My primary aim here is to explore the ways in which Hartley provided an initial theoretical framework for the literary integration of sensation and cognition that Alan Richardson calls "embodied universalism" in *British Romanticism and the Science of the Mind* (2001, 152). Like Richardson, I believe that "some Romantic-era writers [looked] to the body with its nervous system, brain, and 'organic' mind rather than to a disembodied Reason as the ground for human uniformity and equality" (177).[1] I suggest here that Barbauld and Wordsworth were two of the writers working in this mode, and make an attempt to illustrate (albeit briefly) the ways in which they may have adopted — and adapted — Hartley's principles in order to generate poetic structures that could experientially engage and activate the minds of readers.

Hartley's theory of mind centered on the idea that the mind emerged from, and was integrally wedded to, physiological processes. To explain that emergence, he worked from two "doctrines": a theory of vibrations and a theory of associations. Following Isaac Newton, he began with a view of matter suspended in space — particles held together by forces in field-like interaction. So he believed that sensory impressions were transmitted through nerve tissue by vibrations of those particles in space. The stronger the impression, the more displacement of the particles and the stronger the resulting vibration — creating wave-like movements along the nerves toward the brain.

In his system, sensory impressions are always primary and most forceful. They are the initial source of the vibrations that generate mental activity. When they enter the "medullary substance" of the brain, these vibrations are characterized by their location, direction, and strength. Sensory impressions thus generate simple ideas of sensation.

From there, the doctrine of association takes over. Simple ideas of sensation are associated with each other, and with states of the body, and by virtue of their associations they can generate or regenerate those states of mind and body. Their association also leads to complex ideas and actions, and eventually at a higher level of abstraction to what Hartley called "decomplex" ideas and actions. Hartley uses a central analogy in which simple, complex, and de-complex ideas are related to letters, words, sentences, and so on.

> As simple ideas run into complex ones by association, so complex ideas
> run into decomplex ones by the same. But here the varieties of the associa-
> tions, which increase with the complexity, hinder particular ones from being
> so close and permanent, between the complex parts of decomplex ideas, as
> between the simple parts of complex ones: to which it is analogous, in lan-
> guages, that the letters of words adhere closer together than the words of sen-
> tences, both in writing and in speaking. (Hartley 1998, 77)

Associations thus "fan out" from sense impressions to primary associations emerging from sensory impressions to secondary associations emerging from primary associations and so on. Primary associations are strongest, and the further one proceeds down the web the weaker the associations become.

Yet despite the weakening of associations at a distance from sensory impressions, Hartley theorized that patterns of association persist fairly strongly through time. Hartley believed that reactivation of vibratory patterns actually re-creates earlier states of mind and regenerates ideas. Wave-like patterns are strengthened by attention and repetition. Once associations are formed, they rapidly become habitual or automatic. Thus, for followers of Hartley, early associations (and, of course, the educational practices that *form* such early associations) are considered vitally important. Richardson reminds us, "Working from associationist premises, social theorists as diverse as Godwin, Adam Smith, Wollstonecraft, Robert Owen, and James Mill saw early education as crucial in forming (or reforming) society" (Richardson 1994, 12). The new emphasis on "'habit,' 'association,' and internalized discipline" reflected "a shift in educational practice from the instilling of formal precepts to the imposition of 'living rules,' making part of a more general cultural shift which saw social power take less coercive and more consensual, individualistic forms" (Richardson 1994, 60).

Richardson cites an educational shift, in theory, from dialectical argumentation toward "an emphasis on the formation of proper intellectual and moral 'habits,' the development of independent reasoning, and the internalization of authority" (Richardson 1994, 64). This shift was exemplified in the inquiry-centered teaching practices of Joseph Priestley at Warrington (Sullivan 2007; para. 5). However, the theory and the practice did not always match. "In actual practice," writes Richardson, "dialectic tended to yield to the mechanical production of set answers, obedient behavior within the educational setting, and (for the lower classes) passive literacy" (64). Independent reasoning and good "habits of mind" may have been the broader aim, but correct response and good habits of behavior often became the central didactic thrust.

Here we see that "habit" is a term that encompasses everything from "scientific method," which is a habitual *form* of inquiry used to generate *new* ideas about nature, to what Richardson calls "catechistic practices," which were meant to enforce orthodoxy and manage behavior. It can refer to mindful practice or mindless repetition. As such, it was a source of both hope and worry for early Romantic poets. How can poetry form good *habits* of mind without exerting control over the *contents* of readers' minds? How can it *change* existing habits of mind that are deeply entrenched? The goal for these authors was not the mechanical reproduction of beliefs, but the empowerment of each mind as an agent of understanding, and by extension, change. Their dilemma was how to *stimulate* their readers' minds without (a) *ruling* them or (b) making them feverish and fretful. Wordsworth repeatedly returns to "excitement" and "sensation" and "pleasure" in his "Preface." For him, the poems are a stimulus, a "charge" to the system of the reader, not a conveyance of preexisting ideas. The reader is invited to enter a process by which his or her associations may well be altered. The experiment, then, is with ways poetry can deliver a charge to readers without deranging them. Balance and modulation are stressed as well as excitement. Reflection and long thought are stressed as well as "spontaneous overflow of powerful feeling." Changing a culture requires changing minds; changing minds requires more than a rational argument that demands assent.

Anna Barbauld reveals her awareness of the inertial force of existing associations in her essay "On Prejudice" (1800). Here she begins by defining prejudice as "pre-judging; that is, judging previously to evidence" (Barbauld 2002, 335). But instead of expecting us to *eradicate* prejudice (the idealistic course pursued by Godwinian rationalists), Barbauld suggests that we should *accept* prejudice as part of human nature and try to work *with* it and *on* it:

> Let us confess a truth, humiliating perhaps to human pride: a very small part only of the opinions of the coolest philosopher are the result of fair reasoning; the rest are formed by his education, his temperament, by the age in which he lives, by trains of thought directed to a particular track through some accidental association—in short, by *prejudice*. (338)

Here she clearly suggests that reason and rational thinking are limited by our habits and (echoing Hartley) "associations."

Wordsworth amplifies these ideas in his "Essay on Morals" (1798). In this suggestive and interesting fragment, he insists that our habits are not changed by abstract propositions and arguments, but by experiences that move us:

> Can it be imagined by any man who has deeply examined his own heart that an old habit will be foregone, or a new one formed, by a series of propositions, which, presenting no image to the [? mind] can convey no feeling which has any connection with the supposed archetype or fountain of the proposition existing in human life? (Wordsworth 1974, 103)

Here we see the importance of the *image* and *feeling* in the process of motivating action. Imagination presents us with a perception of what *might be* that stirs our feelings enough to provoke action. In Hartley's formulation it assembles sense impressions and makes all higher levels of association possible. Wordsworth's "Essay on Morals" seems to provide a Hartley-grounded critique of the Godwinian abstractions that he had formerly found so appealing. Apparently both Wordsworth and Barbauld follow Hartley in their belief that reason and rational thinking are by necessity *always* secondary to immediate sensory input and accumulated life experience.

So it makes sense that both authors would attempt to employ literary imagination as a "bridge" that, by tapping an accessible field of experiential reference and generating immediate sensory pleasure, might have the power to connect minds and (re)shape associations. Hartley did not provide much analysis of the imagination in his *Observations*, but he did place it suggestively between "Sensation" and "Ambition" on his ascending ladder of human responses. In a series of reciprocal relationships, he writes, "imagination will new-model sensation; ambition, sensation and imagination" and so on (369). Imagination can be seen as the stream of images in the mind: images that may originate in primary and immediate sense experience, or reappear in memory, or emerge from a variety of internal stimuli or combinatory activities taking place either in consciousness or in the unconscious mind. As such, it serves as the interface between "sense impressions" and the worlds of self-representation, fantasy, literary production, and dreaming.

Rhetorically speaking, imagination plays a vitally important role in persuasion because it provides a dynamic link between the listener's experiential knowledge and the speaker's vision of possible actions, meanings, and realities. Hartley does not credit imagination directly, but stresses the importance of experiential knowledge in the process of giving "assent" (being persuaded). In his formulation, "practical assent" emerges from lived experience and is closely allied to our sense impressions. "Rational assent" emerges from secondary associations and deliberation on those associations. Thus rational assent is logical, concerned with systems and abstracted relationships. Practical assent, on the other hand, "arises from the ideas of importance, reverence, piety, duty, ambition, jealousy, envy, self-interest, etc. which intermix themselves in these subjects, and, by doing so, in some cases add great strength to the rational assent; in others, destroy it, and convert it to its opposite" (332).

Thus, by speaking to the experiences of listeners, the speaker (or poet) can establish practical assent that enables those listeners to envision new possibilities that might emerge from their existing field of experiences (and associations). Hartley himself writes (sounding very like Wordsworth in the "Preface"):

> the frequent recurrency of an interesting event, supposed doubtful, or even fictitious, does, by degrees, make it appear like a real one, as in reveries, reading romances, seeing plays, &c. This affection of mind may be called the practical assent to past facts; and it frequently draws after it the rational, as in the other instances above alleged. (331)

Such "practical assent" might prove to be misleading when fiction is its guide. But the interesting idea here is that "practical assent" can perhaps be "harnessed" constructively by fictitious renderings of interesting and compelling events. In short, the literary imagination may be able to engage readers in such a way as to gain their "practical assent" and to shift their views.

With this context in mind, we can consider many of the poetic efforts of Barbauld and Wordsworth as experiments with literature as a source of associations and counter-associations that could shape and reshape human "states of mind." In addition to using poetry and poetic language to form "impressions" and "associations" that would lead to wonder, joy, and hope, these authors wrote many poems that are structured to "jar" the reader's associations with new sense impressions. Hartley insisted that direct sense impressions created the strongest vibrations and had the greatest power to generate nervous system activity. He considered language to be a kind of algebra by which direct sensory impressions were replaced by words and "shadow associations." So it makes sense that poets would attempt to use experience itself rather than abstract propositions, and accessible language rather than artificial "poetic diction," to attempt to engage and *move* their readers.

First and foremost, early Romantic poets sought to address people's "habits of mind" in an experientially compelling manner. While they sometimes construct poetic arguments, sometimes resort to abstractions, and sometimes have clearly defined didactic aims, both poets almost always couch their arguments and lessons in immediate, particular, and often *personal* experiences that can engage the readers' imaginations, establish practical assent, and enable persuasion.

In the world described by Newlyn and Hewitt—a world of individual minds pursuing individual ends—the poet *must* engage readers somehow in order to create shared moments of recognition or understanding. Barbauld and Wordsworth developed similar strategies to *invite*—or even *challenge*—their readers to participate. Barbauld, for instance, often addresses her readers directly by ostensibly writing to a particular person or group of people. By using a direct form of address ("you" and "your," "thou" and "thine," for instance) she places the reader in the position of the purported addressee of her poems. For instance, she addresses Joseph Priestley in "The Mouse's Petition" when she begins the poem: "Oh! hear a pensive prisoner's prayer / For liberty that sighs; / And never let thine heart be shut / Against the wretch's cries" (70–71). But the lines also address the reader, who is indirectly enjoined to pay attention, to open her ears and her heart. In similar fashion, Barbauld constructs her poem "The Invitation" in such a way as to invite us all, along with her friend Elizabeth Belsham, to "admire the achievements of liberal progress" (49n).

In some cases, the direct address is categorical rather than individual: to women in "The Rights of Woman," to outsiders and impoverished people in

"To the Poor." But the reader remains "in the poem" by virtue of the second-person constructions used. Barbauld also creates situations in which multiple audiences are addressed by way of direct and secondary appeals. In "To the Poor," for instance, she addresses the poor but includes the not so poor as a secondary audience that overhears both her encouragements and her criticisms: "Nor fear the God whom priests and kings have made" (140).

In "Inscription for an Ice-House," Barbauld issues an invitation bordering on a command: "Stranger, approach!" (140). These strategies encourage— even demand—the reader's attention and personal involvement. Rather than speaking in broad, general terms about "objective" subject matter, Barbauld's openings often place the reader in a position of relationship with both the speaker and the posited listener of the poems.

Wordsworth, too, issues invitations and challenges in many of his poems. In "Michael," the invitation is subtle: "If from the public path you turn your steps," he writes, you will find yourself in another world altogether, "alone / With a few sheep, with rocks and stones, and kites / That overhead are sailing in the sky" (Wordsworth 1969, 104). In this "utter solitude," however, you will find something significant: "one object which you might pass by, / Might see and notice not. Beside the brook / Appears a straggling heap of unhewn stones! / And to that simple object appertains / A story" (104). As readers, we are invited to redirect our attention, to leave the "public path" and make a discovery with the poet. Once there, the story of Michael unfolds.

Another kind of invitation appears in Wordsworth's "Power of Music," in which he begins with an exclamation, then situates his subject by placing the reader in the scene as well:

> *An Orpheus! An Orpheus! Yes, Faith may grow bold,*
> *And take to herself all the wonders of old;—*
> *Near the stately Pantheon you'll meet with the same*
> *In the street that from Oxford hath borrowed its name.* (Wordsworth 1969, 149)

This poem begins with rapture, then, by *drawing attention* to an ongoing source of such rapture, invites the reader to join the dance.

Wordsworth sometimes ventures beyond invitation and issues more direct, blunt challenges to his readers. In "The Solitary Reaper," he encourages the reader to

> *Behold her, single in the field,*
> *Yon solitary Highland Lass!*
> *Reaping and singing by herself;*
> *Stop here or gently pass!* (Wordsworth 1969, 230)

He constructs the moment as an opportunity for the reader, suggesting that we should either stop to appreciate it or leave "untouched." And in the sonnet "Composed upon Westminster Bridge," the speaker goes so far as to say "Dull would he be of soul who could pass by / A sight so touching in its majesty" (Wordsworth 1969, 214). We should wake up, or be doomed to such dullness.

Participation, rather than observation, is the aim of such points of entry. The reader is encouraged—even provoked—to actually *enter* the poetic landscape, and to *share* in the experience, rather than simply hearing about it "second-hand." Once a reader is engaged, and his or her attention focused, the poem can deliver the "charge" that will generate new associations or disrupt existing prejudices (or both). By engaging, disrupting, and re-forming the associations of the reader, Barbauld and Wordsworth sometimes seek to teach particular lessons and sometimes aim to provoke reflection or inquiry. Like the best educators, Barbauld and Wordsworth both inculcate habits of mind and encourage independent thinking.

Returning to Kenneth Burke's broad understanding of rhetoric, we see just how rhetorical the personal poetry of early Romanticism can be. Burke insists that all persuasion begins in *identification*, or in the establishment of common ground between author and reader, speaker and audience. "You persuade a man," Burke claims, "only insofar as you can talk his language by speech, gesture, tonality, order, image, attitude, idea, *identifying* your ways with his" (55). Taking this a step further, we can acknowledge that *identification* is founded on *shared experiences and assumptions* to an even greater degree than on *shared ideas*. There is a recognition of worldview that occurs when we feel that someone else is "telling it like it is" or "speaking our language" or "making sense." That recognition emerges from the intuited belief that we have experienced similar things, understand our experiences in similar ways, and make sense of the world in a similar fashion. Burke insists that persuasion begins in *established* commonality and leads toward *renewed and extended* commonality: "the rhetorician may have to change an audience's opinion in one respect; but he can succeed only insofar as he yields to that audience's opinions in other respects. Some of their opinions are needed to support the fulcrum by which he would move other opinions" (56). Thus commonality is both the point of origin and the aim of rhetoric: the rhetor speaks a common language and begins with common assumptions and experiences in order to enter the world of debate and difference clothed with (perhaps sometimes "cloaked in") eunoia and ethos. By such means, new ideas and approaches are made accessible to the audience and a new and broader agreement can be forged between speaker and listener.

In general, the poetic strategies of Barbauld and Wordsworth work in just such a way. They intermix the ordinary and the extraordinary, the familiar and the unfamiliar, in ways that both *connect with* and *challenge* readers. The poems often begin with personal experiences that can be seen as "common" and then generate experiences that are uncommon and that demand reflection and reconsideration. Sometimes they begin with an uncommon situation and then draw the reader into that situation, creating an unexpected identification that can jar the reader's point of view. Often they move from invitation and engagement to personal experience that can be shared, to a call for reflection, action, or renewed vision. They are built to do real cognitive work.

Barbauld's "The First Fire" offers an excellent example of the use of engagement and disruption to lead readers from their existing position to a new point of view. Barbauld invites us into the poem by establishing a comfortable, friendly tone:

> Ha, old acquaintance! Many a month has past
> Since last I viewed thy ruddy face; and I,
> Shame on me! had mean time well nigh forgot
> That such a friend existed. Welcome now! — (Barbauld, 176–77)

Here Barbauld uses a direct, intimate form of address that—though it is directed at the fire—engages the reader immediately. She generates additional interest in this case by placing the reader in the position of determining just who the "old acquaintance" is.

The open question encourages close attention to the lines that follow; in those lines we are gradually able to grow fairly certain that the fire is the object of the speaker's address. By the time we reach "breath sulphureous, generating spleen" (Barbauld, 177) we can be pretty confident that this is not a *human* friend. But why is this woman speaking to the fire? The situation provokes engagement.

The fire's importance is magnified at this point in the poem. It is a "magnet" of "strong attraction," a "shrine." The readers of the poem, who are people of means and some social standing, are drawn in and join the "close circle" of "friends, brethren, kinsmen, variously dispersed" that forms around the fire. They are encouraged to feel safe and warm there, though threats lie without.

> Here a man might stand,
> And say, This is my world! Who would not bleed
> Rather than see thy violated hearth
> Prest by a hostile foot? The winds sing shrill;

Heap on the fuel! Not the costly board,
Nor sparkling glass, nor wit, nor music,
Cheer without thy aid. (Barbauld, 177)

Barbauld begins to disrupt her reader's expectations even here by counterbalancing the language of security and warmth with language suggesting dangerous things that lie "outside" the circle of comfort—threats of invasion, "shrill" winds, and the loss of both means ("costly board" and "sparkling glass") and culture ("wit" and "music"). The reader is encouraged to appreciate the fire more fully.

Then Barbauld leads her readers through a series of vignettes or scenes, each centered on the fire. We begin with the "belated traveller" relieved and comforted by his return to the "cheerful scene within!" That scene includes an entire family, from the aged "sire" to the children eagerly gathered around the fire, to the "matron sage." In an extended scene of twenty-one lines, we again enter the "circle" of the fire's warmth and the community "inside." We remain safe from "Winter," who "spends without his idle rage" (Barbauld, 178). But then Barbauld moves us a bit further "outward," into the world of the "solitary man, / From gayer scenes withheld!" and "the bashful poet." And as the poem draws to its close she places us even further away from the center of warmth and security and community, in the world of the prisoner "[i]n narrow cell immured" and the "dweller of the clay-built tenement, / Poverty-struck" (178–79). The expectations of comfort and delight established early in the poem have given way to a vision of a reality that would have seemed completely foreign to the well-to-do reader at the beginning of the poem. By centering our attention on the fire and its powers, then leading us further and further away from its "purifying influence," Barbauld leads us to a position of receptiveness to the final call in the poem:

Assist him, ye
On whose warm roofs the sun of plenty shines,
And feel a glow beyond material fire! (179)

We are encouraged to reflect on fire, on the absence of fire, and on what the fire might mean. Whether it stands for physical warmth and means of subsistence, or community warmth and inclusiveness, or knowledge ("enlightenment"), or spiritual connection or understanding, it is vital to life. We are left to ponder what it means to lack "fire" in its many manifestations, and encouraged to feel responsible for sharing it.

Wordsworth's "Nutting," like "The First Fire," uses a common experience to create uncanny new perceptions and reflections charged with meaning. The poem is even more personal, of course, since it consists of one person's recollection and reflections. It recounts a day—just a day like the day on which the first fire was lit—that somehow yielded special insight. We all know such days, and often long for them. Wordsworth invites us into the world of a boy out for adventure:

> *It seems a day,*
> *(I speak of one from many singled out)*
> *One of those heavenly days that cannot die,*
> *When in the eagerness of boyish hope,*
> *I left our cottage-threshold, sallying forth*
> *With a huge wallet o'er my shoulders slung,*
> *A nutting-crook in hand; and turned my steps*
> *Tow'rd some far-distant wood, a Figure quaint,*
> *Tricked out in proud disguise of cast-off weeds.* (Wordsworth 1969, 147)

By using recollection, the mature Wordsworth can both invite us into an experience that we all have shared—going nutting, blackberrying, "roughing it" in a variety of ways—and encourage us to view the experience from a more reflective position.

As it turns out, the poem dramatizes the pleasures and risks of roughing it. Early in the poem, the boy is thoughtless; he pushes through the woods in search of the nuts he seeks ("Forcing my way"). His initial aim is pragmatic and end-oriented: to fill his wallet with nuts. But suddenly he stumbles into a clearing that gives him pause:

> *I came to one dear nook*
> *Unvisited, where not a broken bough*
> *Drooped with its withered leaves, ungracious sign*
> *Of devastation; but the hazels rose*
> *Tall and erect, with tempting clusters hung,*
> *A virgin scene!* (147)

As readers, we share the boy's sense of delight at this discovery. We also may share the complications of purpose that develop as he witnesses this "dear nook" and considers his relationship with it. At first he sees primarily the bounty waiting to be enjoyed, and "eye[s] / The banquet" before him. The pleasure here is anticipatory, even predatory. But then a different kind of pleasure intrudes. This "dear nook" is a kind of magical place, far from human influence—a place where "fairy water-breaks do murmur on / For ever." Its pleasure evokes something besides the initial desire for "treasure" and gain. Whether the older persona or the boy senses this, we do not know. But as readers we are faced with a cognitively challenging moment: Are we here to complete our task of nutting? Or simply to experience this beautiful place? The boy, or the man remembering, becomes still as he witnesses:

> *I heard the murmur and the murmuring sound,*
> *In that sweet mood when pleasure loves to pay*
> *Tribute to ease, and, of its joy secure,*
> *The heart luxuriates with indifferent things,*
> *Wasting its kindliness on stocks and stones,*
> *And on the vacant air.* (147)

The attention of the boy/man/reader has been shifted from the search for nuts to an open appreciation of the "dear nook."

But again, in another sudden shift, the boy remembers his purpose for being there, and completes his task:

> *Then up I rose,*
> *And dragg'd to earth both branch and bough, with crash*
> *And merciless ravage; and the shady nook*
> *Of hazels, and the green and mossy bower,*
> *Deform'd and sullied, patiently gave up*
> *Their quiet being.* (147)

The contrast here is remarkable, and of course purposeful. The language suggests rape, pillage, and destruction: "crash and merciless ravage" lead to a bower that is "Deform'd and sullied." The boy has his nuts, but he has lost the magical moment that had entranced him. In "Nutting," as in "The First Fire," we are invited into a familiar scene that then transforms into something unfamiliar, unexpected, and even extraordinary.

I will close with Wordsworth's "A Night-Piece"—a poem that is emblematic of the strategies I have discussed here. This poem is written in the present tense, inviting us to participate directly in the experience, and opens without any introduction:

> *—The sky is overcast*
> *With a continuous cloud of texture close,*
> *Heavy and wan, all whitened by the Moon,*
> *Which through that veil is indistinctly seen,*

> *A dull, contracted circle, yielding light*
> *So feebly spread, that not a shadow falls,*
> *Chequering the ground—from rock, plant, tree, or tower.* (Wordsworth 1969, 146)

Note the detailed opening that sets the stage. We are offered a view of the scene and given a moment to enter that scene. Then we are "startled," like the "pensive traveller," by a sudden intrusion of new and unexpected sensations:

> *At length a pleasant instantaneous gleam*
> *Startles the pensive traveler while he treads*
> *His lonesome path, with unobserving eye*
> *Bent earthwards; he looks up—the clouds are split*
> *Asunder,—and above his head he sees*
> *The clear Moon, and the glory of the heavens.*
> *There, in a black-blue vault she sails along,*
> *Followed by multitudes of stars, that, small*
> *And sharp, and bright, along the dark abyss*
> *Drive as she drives: how fast they wheel away,*
> *Yet vanish not!* (146)

A new vista opens before us, and the poem facilitates that by placing us in the position of being "the pensive traveller." We have experienced such moments, but may not have made much of them. The poem dramatizes the moment, and invites us to participate in it fully.

Once we are part of the poetic landscape, we can feel the spatial effect of the next lines. The stars

> *are silent;—still they roll along,*
> *Immeasurably distant; and the vault,*
> *Built round by those white clouds, enormous clouds,*
> *Still deepens its unfathomable depth.* (146)

The perceptual movement outward is accompanied by a change of perspective: the "vault" is represented as a window into eternity. Vision becomes visionary experience. Imagination, aided by the poetic structure provided, enables the leap.

Then, finally, we are returned to a moment of reflection on the experience we have just had:

> *At length the Vision closes; and the mind,*
> *Not undisturbed by the delight it feels,*

Which slowly settles into peaceful calm,
Is left to muse upon the solemn scene. (146)

Notice that the final lines are directed to "the mind" and not the traveler. Now the blending of reader and traveler is complete, and both are "mind experiencing."

This poem offers a very Hartleyan moment. Pleasure is amplified by the sensations produced in the poem, "disturbing" the traveler (and by way of identification, the reader). Like a rock thrown into a pond, the poem "makes waves" within the nervous system of the reader, which then gradually settles back into equilibrium. But as Hartley suggested, enough experiences of this type will *gradually* change the equilibrium of the nervous system itself. "A Night-Piece" nicely illustrates the process of a sensory "intrusion" jarring, unsettling, or disturbing the associations of a pensive, closed mind. Here Wordsworth's "language of the sense" truly "excites" the mind "without the application of gross and violent stimulants." The reader, like the traveler, is left to "muse" on the experience and to make something of it.

CONCLUSION

My position in this essay is that the later Barbauld and the early Wordsworth often work from a general commitment to what Alan Richardson has aptly called "embodied universalism": the belief that we are all connected not by abstract, conceptual "truths," but by the physiological, perceptual, and cognitive processes by which we arrive at those truths. Our conceptual truths may be very different. But we can all "reach" each other experientially—with stories, examples, analogies, metaphors, parables, poems, and so on. The problem, of course, is that our concepts interfere with our ability to perceive new patterns of meaning. As George Lakoff and Mark Johnson remind us in *Metaphors We Live By* (1980):

> The concepts that govern us are not just matters of the intellect. They also govern our everyday functioning, down to the most mundane details. Our concepts structure what we perceive, how we get around in the world, and how we relate to other people. Our conceptual system thus plays a central role in defining our everyday realities. (3)

Learning how to cultivate what Wordsworth called a "wise passiveness"—a receptiveness to perceptual experience—is thus key to discovering new truths or meanings. If we do not "open" ourselves, each experience looks like we expect it to.

Early Romantic poets were aware of this problem and generated poetic structures that aimed to change readers' frames of mind—perhaps shaping what Merlin Donald has called the "temporary functional architectures" (Donald 2001, 189) by way of which readers perceive and act—rather than to change the ideas that readers already held as "true." Wordsworth claimed in the Preface to *Lyrical Ballads* (1800) that his early poems were "experiments": much of Barbauld's later poetry should be seen in a similar light. Their poetry strives toward an emergent cognitive rhetoric—aiming to create new stories that reshape old ones, to create unexpected identifications that shift readers' frames of mind, and to jar readers into renewed encounters with experience. For them, the processes of imagination are the bridge between what is and what may be, between existing associations and new (and better) associations, between memory and lived experience and future action. Mark Turner argues in his landmark book *The Literary Mind* (1996) that literature is an extension of the basic "storying" functions of mind itself. As such, it can engage imagination in ways that may have a shaping effect on people's states of mind and, over time, capabilities of mind. Our study of early Romanticism and of literature in general will be much enhanced if we highlight and explore the "pragmatic imagination," the moderate forms of affect employed to engage it, and the practically grounded idealism that it enables.

NOTE

1. Richardson deals more extensively with human universals and "embodied universalism" in his recent book *The Neural Sublime: Cognitive Theories and Romantic Texts* (2010), employing them to provide historically contextualized understanding of Romantic cruxes such as the nature of sublime experience, the process of image making, and others.

WORKS CITED

Barbauld, Anna Letitia. 2002. *Selected poetry and prose*. Edited by William McCarthy and Elizabeth Kraft. Peterborough, ON: Broadview Press.

Burke, Kenneth. 1962. *A rhetoric of motives*. Berkeley: University of California Press.

Damasio, Antonio. 1994. *Descartes' error: Emotion, reason, and the human brain*. New York: Putnam.

———. 1999. *The feeling of what happens: Body and emotion in the making of consciousness*. New York: Harcourt Brace.

Donald, Merlin. 2001. *A mind so rare: The evolution of human consciousness*. New York: W. W. Norton.

Hartley, David. 1998. *Observations on man, 1791*. Facsimile of the 1791 ed. Washington, DC: Woodstock Books.

Hayden, John. 1984. Wordsworth, Hartley, and the revisionists. *Studies in Philology* 81, no. 1: 94–118.

Hewitt, Regina. 1990. *Wordsworth and the empirical dilemma*. New York: Peter Lang.

Lakoff, George, and Mark Johnson. 1980. *Metaphors we live by*. Chicago: University of Chicago Press.

Nabholtz, John R. 1986. *"My reader, my fellow labourer": A study of English Romantic prose*. Columbia: University of Missouri Press.

Newlyn, Lucy. 2000. *Reading, writing, and Romanticism: The anxiety of reception*. New York: Oxford University Press.

Peckham, Morse. 1970. *The triumph of Romanticism: Collected essays*. Columbia: University of South Carolina Press.

Richardson, Alan. 1994. *Literature, education, and Romanticism: Reading as social practice, 1780–1832*. New York: Cambridge University Press.

———. 2001. *British Romanticism and the science of the mind*. New York: Cambridge University Press.

———. 2010. *The neural sublime: Cognitive theories and Romantic texts*. Baltimore: Johns Hopkins University Press.

Sullivan, Brad. 2000. *Wordsworth and the composition of knowledge: Refiguring relationships among minds, worlds, and words*. New York: Peter Lang.

———. 2007. Cultivating a "dissenting frame of mind": Radical education, the rhetoric of inquiry, and Anna Barbauld's poetry. Romanticism on the Net 45 (February). http://id.erudit.org/iderudit/015817ar (accessed October 4, 2009).

Turner, Mark. 1996. *The literary mind*. New York: Oxford University Press.

White, Daniel E. 1999. The "joineriana": Anna Barbauld, the Aikin family circle, and the dissenting public sphere. *Eighteenth-Century Studies* 32, no. 4: 511–33.

Wordsworth, William. 1969. *Poetical works*. Edited by Thomas Hutchinson. New ed. revised by Ernest de Selincourt. New York: Oxford University Press.

———. 1974. *The prose works of William Wordsworth, volume 1*. Edited by W. J. B. Owen and Jane Worthington Smyser. Oxford: Clarendon Press.

CHAPTER 12

LEAFY HOUSES AND ACORN KISSES:
J. M. BARRIE'S NEVERLAND PLAYGROUND

GLENDA SACKS

IN THE FIRST CHAPTER OF *Peter and Wendy* (1911) by J. M. Barrie, now popularly known as *Peter Pan* (PP), there is a curious description of Mrs. Darling tidying up:

> Occasionally in her travels through her children's minds Mrs. Darling found things she could not understand, and of these quite the most perplexing was the word Peter. She knew of no Peter and yet he was here and there in John and Michael's minds, while Wendy's began to be scrawled all over with him. (PP, 1:7)

Earlier in the chapter we learn that Mrs. Darling "first heard of Peter when she was tidying up her children's minds. It is the nightly custom of every good mother after her children are asleep to rummage in their minds and put things straight for the next morning" (PP, 1:5). These idiosyncratic descriptions create a nexus for the reader, where the fantastic image of a mother rifling through her children's minds converges with the acknowledgement that children have inner worlds inhabited by imaginary friends. By opening his story with an enchanting description of children's minds as a playroom to be tidied or a toy box to be packed, Barrie focuses the story's plot on the imaginative adventures of the Darling children, a fantasy nesting in a fantasy. As the story progresses, the children indeed do fantastic things: they fly with Peter to the fantastic island of Neverland, and partake in glorious adventures over there like hunting "redskins," playing with mermaids, and being captured by pirates. However, on closer examination the adventures are a series of child games, similar to contemporary pretend games of "House House," "Doctor Doctor," hide-and-seek, and follow-the-leader, to name a few.

According to cognitive psychologist Derek Bolton (1995), children's pretend play can be used to experiment with diverse circumstances, emotions, capacities, and tasks, to try out contexts and activities different from the child's own (220). In their adventures or games on the island of Neverland, the Darling children, together with Peter and the lost boys, investigate gender roles and experiment with intrapersonal relationships found in the adult world (like playing Mommy and Daddy). They safely experience the bumpiness of life with all its physical and emotional traumas, without the interference of parents. Developmental psychologist Paul Harris (2000) claims that the imagined encounters of childhood pretend games, like actual encounters, "can evoke feelings of dissatisfaction or satisfaction, disappointment or relief, fear or excitement, as the case may be" (190). Concurring with this view, Marjorie Taylor, Bridget S. Cartwright, and Stephanie M. Carlson (1993) observe that there is no question that young children have strong emotional responses to fantasy material. They note that for both children and adults, fantasy is often emotionally charged, and that through fantasy we can confront dangerous thoughts (161).

Focusing on the insights of developmental and cognitive psychologists such as Bolton, Harris, Taylor, and others encourages a new reading of J. M. Barrie's groundbreaking play and novel about Peter Pan, the boy who refuses to grow up. When viewed through the prism of cognitive development theories, both the novel and the play can be read as a mapping out of the cognitive processes that constitute children's imaginative play. It is my claim that on the island of Neverland, which is a metaphor for the mind or brains of the Darling children, Barrie creates an imaginary space where they can simulate, experiment, empathize, and experience adult life. Furthermore, within the framework of cognitive development, I will show how the character of Peter Pan is a typical imaginary companion (IC) of the Darling children and the lost boys.

Popularly thought to be a story about a boy who wouldn't grow up, *Peter Pan* on one level embodies contradictory childhood fantasies like having exciting adventures and yet being perfectly safe, with one's parents close at hand (Lurie 1990, 131). However, critics in the late twentieth century have produced alternative, adult-orientated readings of the text. According to Jacqueline Rose's (1984) canonical Freudian reading of *Peter Pan*, at the heart of children's fiction is the problem of the relationship between adult and child. Rose focuses on the psychological aspects of language in children's fiction and in so doing she sexualizes many aspects of the narrative when she writes that "behind *Peter Pan* lies the desire of a man for a little boy (or boys)" (3). James Kincaid (1992) puts forward the Foucauldian idea that the child is constructed from a range of cultural discourses, and as a result the child becomes the site of fantasy born out of an erotic flaneurism. Both Rose and Kincaid demonstrate latent eroticism within literature for children, thus subverting notions of children's sexual innocence in these texts.

In opposition to critical approaches that focus on the adult subconscious, a cognitive reading that places *Peter Pan* in a sociocultural context will show how Barrie creates an imaginary environment that allows the Darling children and the lost boys to challenge the lingering presence of strict Victorian attitudes to children's upbringing that continued to hold sway in the Edwardian nursery.[1] Lurie notes that Victorian literary fairy tales tended to have a conservative moral and political bias. She writes that "under their charm and invention is usually an improving lesson: adults know best; good, obedient, patient, and self-effacing little boys and girls are rewarded by the fairies, and naughty assertive ones are punished" (1990, 99). Granted, an Edwardian adult would never need to fend off pirates or hunt bears in his everyday world, but the dangers presented by these imaginary activities on Neverland provide the children with the tools to deal with their own varied emotions and to experiment with different points of view. By challenging the rules, the children subvert Victorian and Edwardian notions of what constituted a "good, obedient, patient, and self-effacing" child.

I. NEVERLAND AS A METAPHORICAL MIND/BRAIN AND SITUATED COGNITION

The island of Neverland has been regarded variously as a textual space in which reality is fictively recomposed for the benefit of its inhabitants, the site of a reductive colonial discourse where English lost boys are in constant conflict with the indigenous tribe of Neverland, or charted as the "other" in opposition to the political structure of Edwardian England (Fox 2007, 253–54). Clearly the island of Neverland creates a textual nexus for a myriad of literary interpretations. The claim posited here is that the island is a literary analogy of a child's mind—a claim that is supported by Barrie's description of a map of a child's mind in the first chapter of *Peter Pan*. He writes, "There are zigzag lines on it, just like your temperature on a card, and these are probably roads in the island; for the Neverland is always more or less an island, with astonishing splashes of color here and there" (PP, 1:6). In this description, Barrie starts off with a description of a map of a child's mind and ends with a reference to the island of Neverland.[2]

Barrie goes on to describe the island of Neverland as a place where gnomes and savages live in lonely lairs, but "there is also first day at school, religion, fathers, the round pond, needlework, murders, hangings, verbs that take the dative, chocolate pudding day, getting into braces . . . and so on" (PP, 1:6–7).

Like one's experience of consciousness, where the chaos of thoughts and daily events swirl around together with fantastic imaginings, these banal and extraordinary events occur on or in this island brain nestling in the Darling children's minds. But Barrie differentiates between the Darling children's islands. Although all of them conjure up the Neverland in their minds, each of the three Darling children imagines a different place and therefore their islands never perfectly "match up." John, for instance, "lived in a boat turned upside down on the sand, Michael in a wigwam, [and] Wendy lived in a house of leaves deftly sewn together" (PP, 1:7). The geography of the island is difficult to pinpoint as it shifts and changes according to each imaginer. Barrie writes, "[B]ut on the whole, the Neverlands have a family resemblance, and if they stood in a row you could say of them that they have each other's nose and so forth" (PP, 1:7).

Barrie's use of the plural "Neverlands" in the sentence expresses simultaneously the differences yet sameness between the children's island minds, highlighting for the reader the shared nature of imaginative play. Colleen Siefert's (1999) definition of the perspective of situated cognition is helpful here. She observes:

> This perspective emphasizes that individual minds usually operate within environments that structure, direct and support cognitive processes. [It] argues that the nature of cognitive processing is uniquely determined within its context and that it cannot be studied in isolation without destroying its defining properties . . . [Furthermore] the social environment also influences cognition through the presence of other minds to influence, assist, mislead, demonstrate, question and raise other perspectives. (767)

Siefert emphasizes the importance of the social environment for cognitive processing and the important role of other minds in assisting cognitive processes. Whereas each Darling child lives in his and her own abode, it is their shared imaginative games that help them test other frames of reference. By hunting the "redskins" with Peter and the lost boys, a version of the game of hide-and-seek, Michael and John Darling experience the fear that soldiers would feel when threatened by an unseen enemy. However, unlike real soldiers, the boys are able through imaginative play to experience the outlook of their enemies. While hunting the "redskins" at Slightly Gulch, Peter would suddenly change sides in the middle of a fight:

> He called out, "I'm redskin to-day; what are you, Tootles?" And Tootles answered, "Redskin; what are you, Nibs?" and Nibs said, "Redskin; what are you, Twin?" and so on; and they were all redskin; and of course this would

have ended the fight had not the real redskins, fascinated by Peter's methods, agreed to be lost boys for that once, and so at it they all went again, more fiercely than ever. (PP, 7:82)

Barrie himself took part in pretend hunting and fighting with the Llewelyn Davies boys, George, Jack, and Peter, at Black Lake Cottage in the summer of 1901. In both the play and the novel these pretend games have been transformed into a fight between the lost boys and the "redskins" on Neverland. The intersubjective nature of pretend play with the exchanging of identities midway through the fight highlights an important function of pretend play, which is to experiment with the emotions, capacities, and tasks of others (Bolton 1995).

II. LEAFY HOUSES AND SHIFTING FIREPLACES: IMAGINATIVE PLAY AND COGNITION

Thus the metaphorical children's mind/brain that is the island of Neverland provides the perfect environment for pseudo-adult play. The social nature of the children's games on the island constitutes what Colwyn Trevarthen (1999) terms "intersubjectivity." Trevarthen defines intersubjectivity as the process in which mental activity, including conscious awareness, motives and intentions, cognitions, and emotions, is transferred between minds and manifests itself as an immediate sympathetic awareness of feelings and consciousness in others. Trevarthen observes, "On it depends cultural learning and the creation of a 'social reality' of conventional beliefs, languages, rituals and technologies" (1999, 415–16). The nature of children's games, with their agreed-upon imaginary spaces and props, requires intersubjective thought processes. They are situations where a child needs to understand the motives and intentions of other children in order that the games be played successfully. An example of such intersubjective thinking about Neverland can be seen when the children and the lost boys play the game of "House House" after Wendy arrives on the island. The boys ask Wendy to "sing" a house into existence, after which they quickly "rattle up a little house," and, when Wendy asks for roses, "quickly they made believe to grow the loveliest roses up the walls" (PP, 6:72).[3] Being the work of the imagination that it is, nothing is stable in Wendy's leafy home, which has a Never tree which grows in the center of the room and gets sawed down every day, and an "enormous fireplace which was in almost any part of the room where you cared to light it" (PP, 7:77).

Although the story is a fantasy, Barrie continually reminds both the readers of his story and the audience of the play upon which his story is based that his literary and dramatic characters are in fact playing games. He directs his cast in the fifth act of *Peter Pan, or The Boy Who Would Not Grow Up* (1904) that "it is a pretend meal this evening with nothing whatever on the table, not a mug, nor a crust, nor a spoon" (Barrie 1928, 61). In the book he cites a list of delicious food for dinner and then writes that "you never exactly knew whether there would be a real meal or just a make-believe, it all depended upon Peter's whim . . . Make-believe was so real to him that during a meal of it you could see him getting rounder" (PP, 7:78–79). The practice of miming here is one aspect of pretend play that is based on the notion of simulation, when the child is able to construct a make-believe situation which can be fed into the child's own knowledge and planning system. According to Harris, "The output of this system can then be translated into a pretend action or statement" (2000, 35). Pretending to cook and prepare meals and then eating them is a popular child's game, simulating an ordinary activity that usually takes place under adult supervision. Feeding oneself in a child's world is a developmental milestone, and therefore the simple act of eating an imaginary meal prepared and cooked by a child transports that child into an adult world. Furthermore, the children demonstrate what Trevarthen describes as intersubjectivity in their understanding of their friends' emotions and activities while participating in a mimed communal meal, thereby demonstrating a successful response to the problem of shared meaning in imaginary play.

It is evident that the story relies heavily on the rituals and ceremonies of children's make-believe games. Once ensconced in her new house, the lost boys ask Wendy to be their mother: "O Wendy lady, be our mother." She replies: "Of course it's frightfully fascinating, but you see I am only a little girl. I have no real experience" (PP, 6:74). Wendy is aware of the incongruity of being a mother at her age, nevertheless she enters into pseudo-adult play and becomes the stereotypical female nurturer in the game of "House House"— cooking, cleaning, sewing, and telling the lost boys and her brothers bedtime stories.[4] She organizes the boys' lives the way she remembers her life to be in her nursery back home, an orderly existence with strictly observed meal times, bath times, and bed times. The importance of rules is seen in Barrie's copious instructions for Act 5 in the play where he writes that at dinner time "Wendy . . . smiling complacently at their captivating ways, but doing her best at the same time to keep the rules about hands-off-the-table, no-two-to-speak-at-once, and so on" (Barrie 1928, 61). The hyphenation of the rules highlights the repetitive nature of their usage, both by Wendy in her pseudo-mother role play and her remembrance of them from her own social reality back home. Nevertheless, the lost boys adore their new pretend parent, who on the one hand is a little girl with no real authority over them, but on the other hand does all the motherly things that they love.

Wendy's new role as mother epitomizes what Lev Vygotsky (1978) terms "symbolic play." Vygotsky theorized that play enables the child to act in a purely cognitive realm, and provides a critical bridge between perceptual/ situational constraints of childhood and adult thought that is totally free of situational constraints. He observes:

> In play a child behaves beyond his average age, above his daily behavior; in play it is as though he were a head taller than himself . . . play contains all developmental tendencies in a condensed form and is itself a major source of development . . . From the point of view of development, creating an imaginary situation can be regarded as a means of developing abstract thought. (102–3)

Despite being a child herself and thirsting for adventure, Wendy conforms (most of the time) to the rules of the game, and continues her curtailed existence as a mother minding the house: "really, there were whole weeks when, except perhaps with a stocking in the evening, she was never above ground" (PP, 7:78). Vygotsky would see this self-regulation as a central developmental function, where children act against their immediate impulses and instead follow the "rules of the game." The lost boys and the Darling brothers, on the other hand, sometimes play along at being Wendy's children, especially at mealtime and bedtime, when a mother figure is usually present, but at other times their behavior is more pseudo-adult, being then what Vygotsky terms "taller than themselves." They do this by dodging Captain Hook and his fierce pirates, and by appearing to be brave when confronted with the specter of being attacked by the wild beasts that inhabit the island. In this way the children's adventures provide them with a gamut of imaginative experiences, allowing them to develop their ability to think in the abstract. Although late Victorian and Edwardian views of children had softened, children then were still very restricted by adults in what they could say and do. Wendy unconsciously takes this restrictive adult view of her "children" when she instructs them to wash and put on their nighties before they can dance (PP, 10:110). Apparently the boys have to act against their immediate impulses to do what they want (as Vygotsky notes, this is a central developmental function), and instead they practice self-regulation by following the strict rules of their Edwardian "mother" before they indulge in the wildness and freedom of dance.

III. HAPPY DEATH ON NEVERLAND

Everyone is being hunted on the island of Neverland, in an altered game of hide-and-seek where being caught carries with it a death sentence. Barrie writes:

The lost boys were out looking for Peter, the pirates were out looking for the lost boys, the redskins were out looking for the pirates, and the beasts were out looking for the redskins. They were going round and round the island . . . All wanted blood except the boys. (PP, 5:51–52)

Violence, death, and blood are part of the Neverland world, where "the boys on the island vary, of course, in numbers, according as they get killed" (PP, 5:52). The game of dying is patently a part of children's pretend play, as can be seen at the end of Act 3 in the play when Peter Pan and Wendy are "trapped" on an island, with rising waters bubbling around their feet. The inability to understand the finality of death is explicitly articulated by Peter Pan in the play when he turns to the audience and says, "To die will be an awfully big adventure" (Barrie 1928, 59). The threat of death and dying is part of the children's experience of Neverland, although diluted and tempered down: the lost boys shoot Wendy but she miraculously survives, and the clapping audience saves Tinker Bell after she drinks poison and after the Peter Pan character famously appeals to the audience's belief in fairies at the end of Act 4, "If you believe, clap your hands!" (72). Harris (2000) proposes that when someone is absorbed in an imagined world, the events within that world are processed in the same way as real events. He notes that children involved in group play based on a story are more "likely to increase their psychological proximity to the perspective of the protagonist and their absorption within the make-believe framework" (Harris 2000, 76). One way that older children deal with fear is to remind themselves that the material is simply imaginary, and so they recruit an appropriate strategy (like telling themselves it's "just a game") whenever their emotional reaction becomes too intense (Harris 2000, 78–79). Unmistakably, the lost boys experience terrible anxiety after they shoot Wendy and she lies dead on the floor in front of them: "Tootles' face was very white" (PP, 6:66). Their anxiety is made evident in their response to Peter's question about whether Slightly is a doctor. Here Barrie describes the different levels of make-believe that Harris delineates when talking about extreme emotions:

The difference between him [Peter] and the other boys at such a time was that they knew it was make-believe, while to him make-believe and true were exactly the same thing. This sometimes troubled them, as when they had to make believe that they had had their dinners. If they broke down in their make-believe he rapped them on the knuckles. (PP, 6:70–71)

Obviously the children are able to differentiate between levels of make-believe play. Sometimes they are more consumed by the game and at other times less

involved with the make-believe game. Later, when Wendy miraculously revives, they "gurgled with joy" and "broke into song" (PP, 6:72). For the Darling children and the lost boys, the game of dying allows them in quick suc-
cession to experience deep fear and its antidote—euphoric relief. Clearly they
are adroit at modulating their emotional reactions to their pretend play. As
Harris notes, we can reasonably expect children's emotional engagement in
pretend play, whether it is fear or distress, to decline with age as they become
more adept at recruiting an appropriate strategy "whenever their emotional
reaction becomes too intense" (78).

IV. WENDY'S IMAGINARY COMPANION

The literary character of Peter Pan has alternately been considered to be a symbol of death (Wiggins 2006), as epitomizing transformation, reformation and
regeneration (McGavock 2006), and, as previously stated, a symbol of adult
desire (Rose 1984; Kincaid 1992). However, the cognitively based analysis of
child's pretend play taken here encourages an interpretation of the character
of Peter Pan as an imaginary companion. According to Taylor, Cartwright,
and Carlson (1993), the characteristics of imaginary companions (ICs) are that
they are propelled into space and occupy specific spaces rather than thought
of being in the head of the imaginer, play a daily role in children's fantasy
life, and are spontaneous products of a child's own imagination; further, children are willing to involve others in the imaginary world of their ICs (276).
Mrs. Darling, who in the curious opening paragraph of this essay finds the
word "Peter" scrawled all over her children's minds, knows that they cannot
have encountered Peter in her world as "she knew of no Peter." It is Wendy
who first "sees" Peter, awakens her brothers at the start of the adventure,
and shares him with her brothers throughout the story. Sharing imaginary
companions is a characteristic of ICs, and Peter Pan fits the description of an
imaginary companion for Wendy, as it is she who speaks about him first, and
it is through her that he interacts with her brothers. She asks Peter whether he
could teach her brothers to fly and when he replies in the affirmative she tells
John and Michael that "Peter Pan has come and he is to teach us to fly" (PP,
1:34). Here she informs her brothers of the presence of her imaginary companion, and then she instructs them on how to proceed with the game. It is
clear that Wendy is prepared to include her brothers in her imaginary world
that Peter Pan inhabits.

    In her 2002 study of ICs, Tracy Gleason notes that there are sex differences
between the type of imaginary companions boys and girls create. Whereas
girls tend to create imaginary companions who are less competent than themselves, boys try to emulate a heroic figure, whether it is someone they know or

a fantasy figure in comics or fairy tales (981). When Wendy first meets Peter, he is unable to stick to his shadow and she finds him sitting on the floor sobbing. Here the image of Peter Pan as a helpless creature conforms to Gleason's observation that girls create less competent imaginary companions than boys do (981). Wendy promptly sews Peter's shadow back onto his foot, solving the problem for him. Later, in Neverland, she extends her nurturing role by cleaning and cooking for him and the lost boys, and so Peter Pan provides for Wendy the perfect opportunity to try out the adult female role of mothering.

Furthermore, in accordance with Gleason's findings, Wendy's brothers and the lost boys regard Peter Pan as a heroic figure; they swear oaths of loyalty to him, go hunting with him, and are afraid when he isn't around. They are so loyal to him that the lost boys don't question Tinker Bell's instruction that "Peter wants you to shoot the Wendy," as it is not in the nature of the lost boys to question anything that Peter orders. They immediately fetch their bows and arrows ("Let us do what Peter wishes") in order to do his bidding (PP, 5:63). Their loyalty to Peter is shown when, together with the Darling brothers, they bravely fight and outwit a group of adults on the island—Captain Hook and his pirates. It would seem that on Neverland the boys experiment with the male adult role as protector and defender, while their humiliation of the pirates allows the children to flout Victorian and Edwardian rules about honoring adults.

So it is under the direction of the IC, Peter Pan, that the Darling children freely explore agency not available to them back home in their Edwardian nursery. He provides them with the excuse to indulge in bad behavior: going on the rampage, staying up after supper, and talking back to adults. He is especially a liberating companion for Wendy who, as a girl, was far more restricted in the range of her behaviors than the boys. While Peter encourages her to be a mother on Neverland, he also shows her to how to fly, swim, and dive.

Gillian Brown (1999) observes that during the nineteenth century toys and games designed for girls stressed domestic concerns, whereas accounts of boyhood advanced the values of pleasure and carelessness in childhood. Brown surmises that "whereas boys embody the radical difference and distance of childhood, girls embody the continuity between children and adults" (89). In Edwardian England, gender roles were rigidly defined and girls were taught to be ladies and encouraged to restrain their behavior accordingly. Peter Pan therefore can be seen as an ideal imaginary companion for Wendy, creating nurturing opportunities for her feminine side and allowing her to be more boyish when she gets caught up in the more boisterous games played on Neverland. However, when Wendy attempts to be flirtatious and tries to kiss Peter, he quickly withdraws from the games.

V. ACORN KISSES: THE FAILURE OF NEVERLAND

The acorn button that Peter Pan gives Wendy, thinking that this gesture constitutes kissing, indicates the gap in his (and the children's) knowledge about human sexual behavior. Later in the story, while playing with Wendy at being pseudo-parents, Peter Pan worriedly asks Wendy, "It is only make-believe, isn't it, that I am their real father?" After skirting the troubling subject of fatherhood, Peter Pan tells Wendy that he is confused by Tiger Lily because "there is something that she wants to be to me, but she says it is not my mother," to which Wendy replies, "It isn't for a lady to tell" (PP, 10:110–11). Sexual activity is an important part of the adult experience, and it is in this puzzled conversation between Wendy and Peter Pan that their role-play falls apart. The island here could be viewed as a kind of pastoral environment, away from restraints of civilization, a place in which, according to Ellen Spolsky (2003), bodily self-knowledge can take place without architectural barriers or closed doors, but with many leisure hours to play, dream, and play musical instruments (83). Nevertheless, the Darling children and the lost boys fail to learn by kinesis or bodily analogy anything about their own or other bodies, and remain hazy and confused about the subject of sex. Referring to Longus' *Daphnis and Chloe* (second century AD), Spolsky observes that as the children grow, the reader is shown how much physical knowledge is learned directly by imitating nature. They learn by kinesis or bodily analogy about sexual knowledge in their pastoral surroundings (Spolsky 2003, 90). In *Peter Pan*, Wendy and Slightly play a chaste game of "Doctor Doctor" after Tootles accidentally shoots her. Wendy lies dead on the ground while Slightly mimes putting a glass thermometer in her mouth: "'I will put a glass thing in her mouth,' said Slightly; and he made believe to do it" (PP, 6:71). Slightly, pretending to be a doctor who is treating his patient, states that "this has cured her" and prescribes the patient a cup of beef tea. In this scene Siefert's concept of situated cognition is played out, where the social environment can be said to influence cognition by raising new perspectives. Here it is the lost boys who experiment with the girlish perspective of nurturer, and who have to make sure that their patient recovers by feeding her healthy beef tea.

Although they are playing the game of "Doctor Doctor," with its inevitable focus on the body (here in pastoral surroundings), sex is unknowable to them, and the more visible aspects of adult sexuality such as flirting and kissing are attempted with strange results. The technicalities of sex and the knowledge about how babies are made remain a great puzzle for the children. Peter doesn't know what kissing is, and to not embarrass him Wendy gives him a thimble. In return, Peter Pan gives her an acorn button in place of a kiss. In the play he is completely asexual: "You mustn't touch me," he cries to Wendy in Act 1, "No one must ever touch me" (Barrie 1928, 30). Moreover, when Wendy talks about her parents having descendents, Nibs, one of the lost boys, thinks that they gave birth to white rats, and Peter Pan tells everyone that babies come from birds. Apparently, the children confuse human with animal procreation, ascribing the appearance of babies to rats or the stork of fairy tales rather than the realism of human biology. Aside from the clarity of the nurturing role assigned to mothers in Neverland, other aspects of male and female sexual behavior are confused, blurred, or just plain wrong. There is no strong father figure on the island, just Captain Hook and his motley crew of pirates who behave like overgrown boys rather than mature men, as evidenced by their need of a mother. After all, it is Captain Hook's idea to capture the Darling children, make the boys walk the plank, and make Wendy his mother (PP, 8:92). Moreover, the description of James Hook hovers between the masculine and the feminine. He has long curls "which at a distance looked like black candles . . . His eyes were of the blue of the forget-me-not and of a profound melancholy . . . In dress he somewhat aped the attire associated with the name of Charles II" (PP, 5:55). This dandyish description undermines the swashbuckling image of what a pirate is supposed to be. The effeminate image of a pirate highlights the laughable notion that pirates would capture a woman to be their mother, and the fear that Hook shows at the sound of a ticking clock in the crocodile shows cowardice instead of heroism. In fact, the bravest figure on the island aside from the irresponsible and forgetful Peter is a woman, Tiger Lily, princess of the Piccaninny tribe, who doesn't even snivel when she is about to die. It would seem that gendered roles are interchangeable on Neverland, where grown men want a mother and whimper at the sound of a clock ticking, and young girls bravely face death.

Consequently, Barrie subverts traditional notions of gendered feminine and masculine traits in Neverland when it comes to sexuality and sexual attraction. Males are deprived of their masculinity in the form of the neutering of their desire for women (they want mothers), and their lack of courage. They are no kind of role model for growing boys. Furthermore, the only overtly sexual female on the island, Tinker Bell, is a tiny fairy rather than a fully grown woman, and she is shown to be unladylike in her pinching, pulling of hair, insult throwing, and swearing. She is simply an awful role model for a well-brought-up Edwardian girl like Wendy. The only other female on the island is Tiger Lily, who is "coquettish, cold and amorous by turns . . . (and) staves off the altar with a hatchet" (PP, 5:56). How comforting for the immature men on the island to know that they will not be forced to deal with the amorous advances of a lady; they would rather face a hatchet than a kiss.

CONCLUSION

Barrie himself struggled with his own identity and sexuality, possibly remaining celibate his whole life, and probably regarded the story of *Peter Pan* and the island of Neverland as a kind of safe haven for children, where their wishes all came true, and nobody died or grew up either. Therefore, for Barrie, the story of *Peter Pan* could be seen as indulging in wishful thinking, a kind of counterfactual thought process, which, according to Harris (2000), can offer "a way to liquidate—at least in the imagination—the unpleasantness of reality" (139). Harris hypothesizes:

> Once we enter that state of absorption, it is the events occurring within the imagined world that drive our emotional system. Indeed our emotional response to those events is heightened by their being viewed alongside, or from the perspective of, the main protagonists. We share their aspirations and disappointments. (65–66)

Barrie, as the author of *Peter Pan*, can be seen simultaneously as its emotional and involved reader, encountering and re-experiencing a pseudo-childhood through imaginary games and make-believe. However, as the author of the story, he blurred over what he saw to be the ugliness of adult sexuality and the dullness of adult life. Instead he created the flexible imaginary space of Neverland in direct opposition to the narrow confines of the Edwardian nursery with its rules and routines. In this child-orientated alternative world, the Darling children and the lost boys could safely negotiate pseudo-adult experiences and wild adventures with the encouragement of their perfect imaginary friend Peter Pan, yet never have to grow up to experience the real, undiluted traumas of adulthood.

NOTES

1. According to Jackie Wullschläger (1995), the Edwardian decade focused on the concept of the Edwardian child as hedonist. She claims that the idealization of childhood, which around the Victorian age remained central to English culture, underwent a change around 1880, from an emphasis on the child as moral icon, an emblem of purity, to a craze for the child as a fun-loving hero. She notes that virile, outward-bound young men are the cult figures of the 1890s and first decade of the twentieth century, and asserts that a sense that life beyond youth was not worth living contributed to the fervor for youthful martyrdom that came in 1914 (109). However, Victorian morals and ideas still continued to hold sway over the English nursery long after the Edwardian age was over.

2. Lisa Chaney (2005) surmises that the name "Neverland" referred to an Australian Aboriginal area in the Northern Territory. She notes that it would have been entirely appropri-

ate if this had inspired Barrie's name, as the Aboriginals who lived there "gave to the repository of their understanding of themselves the name of the Dream Time" (226).

3. Anne Varty (2007) notes that the creation of the Wendy house can be seen to have a personal origin in Barrie's castaway games with the Llewelyn Davies boys, and a public origin in survival games inspired by Daniel Defoe and others. Varty points out that amongst the more formal, rule-bound outdoor games, such as "Prisoners" or "Den," there was also a place for learning survival skills, thereby perpetuating the lessons of Defoe and anticipating the ideas of Robert Baden-Powell, the creator of the English Scouts movement, through fantasy (397).

4. Alison Lurie (1990) surmises that Wendy, "the little mother," may also be an idealized version of Sylvia Davies, the mother of the Llewelyn Davies boys with whom Barrie played pirate games at his Black Lake Cottage in Sussex. Another theory that Lurie puts forward about the basis of Wendy's mothering role is the image of the mother based on Barrie's own mother's childhood as described in *Margaret Ogilvy* (1896): "She was eight when her mother's death made her mistress of the house and mother to her little brother, and from that time she scrubbed and mended and baked and sewed" (qtd. in Lurie, 129).

WORKS CITED

Barrie, J. M. [1911] 1994. *Peter Pan*. London: Penguin.

———. 1928. *The plays of J. M. Barrie in one volume*. New York: Scribner.

Bolton, Derek. 1995. Self-knowledge, error and disorder. In *Mental simulation: Evaluations and applications*. Edited by Martin Davies and Tony Stone. Cambridge, MA: Blackwell.

Brown, Gillian. 1999. Child's play. *Differences: A Journal of Feminist Cultural Studies* 11, no. 3: 76–106.

Chaney, Lisa. 2005. *Hide-and-seek with angels: A life of J. M. Barrie*. London: Hutchinson.

Fox, Paul. 2007. Other maps showing through: The liminal identities of Neverland. *Children's Literature Association Quarterly* 32, no. 3: 252–68.

Gleason, Tracy. 2002. Social provisions of real and imaginary relationships in early childhood. *Developmental Psychology* 38, no. 6: 979–92.

Kincaid, James R. 1992. *Child-loving: The erotic child and Victorian culture*. London: Routledge.

Harris, Paul. 2000. *The work of the imagination*. Oxford: Blackwell.

Lurie, Alison. 1990. *Don't tell the grown-ups: Subversive children's literature*. London: Bloomsbury.

McGavock, Karen. 2006. The riddle of his being: An exploration of Peter Pan's perpetually altering state. In *J. M. Barrie's Peter Pan: In and out of time*. Edited by Donna R. White and C. Anita Tarr. Lanham, MD: Scarecrow Press.

Rose, Jacqueline. 1984. *The case of Peter Pan, or The impossibility of children's fiction*. Philadelphia: University of Pennsylvania Press.

Siefert, Colleen. 1999. Situated cognition and learning. In *The MIT Encyclopedia of the Cognitive Sciences*. Edited by Robert A. Wilson and Frank C. Keil. Cambridge, MA: MIT Press.

Spolsky, Ellen. 2003. *Satisfying skepticism: Embodied knowledge in the early modern world*. Aldershot, UK: Ashgate.

Taylor, Marjorie, Bridget S. Cartwright, and Stephanie M. Carlson. 1993. A developmental investigation of children's imaginary companions. *Developmental Psychology* 29, no. 2: 276–85.

Trevarthen, Colwyn. 1999. Intersubjectivity. In *The MIT Encyclopedia of the Cognitive Sciences*. Edited by Robert A. Wilson and Frank C. Keil. Cambridge, MA: MIT Press.

Varty, Anne. 2007. Locating Neverland: Peter Pan and parlour games. *New Theatre Quarterly* 92, no. 4: 393–402.

Vygotsky, Lev. 1978. *Mind in society*. Cambridge, MA: Harvard University Press.

Wiggins, Kayla McKinney. 2006. More darkly down the left arm: The duplicity of fairyland in the plays of J. M. Barrie. In *J. M. Barrie's Peter Pan: In and out of time*. Edited by Donna R. White and C. Anita Tarr. Lanham, MD: Scarecrow Press.

Wullschläger, Jackie. 1995. *Inventing wonderland: The lives and fantasies of Lewis Carroll, Edward Lear, J. M. Barrie, Kenneth Grahame, and A. A. Milne*. London: Methuen.

THE PSYCHOLOGY OF FICTION:
PRESENT AND FUTURE

KEITH OATLEY, RAYMOND A. MAR, AND MAJA DJIKIC

INTRODUCTION

The formation of separate university departments of literature and psychology in the nineteenth century seems to have contributed to an antagonism in which many literary scholars regard psychology as reductive and trivializing, whereas many psychologists regard fictional literature as description that lacks reliability and validity. These positions ensure that although literary scholars and psychologists might be interested in similar topics such as character and emotion, they tend to take no notice of each other.

The founding discussion of fiction in the West was Aristotle's *Poetics* ([ca. 330BC] 1970), which combines literary theory and psychology. With the antagonism between literary studies and psychology, integration might have died. But integrative thinking has continued, although in a rather backroom way. For instance, in literary studies it can be seen in a work that people in departments of literature hold in high regard, Erich Auerbach's *Mimesis* (1953). About researches of the kind he presents in that book, Auerbach has said: "For when we do understand the past what we understand is the human personality, and it is through the human personality that we understand everything else. And to understand a human existence is to rediscover it in our own potential experience" (1965, 102).

Integrative thinking can be seen, too, in psychology, for instance in a book by Jerome Bruner (1986), who wrote: "There are two modes of cognitive functioning, two modes of thought, each providing distinctive ways of ordering experience, of constructing reality. . . . A good story and a well-formed argument are different natural kinds. . . . The one verifies by eventual appeal to procedures for establishing formal and empirical truth. The other establishes not truth but verisimilitude" (11). Bruner calls these modes, respectively, "paradigmatic" and "narrative."

His argument might be thought to justify the separation of university departments that treat the different modes. But for both literary theorists and psychologists, the real implication is the opposite, because it includes an invitation to investigate how narrative thinking works. In carrying out this investigation, dialogue between the humanities and cognitive science is essential. The cognitive approach to literature, which this volume—with its contributors from both literature and psychology—so admirably presents, is one of the products.

Our argument in this chapter is that, with the growing integration between the humanities and cognitive approaches, this is a propitious time for the psychology of fiction. Members of departments of language and literature, feeling perhaps a vacuum after the wars between traditionalists and postmodernists, now take an interest in psychological issues. At the same time, cognition has become important in psychology, with its applications to problems that include those of understanding what goes on in the minds of people as they engage with fiction.

I. SHIFTING THE PREMISES

With the coming of cognitive science and its interdisciplinary structure that includes psychology, linguistics, and artificial intelligence, older attitudes have shifted. Cognition is about knowledge (conscious and unconscious, concerning the physical and social world), how it is organized in the mind, and how it is used in such activities as perceiving, remembering, thinking, reading, and imagining. Literature, too, is on this agenda, and the approach is described by Jaén and Simon (this volume).

We (the authors of this article) propose that this movement can be pressed further. Strictures by postmodernists such as Derrida (1976), who proposed that text cannot represent anything outside itself, and by psychologists who argue that fiction is flawed description, are jejune: both derive from the assumption that art is imitation or copying, the usual translations of *mimesis*, the central term in Aristotle's *Poetics*. This family of meanings is, however, the lesser part of what Aristotle wrote about. As Halliwell (2002) has shown, the Greek word *mimesis* had a second family of meanings, which is often ignored. This family has to do with model building, and with imagination. As Halliwell puts it: "Reduced to a schematic but nonetheless instructive dichotomy, these varieties of mimetic theory and attitude can be described as encapsulating a difference between a 'world-reflecting' [conception] (for which the mirror has been a common though far from straightforward metaphorical emblem), and, on the other side, a 'world simulating' or 'world creating' conception of artistic representation (22)."

This second family of meanings is more important for fiction. Literary art is not, therefore, to be judged entirely by criteria of a correspondence theory of truth, but principally by coherence (one of Aristotle's themes in *Poetics*).

The metaphor that Shakespeare (for example, *A Midsummer Night's Dream*) and Coleridge ([1794–1820] 2000) used for the world-simulating or world-creating aspect of fiction was the dream. As we take up a novel or go to the theater or cinema, we mentally enact a version of the dream into which the author conducts us. Alice-like, we pass through the looking glass into a created fictional world. Dream is a good metaphor because it summons a state of mind that is both familiar and different from the ordinary one. At the same time, the question of the properties of this state is sharpened. The modern metaphor is simulation. Pieces of fiction are simulations of selves in the social world. Fiction is the earliest kind of simulation, one that runs not on computers but on minds (Oatley 1992, 1999). One of the virtues of taking up this idea from cognitive science is that we can think that just as if we were to learn to pilot an airplane we could benefit from spending time in a flight simulator, so if we were to seek to understand ourselves and others better in the social world we could benefit from spending time with the simulations of fiction in which we can enter many kinds of social worlds, and be affected by the characters we meet there.

With this shift, an interdisciplinary dialogue can take place without literary scholars having to sacrifice anything to trivialization or reductionism, and without psychologists and cognitive scientists having to sacrifice anything to inadequate methodology.

II. TESTING LITERARY THEORY

Although the theory of fiction as simulation emphasizes coherence (Oatley 1999), questions of correspondence remain. In particular, empirical tests of statements made in literary theory are important. An early example was the experiment by I. A. Richards (1929) in which he gave thirteen poems to a set of students of English literature, and asked what they made of each one. The assumption was that educated people understand what they read but, wrote Richards, "readers of poetry frequently and repeatedly *fail to understand it*" (12; emphasis in original). Richards did ask what people were doing when they read a poem, but his intent was to demonstrate their shortcomings. The movement of New Criticism, which derived from the approach, was to teach people to make correct interpretations (for example, Brooks and Warren 1938). It was Rosenblatt (1938), from a different tradition, who started to ask seriously how readers respond to literature, and with her book the movement of reader response criticism began.

An early empirical study of an important literary concept, in the mode of taking an empirical interest in the experience of readers, was by Van Peer (1986), who tested whether defamiliarization—the set of literary techniques designed to bring an idea or observation alive, as proposed by the Russian Formalists—did indeed have effects on the reader of the kind that were claimed. Van Peer uses the term "foregrounding" for this set of techniques, and argued that it is accomplished by creating linguistic variations that are departures from ordinary usage. He asked his participants to read six short poems, the linguistic content of which he had analyzed to determine which phrases were foregrounded. He found that foregrounded phrases were indeed experienced by readers as more striking, more important, and more worthy of discussion than other phrases.

A different kind of empirical test was conducted by Gerrig and his colleagues (Gerrig 1993; Prentice, Gerrig, and Bailis 1997; see also Gerrig, this volume). These researchers tested Coleridge's idea ([1817] 1907) that in fiction there is a "willing suspension of disbelief." The phrase is so resonant that it seems true. Yet, psychologically, Gerrig and his colleagues found it to be misleading. When we read fiction, we don't have to suspend disbelief. Instead we tend often to accept what is said rather easily, and sometimes it may not be true (see also Green and Brock 2000; Marsh and Fazio 2006; Marsh, Meade, and Roedigger III 2003).

Tests have also been made to study tenets of the Romantic theory of literature as proposed by Collingwood (1938). Oatley (2003) has cast these tenets into psychological hypotheses. They include the hypothesis that art is an expression of problematic emotions in languages, such as those of words, music, and painting, in order to explore and understand them. Djikic, Oatley, and Peterson (2006) used Pennebaker, Francis, and Booth's (2001) Linguistic Inquiry and Word Count (LIWC) to analyze the transcripts of interviews of nine writers of fiction and nine physicists. They found that as compared with those of the physicists, the writers' preoccupations were far more concerned with emotions, especially negative emotions.

Studies of these kinds point toward a future in which, rather than accepting assertions from literary theory that seem plausible, these assertions can be investigated so that we know better what readers actually make of poems and stories, and what writers are doing when they write them.

III. LITERARY WORKS IN PSYCHOLOGY

Just as psychology has been applied to testing theories of literary fiction, an equally important movement is taking place in the opposite direction. Literary fiction is starting to provide material for the development of psychological understanding.

An important example of this movement derives from the work of Turner (1996), who has proposed that "[n]arrative imagining—story—is the fundamental instrument of thought" (4). Its function is to give the world meaning. There are two steps. The first is to form a story, a sequence about what someone did and what events occurred. The second is to project this story onto another story—for instance, onto the story we have constructed of our own lives. Turner calls this process parable: the projection of story structure onto the encounters of everyday life, in order to give them meaning. Thus narrative thinking is the stuff of everyday mental life. Turner moves his argument forward using stories from literary sources such as *The Thousand and One Nights*, and the *Odyssey*.

A second way of using literature has been to propose that since works of fiction tend to induce emotions in their readers or viewers, they can be used in psychological experiments. A method of choice has been to use clips from films (Gross and Levenson 1995). It is also worthwhile to consider using whole works. Thus Oatley (2009) has proposed that we can see Shakespeare's *Othello* as a study of resentment in the play's main protagonist, Iago. It is hard to empathize with Iago, and this points to an interesting psychological issue. Why should this be, when most of us have experienced destructive resentments? The psychological point is that since works of literary art enable people to experience emotions, we can use this experience to study the psychology of emotions that arise in reading literature or watching drama, just as in the process of understanding visual perception researchers use demonstrations, such as those of induced movement and stereopsis.

Fiction is imagination and, as Mar and Oatley (2008) have argued, it is a kind of abstraction. Abstraction is necessary to think about anything beyond the immediate and concrete. Suggestive evidence is that a group of people, the Pirahã, who live in Amazonia, have no indigenous fiction and live in a here-and-now world without abstractions (Everett 2005).

"The human imagination remains one of the last uncharted terrains of the mind." So says the jacket of Byrne's (2005) book on how people use their imagination to think about "what if." The best book on the development of imagination we know is that of Harris (2000). Fiction—sometimes known as imaginative literature—is an underexplored means for the study of imagination, although this approach has been used by Gibbs and Matlock (2008). There are plenty of books from literary theorists with "imagination" in their titles. In the future we may hope to see more use of fiction to explore psychological accomplishments of imagination.

IV. PSYCHOLOGICAL PROCESSES IN LITERATURE

An important but only rather recently implemented movement has been to ask what psychological processes are involved in reading fiction. In studying comprehension, some researchers (for example, Graesser, Olde, and Klettke 2002) pay careful attention to stories and story structure in their work on discourse analysis.

Some psychological processes are drawn upon widely in fiction. Metaphor and metonym are fundamental, as described by Jakobson (1956) and Lodge (1977). Whereas metaphor is a mapping of one domain of meaning onto another, metonymy works by juxtaposition, spreading meaning by implication—for instance, from what someone in a novel or film wears, what they eat, or the manner in which they move, to how we might understand that character. Hogan (2003) has proposed that priming—a basic cognitive process in which one event or perception makes more available a certain interpretation of another event—offers a cognitive explanation of how tropes such as metaphor and metonym work. Further examples of Hogan's work, drawing on basic cognitive processes to understand literary effects, can be seen in his chapter in this volume.

Zunshine (2006) has argued that reading fiction is the pleasurable exercise of our faculties of theory of mind. Theory of mind is a lively topic in psychology in which it has been found that, from about the age of four, children start to be able to infer something of what others are thinking and feeling. Zunshine argues that fiction allows us to apply these skills on fictional characters, often in complex ways, and that writers construct this process to be enjoyable. Some genres such as detective stories indeed require us to work out what is going on in the minds of characters who are trying to conceal what they are thinking and feeling.

A recent innovation in cognitive approaches to literature has been to employ neuroimaging (Mar 2004). This work has provided encouraging evidence for the idea of simulation, rooted within theories of embodied cognition (Barsalou et al. 2003). The embodied cognition approach argues that conceptual knowledge is partially represented in modality-specific regions of the brain, such as motor areas and sensory areas. In line with this idea, action verbs re-

ferring to emotional expressions result in activation of the facial musculature that in turn can shape emotional judgments (Foroni and Semin 2009).
Action words specifically affect areas of the motor cortex associated with the
body part used to perform each action (Pulvermüller, Härle, and Hummel
2001). Work in this area has just started to extend to full-length narratives.
Speer et al. (2009), for example, found that different brain areas appear to
track different aspects of a short story the participants are reading, and these
regions correspond with regions activated when the person performs or observes similar activities. Other neuroimaging studies have begun to uncover
differences between narrative comprehension and sentence-level comprehension (Xu et al. 2005), and how the brain builds models of a story (Yarkoni,
Speer, and Zacks 2008). Of even more interest, we think, is the finding, now
replicated over many studies, that areas of the brain concerned with the comprehension of narrative overlap with areas concerned with theory of mind
and understanding other people (Mar 2011). This is an exciting new area of
research that is likely to be important for future of cognitive approaches to
literature.

V. EXPLORATION ACROSS CULTURES

A conspicuous accomplishment of international journalism of the twentieth
century on war, health, and other human vicissitudes has enabled us to empathize with people in societies and predicaments far distant from our own. Fiction has a similar accomplishment. It is a welcome legacy of post-colonialism
that prose and film fiction from round the world has come to be of great
interest.

In fiction, explorations extend into the contemporary world and into the
past. In the contemporary world, we might think of the novel *Waiting* (1999)
by Ha Jin, a Chinese writer who emigrated to the United States and writes
in English. The novel is about the difficulties of love relationships in Chinese
communist society. If we treat history not as time travel but as culture travel,
we can think of Mary Renault's novels—for example, *The Last of the Wine*
(1956), which brings to life Athens at the end of its Golden Age and allows us
to leap two and a half millennia into the troubles and joys of everyday Athe-
nians. This mental travel in space or time strips off what is eccentric and trivial, and engages us in concerns that are intrinsically human so they become
indistinguishable from our own.

A particularly important contribution to cross-cultural understandings has
been Hogan's book (2003) for which he read stories from all round the world
from before the time of European expansion. He found three kinds of story

to be so common as to be universal. The most common is the love story. In its paradigmatic form, lovers long to be united but they are impeded, most typically by a male relative of one of them. In the tragic version the lovers die, perhaps to be united on another plane. In the comic version they are united and the relative who was impeding them is reconciled. Second most common is the story of conflict. In a typical version this is between brothers, one of whom takes what rightfully belongs to the other—for instance, by displacing him from a throne or a property. There is a fight, in the course of which right is restored, though sometimes with the realization that this has involved the person who has thought himself justified being drawn into evil actions. The third kind of prototypical story is of self-sacrifice, in which a community with severe difficulties is saved by an individual making a sacrifice of his or her life.

In the future, reading literatures of different cultures will enable Western-centric conceptions to be recognized and modified. It will allow the unchallenged assumptions about Western mind, omnipresent to the point of invisibility, to be brought to the foreground and examined as only one among many.

VI. EFFECTS OF LITERATURE

Although in both Western and Eastern traditions it has been accepted that reading or watching fiction has psychological and social benefits, it is only recently that this issue has been tested empirically. In children, use of terms for mental states (desires, emotions, etc.) as well as success in theory-of-mind tasks was studied by Adrian et al. (2005). Children's use of terms for mental states and their abilities in theory of mind were found to be related both to the amount of reading mothers did with them and to the number of mental-state terms that mothers used when they read picture books to their children. Related research by Peskin and Astington (2004) showed that the key was for children to imagine such mental states.

For adults, Stanovich and his colleagues (for example, Stanovich, West, and Harrison 1995) have shown that reading promotes cognitive gains generally. But are there psychological effects specific to fiction? Hakemulder (2000, 2001, 2008) conducted experiments to see whether student readers mentally took on roles of characters in stories, and whether doing so would enable them to be more empathetic. Participants read either a nonfiction essay about the problem of women's rights in Algeria or a chapter from a novel about the life of an Algerian woman. As compared with those who read the essay, those who read the fiction reported that they would be less likely to accept current norms for relationships between men and women in Algeria. In a further study, Hakemulder found that, as compared with readers asked to attend to the structure of a story, readers who were asked to project themselves mentally into the situation of the story showed decreased tolerance for current norms among students.

In our own studies we have found two kinds of effect (Mar, Oatley, and Djikic 2008). In one kind we investigated associations between reading fiction and social abilities. Mar et al. (2006) measured the amount of reading of non-fiction and fiction that participants did, and then gave them two tests of social ability. One was a test of theory of mind and empathy, and the other was a test of interpersonal perception in which participants watched video clips of ordinary people in interaction and answered questions about what was going on. Mar et al. found that fiction reading was associated with better performance on these tasks, whereas nonfiction reading was associated with worse performance. The former association was retested in a larger sample, with the same result, and with an additional finding that the effect was not due to individual differences (Mar, Oatley, and Peterson 2009). Similar results have been found in children (Mar, Tackett, and Moore 2010). In an experimental study, Mar (2007) used a fiction story and a nonfiction piece from the *New Yorker*, and randomly assigned people to read one or the other. Immediately after reading, those who read the piece of fiction did better on a test of social reasoning, though not on a test of analytical reading, than those who read the piece of nonfiction. It was hypothesized that reading fiction put participants into a state of preparedness to reason about the social world.

In a second kind of study we investigated effects of fiction on selfhood. Djikic et al. (2009a) randomly assigned people to read either Chekhov's short story "The Lady with the Little Dog" or a comparison piece in a nonfiction format of the same length and reading difficulty, with the same characters, the same events, and some of the same conversation. Chekhov's story is about a man and a woman at the seaside resort of Yalta who have an affair although they are both married to someone else. The comparison piece was written by one of us (MD) in the nonfiction style of proceedings of a divorce court. Readers found it just as interesting as Chekhov's story, though not as artistic. Before and after reading, we measured readers' emotions, and also their personality using a standard measure of the "Big Five" personality traits. We found that as compared with those who read the court report, those who read Chekhov's story changed their personality in small but measurable ways, and in idiosyncratic directions. These changes were mediated by the changes in emotion that readers experienced in the course of reading. Furthermore, we found that even defensive individuals, whose avoidant style of attachment involved habitual suppression of emotion in everyday life, experienced significantly more emotion reading Chekhov's story than the control text (Djikic et al. 2009b). This leads us to believe that literature could provide a nonintrusive, nonthreatening method of reaching and affecting some people who are usually hard to reach.

When we engage our self in a piece of fiction, we enter a simulation that has the potential to transform that self. How might this work? The reader of Chekhov's "The Lady with the Little Dog" inserts the intentions and plans of the story's protagonists, Gomov and Anna, into his or her own mental planning processor, and thereby becomes affected by the circumstances that affect Gomov or Anna. Chekhov offers cues to start the simulation and keep it running. We experience something of how the two protagonists affect each other and are affected by each other in the intimacy that they realize, and in their inwardness. We readers take on the goals and plans of Gomov and of Anna, but we also remain ourselves. It is we ourselves who experience emotions. These emotions are not those of the characters—these characters are abstractions. The emotions are our own in the frustrations and calm moments and reunions of the story. For each of us the experience is different. We might ourselves be in a relationship that is deadening and wonder how we reached this impasse. We might feel excited or disapproving of the protagonists' affair. We might feel a foreboding, so that we wonder how anything good could come from it, and how it will affect others. As readers with these or other thoughts and feelings, our own emotional experience and our habitual selves can change somewhat.

In the future we envisage more studies of how people's conceptions of others and themselves change in engagement with fiction. We are in the process of testing other stories, and comparing their effects with those of nonfictional essays. We hope also to investigate what kinds of stories have particular kinds of psychological effects. Most importantly we envisage being able to use the studies of effects to see how fiction really works.

VII. EDUCATION AND THERAPY

Now that measurable psychological effects of reading fiction have begun to be shown, there are implications for education and therapy. In education it has been assumed that fiction is worthwhile, and teachers of literature, from primary school to graduate school, use literature in discussions both of understanding others and of understanding oneself. We may perhaps look forward to thinking of how evidence that fiction can promote certain kinds of personal and interpersonal improvements might affect education.

In the area that may broadly be called bibliotherapy, worthwhile programs have emerged. One such is Changing Lives Through Literature, which began in 1991 in discussions between a professor of English literature, Robert Waxler, and a judge, Robert Kane. They agreed that perhaps offenders could be sentenced to probation rather than jail on condition that they attended a seminar on literature. A book has been published on the project: Trounstine and Waxler (2005). An evaluation of the program by Jarjoura and Krumholz (1998) was of seventy-two young, male repeat offenders on probation. There were two groups. In a program group, thirty-two of these men took the Changing Lives Through Literature program (in four eight-person classes, which included the literature seminars, talks from role models, and other rehabilitative input). In a comparison group, forty of these men with comparable criminal records did not take the program. During the study period six of the men in the program group (18.75 percent) committed further offences while eighteen in the comparison group (45 percent) did so. Although this result is encouraging, the report contains no statistical analyses, and there is ambiguity about the active ingredients of the program.

A second kind of program has been to introduce reading circles for teenage single mothers. The first of these, Literature for All of Us (see reference list for website), was founded in Chicago in 1996 by Karen Thomson, and has reached 4,500 young people. In this program, there is a weekly ninety-minute book group, facilitated by an experienced leader, in which discussion of a book that members of the group read is followed by a poetry-writing exercise in which members complete a set of sentences with prompts such as "I am . . ." This exercise encourages members to explore themes they have read about. Another program, based on the same principles, Literature for Life (see reference list for website), was founded in 2000 in Toronto by Jo Altilia and has reached 1,400 young people.

Informally, the website of Literature for All of Us has reported: "Over 65% of book group participants reported reading more often on their own after joining book group," and "Evaluations found significant developments in the use of critical thinking and problem-solving skills, two important goals of Social Emotional Learning. School staff also noted improvements in participants' behavior, which they attributed to the skills learned in book groups." The director of Literature for Life has reported that many of the people who have joined book circles "experience an increase in perspective-taking, empathy, and problem-solving as a result of their participation." A culture of literacy can begin to emerge within young families, and it helps prepare children for schooling. There are empirical indications that when parents read stories to their children, this is helpful for the development of literacy (for example, Neuman 1996). So these reading circles can influence two generations, as well as boyfriends and extended family of the young women involved. Long (1986) found that in reading groups, middle-class women accomplish a valorizing of themselves as women, in ways that are often devalued by society. There is no reason why this kind of effect should be confined to the middle classes.

We do not know of any educational or therapeutic programs that have started to draw on the evidence for effects of fiction that we have discussed in the previous section, but for the future we may look forward to such programs.

CONCLUSION

In the five areas we have reviewed, there is evidence of a lively current interest and strong possibilities for the future. In our view this future needs to be interdisciplinary. Despite shared interests by researchers in the humanities and in psychology in such matters as human character, emotions, and the vicissitudes of the social world, there are barriers between disciplines that have been standing for too long.

WORKS CITED

Adrian, Juan E., Rosa A. Clemente, Lidon Villanueva, and Carollen Rieffe. 2005. Parent-child picture-book reading, mother's mental state language, and children's theory of mind. *Journal of Child Language* 32: 673–86.

Aristotle. [ca. 330BC] 1970. *Poetics*. Translated by G. E. Else. Ann Arbor: University of Michigan Press.

Auerbach, Erich. 1953. *Mimesis: The representation of reality in western literature*. Translated by W. R. Trask. Princeton, NJ: Princeton University Press.

———. 1965. *Literary language and its public in Late Latin antiquity and in the Middle Ages*. Translated by Ralph Manheim. New York: Pantheon.

Barsalou, Lawrence W., W. Kyle Simmons, Aron K. Barbey, and Christine D. Wilson. 2003. Grounding conceptual knowledge in modality-specific systems. *Trends in Cognitive Sciences* 7: 84–91.

Brooks, Cleanth, and Robert Penn Warren. 1938. *Understanding poetry: An anthology for college students*. New York: Holt.

Bruner, Jerome. 1986. *Actual minds, possible worlds*. Cambridge, MA: Harvard University Press.

Byrne, Ruth M. J. 2005. *The rational imagination: How people create alternatives to reality*. Cambridge, MA: MIT Press.

Coleridge, Samuel Taylor. [1794–1820] 2000. *Coleridge's notebooks: A selection*, ed. Seamus Perry. Oxford: Oxford University Press.

———. [1817] 1907. *Biographia literaria*. Edited by J. Shawcross. Oxford: Oxford University Press.

Collingwood, R. G. 1938. *The principles of art*. Oxford: Oxford University Press.

Derrida, Jacques. 1976. *Of grammatology*. Translated by G. C. Spivak. Baltimore: Johns Hopkins University Press.

Djikic, Maja, Keith Oatley, and Jordan Peterson. 2006. The bitter-sweet labor of emoting: The linguistic comparison of writers and physicists. *Creativity Research Journal* 18: 191–97.

Djikic, Maja, Keith Oatley, Sara Zoeterman, and Jordan Peterson. 2009a. On being moved by art: How reading fiction transforms the self. *Creativity Research Journal* 21: 24–29.

———. 2009b. Defenseless against art: Impact of reading fiction on emotion change in avoidantly attached individuals. *Journal of Research in Personality* 43: 14–17.

Everett, Daniel L. 2005. Cultural constraints on grammar and cognition in Pirahã: Another look at the design features of human language. *Current Anthropology* 46: 621–46.

Foroni, Francesco, and Gün Semin. 2009. Language that puts you in touch with your bodily feelings: The multimodal responsiveness of affective expressions. *Psychological Science* 20, no. 8: 974–80.

Gerrig, Richard J. 1993. *Experiencing narrative worlds: On the psychological activities of reading*. New Haven: Yale University Press.

Gibbs, Raymond W., and Teenie Matlock. 2008. Metaphor, imagination, and simulation: Psycholinguistic evidence. In *The Cambridge handbook of metaphor and thought*, 161–76. Edited by Raymond W. Gibbs. New York: Cambridge University Press.

Graesser, Arthur C., Brent Olde, and Bianca Klettke. 2002. How does the mind construct and represent stories? In *Narrative impact: Social and cognitive foundations*, 229–62. Edited by M. C. Green, J. J. Strange, and T. C. Brock. Mahwah, NJ: Erlbaum.

Green, Melanie C., and Timothy C. Brock. 2000. The role of transportation in the persuasiveness of public narratives. *Journal of Personality and Social Psychology* 79: 702–21.

Gross, James, and Robert W. Levenson. 1995. Emotion elicitation using films. *Cognition and Emotion* 9: 87–108.

Hakemulder, Frank. 2000. *The moral laboratory: Experiments examining the effects of reading literature on social perception and moral self-concept*. Amsterdam: John Benjamins.

———. 2001. How to make *alle Menschen Brüder*: Literature in a multicultural and multiform society. In *The psychology and sociology of literature*, 225–42. Edited by Dick Schram and Gerard Steen. Amsterdam: John Benjamins.

———. 2008. Imagining what could happen: Effects of taking the role of a character on social cognition. In *Directions in empirical literary studies: In honor of Willie van Peer*, 139–53. Edited by S. Zyngier, M. Bortolussi, A. Chesnokova, and J. Auracher. Amsterdam: John Benjamins.

Halliwell, Stephen. 2002. *The aesthetics of mimesis: Ancient texts and modern problems*. Princeton, NJ: Princeton University Press.

Harris, Paul L. 2000. *The work of the imagination*. Oxford: Blackwell.

Hogan, Patrick C. 2003. *The mind and its stories: Narrative universals and human emotion*. Cambridge: Cambridge University Press.

Jakobson, Roman. 1956. Two aspects of language and two types of aphasic disturbance. In *Fundamentals of language*, 53–83. Edited by Roman Jakobson and Morris Halle. 'S-Gravenhage: Mouton.

Jarjoura, G. Roger, and Susan T. Krumholz. 1998. Combining bibliotherapy and positive role modeling as an alternative to incarceration. *Journal of Offender Rehabilitation* 28: 127–39.

Jin, Ha. 1999. *Waiting*. New York: Pantheon.

Literature for All of Us. http://www.literatureforallofus.org/home.html (accessed July 23, 2009).

Literature for Life. http://www.literatureforlife.org (accessed July 23, 2009).

Lodge, David. 1977. *The modes of modern writing: Metaphor, metonymy, and the typology of modern fiction*. Ithaca, NY: Cornell University Press.

Long, Elizabeth. 1986. Women, reading, and cultural authority: Some implications of the audience perspective in cultural studies. *American Quarterly* 38: 591–612.

Mar, Raymond A. 2004. The neuropsychology of narrative. *Neuropsychologia* 42, no. 10: 1414–34.

———. 2007. Simulation-based theories of narrative comprehension: Evidence and implications. PhD diss., University of Toronto.

———. 2011. The neural bases of social cognition and story comprehension. *Annual Review of Psychology* 62: 103–34.

Mar, Raymond A., Keith Oatley, Jacob Hirsh, Jennifer dela Paz, and Jordan B. Peterson. 2006. Bookworms versus nerds: Exposure to fiction versus non-fiction, divergent associations with social ability, and the simulation of fictional social worlds. *Journal of Research in Personality* 40: 694–712.

Mar, Raymond A., and Keith Oatley. 2008. The function of fiction is the abstraction and simulation of social experience. *Perspectives on Psychological Science* 3: 173–92.

Mar, Raymond A., Keith Oatley, and Maja Djikic. 2008. Effects of reading on knowledge, social abilities, and selfhood: Theory and empirical studies. In *Directions in empirical literary studies: In honor of Willie van Peer*, 127–37. Edited by S. Zyngier, M. Bortolussi, A. Chesnokova, and J. Auracher. Amsterdam: John Benjamins.

Mar, Raymond A., Keith Oatley, and Jordan B. Peterson. 2009. Exploring the link between reading fiction and empathy: Ruling out individual differences and examining outcomes. *Communications: The European Journal of Communication* 34: 407–28.

Mar, Raymond A., Jennifer L. Tackett, and Chris Moore. 2010. Exposure to media and theory-of-mind development in preschoolers. *Cognitive Development* 25: 69–78.

Marsh, Elizabeth J., and Lisa K. Fazio. 2006. Learning errors from fiction: Difficulties in reducing reliance on fictional stories. *Memory and Cognition* 34: 1140–49.

Marsh, Elizabeth J., Michelle L. Meade, and Henry L. Roediger III. 2003. Learning facts from fiction. *Journal of Memory and Language* 49: 519–36.

Neuman, Susan B. 1996. Children engaging in storybook reading: The influence of access to print resources, opportunity, and parental interaction. *Early Childhood Research Quarterly* 11: 495–513.

Oatley, Keith. 1992. *Best laid schemes: The psychology of emotions*. New York: Cambridge University Press.

———. 1999. Why fiction may be twice as true as fact: Fiction as cognitive and emotional simulation. *Review of General Psychology* 3: 101–17.

———. 2003. Creative expression and communication of emotion in the visual and narrative arts. In *Handbook of affective sciences*, 481–502. Edited by Richard J. Davidson, Klaus R. Scherer, and H. Hill Goldsmith. New York: Oxford University Press.

———. 2009. An emotion's emergence, unfolding, and potential for empathy: A study of resentment by "the psychologist of Avon." *Emotion Review* 1: 31–37.

Pennebaker, James W., Martha E. Francis, and Roger J. Booth. 2001. *Linguistic inquiry and word count (LIWC): LIWC 2001*. Mahwah, NJ: Erlbaum.

Peskin, Joan, and Janet W. Astington. 2004. The effects of adding metacognitive language to story texts. *Cognitive Development* 19: 253–73.

Prentice, Deborah, Richard J. Gerrig, and Daniel S. Bailis. 1997. What readers bring to the processing of fictional texts. *Psychonomic Bulletin and Review* 4: 416–20.

Pulvermüller, Friedemann, Markus Härle, and Friedhelm Hummel. 2001. Walking or talking? Behavioral and neurophysiological correlates of action verb processing. *Brain and Language* 78: 143–68.

Renault, Mary. 1956. *The last of the wine*. London: Longman.

Richards, I. A. 1929. *Practical criticism: A study of literary judgment*. London: Routledge and Kegan Paul.

Rosenblatt, Louise. 1938. *Literature as exploration*. New York: Noble and Noble.

Shakespeare, William. [1600] 1995. *A midsummer night's dream*. Oxford: Oxford University Press.

———. [1602] 1997. *Othello*. London: Thomas Nelson.

Speer, N. K., J. R. Reynolds, K. M. Swallow, and J. M. Zacks. 2009. Reading stories activates neural representations of perceptual and motor experiences. *Psychological Science* 20, no. 8: 989–99.

Stanovich, Keith E., Richard F. West, and Michele R. Harrison. 1995. Knowledge growth and maintenance across the life span: The role of print exposure. *Developmental Psychology* 31: 811–26.

Trounstine, Jean R., and Robert Waxler. 2005. *Finding a voice: The practice of Changing Lives through Literature*. Ann Arbor: University of Michigan Press.

Turner, Mark. 1996. *The literary mind: The origins of thought and language*. New York: Oxford University Press.

Van Peer, Willie. 1986. *Stylistics and psychology: Investigations of foregrounding*. London: Croom Helm.

Xu, J., S. Kemeny, G. Park, C. Frattali, and Allen Braun. 2005. Language in context: Emergent features of word, sentence, and narrative comprehension. *NeuroImage* 25, no. 3: 1002–15.

Yarkoni, T., N. K. Speer, and J. M. Zacks. 2008. Neural substrates of narrative comprehension and memory. *NeuroImage* 41, no. 4: 1408–25.

Zunshine, Lisa. 2006. *Why we read fiction: Theory of mind and the novel*. Columbus: Ohio State University Press.

MAJA DJIKIC is a postdoctoral fellow at the Desautels Center for Integrative Thinking (Rotman School of Management, University of Toronto) and a lecturer at the Psychology Department (University of Toronto). She studies the effect of the arts on personality change, and on the modeling of self and others. Her work has been published in *Psychological Science*, *Creativity Research Journal*, *Journal for Research in Personality*, *New Ideas in Psychology*, *Journal of Adult Development*, and others. She is a coeditor of *OnFiction* (www.onfiction.ca), an on-line magazine on the psychology of fiction.

NIGEL FABB is professor of literary linguistics at the University of Strathclyde. He is an editor of *Journal of Linguistics*, and an author of nine books on literature and linguistics. These include *A Grammar of Ma'di* (2002; with Mairi Blackings), *Linguistics and Literature: Language in the Verbal Arts of the World* (1997), *Language and Literary Structure: The Linguistic Analysis of Form in Verse and Narrative* (2002), and *Meter in Poetry: A New Theory* (2008; with Morris Halle).

MARGARET H. FREEMAN is emeritus professor of English at Los Angeles Valley College. She is a codirector of the Myrifield Institute for Cognition and the Arts in Heath, Massachusetts (www.myrifield.org). Her research interests lie in the field of cognitive aesthetics, with a particular focus on poetic iconicity. She also specializes in the study of Emily Dickinson's poetry. She has given presentations at conferences and workshops throughout the world and has published articles on cognitive approaches to poetry in several journals and anthologies.

RICHARD J. GERRIG is professor of psychology at Stony Brook University. He holds a PhD in cognitive psychology from Stanford University and his research largely centers on readers' experiences of narratives. He is the author of *Experiencing Narrative Worlds* (Yale University Press 1993). His recent publications include, with Giovanna Egidi, "How Valence Affects Language Processing: Negativity Bias and Mood Congruence in Narrative Comprehension" (*Memory and Cognition*) and, with Matthew Jacovina, "How Readers Experience Characters' Decisions" (*Memory and Cognition*). Gerrig's introductory psychology textbook, *Psychology and Life*, coauthored with Philip Zimbardo, has been translated into ten languages.

MORRIS HALLE is institute professor and professor of linguistics (emeritus) at MIT. He is the author of many articles and books, including *Preliminaries to Speech Analysis* (1952; with Roman Jakobson and Gunnar Fant), *The Sound Pattern of English* (1968; with Noam Chomsky), *English Stress: Its Form, Its Growth, and Its Role in Verse* (1971; with Samuel Jay Keyser), and *From Memory to Speech and Back: Papers on Phonetics and Phonology 1954–2002* (2002).

F. ELIZABETH HART is associate professor of English at the University of Connecticut. She has published essays on the intersection of cognitive theory and literature in the journals *Mosaic*, *Configurations*, *Philosophy and Literature*, and *College English*, and in the essay collections *The Work of Fiction: Cognition, Culture, and Complexity* (2004) and *Performance and Cognition: Theatre Studies and the Cognitive Turn* (2006; for which she also served as co-editor). Among her recent publications are two essays in volumes edited by David Herman, *The Emergence of Mind* (2011), and Bryan Reynolds and Paul Cefalu, *The Return of Theory in Early Modern Studies* (2011).

PATRICK COLM HOGAN is a professor in the Department of English and the Program in Cognitive Science at the University of Connecticut. He is the author of thirteen books, including *Cognitive Science, Literature, and the Arts: A Guide for Humanists* (Routledge 2003), *The Mind and Its Stories: Narrative Universals and Human Emotion* (Cambridge University Press 2003), and *What Literature Teaches Us about Emotion* (Cambridge University Press 2011). He recently edited *The Cambridge Encyclopedia of the Language Sciences* (Cambridge University Press 2011).

NORMAN HOLLAND retired in 2008 from the Marston-Milbauer Eminent Scholar's Chair at the University of Florida, where he was also a faculty member of the McKnight Brain Institute. At Florida, he founded the Institute for Psychological Study of the Arts, the online discussion group PSYART, the online journal *PsyArt*, and the PsyArt Foundation. His latest book is *Literature and the Brain*, available at www.literatureandthebrain.com. His earlier books include such titles as *Laughing*; *The I*; *The Brain of Robert Frost*; and *Meeting Movies*. He is currently developing a website of essays on film at www.asharperfocus.com.

ISABEL JAÉN is assistant professor of Spanish at Portland State University where she teaches early modern Peninsular literature. She has published articles on Spanish literature, comparative literature, and literature and cognition, and currently works on Golden Age Spanish literature and medical philosophy, exploring the ideas of Hippocrates, Galen, Vives, and Huarte de San Juan in relation to Cervantes and Calderón de la Barca. She is an executive committee member of the Modern Language Association Cognitive Approaches to Literature Discussion Group. In 2005 she cofounded with Julien J. Simon the Literary Theory, Cognition, and the Brain working group at the Yale University Whitney Humanities Center.

RAYMOND A. MAR is an assistant professor of psychology at York University (Toronto) who uses the methods of neuroscience, personality psychology, social psychology, and developmental psychology to research the relationship between story processing and social processing. His work has been published in the *Journal of Research in Personality*, *Perspectives on Psychological Science*, *Neuropsychologia*, and *Social Cognitive and Affective Neuroscience*. Mar is a coeditor of *OnFiction* (www.onfiction.ca), an online magazine on the psychology of fiction.

AARON MISHARA is a clinical core faculty member at the Chicago School of Professional Psychology where he teaches phenomenologic-holistic approaches to neuroscience, psychopathology, and psychotherapy. He conducted neuropsychological and functional neuroimaging research of schizophrenia at NIMH and Yale University School of Medicine, and taught medical and philosophical courses (in German) at the Julius-Maximilians University of Würzburg (Germany). He collaborates internationally with Cambridge University and Hannover Medical School and co-directs the Literary Theory, Cognition, and the Brain working group at the Yale University Whitney Humanities Center. He is on the advisory board of several international journals, has published numerous articles and book chapters, and is currently editing the book *Phenomenological Neuropsychiatry, How Patient Experience Bridges Clinic with Clinical Neuroscience* (forthcoming).

JOSEPH MURPHY is associate professor and associate chair of the Department of Languages, Literatures, and Cultures at the University of Florida. He has a BS degree in mechanical engineering and advanced degrees in East Asian literature and film studies. He is author of *Metaphorical Circuit: Negotiations between Literature and Science in 20th-Century Japan* (2004), and coeditor of *The Theory of Literature and Other Critical Writings of Natsume Soseki* (2008), winner of the MLA Scaglione Prize for literary translation.

KEITH OATLEY is emeritus professor of cognitive psychology at the University of Toronto. He is a fellow of the Royal Society of Canada, and a fellow of the British Psychological Society. His principal research has been on emotions and on the psychology of reading and writing fiction. He has recently published *Such Stuff as Dreams: The Psychology of Fiction* (Wiley-Blackwell 2011). He is the author of three novels and a coeditor of *OnFiction* (www.onfiction.ca), an online magazine on the psychology of fiction.

CLAIBORNE RICE is assistant professor of English at the University of Louisiana at Lafayette. He received his PhD in English from the University of Georgia in 2002. His research focuses on how contemporary theories of linguistics, especially cognitive linguistics, can be used to understand poetic language and practice. His recent projects involve both cognitive and corpus linguistics, examining how poetic practice in experimental poetry might be modeled using linguistic corpora of different genres.

GLENDA SACKS teaches at the Academic Institute for Arab Teacher Training, Beit Berl College, Israel, and the Interdisciplinary Center, Herzliya, Israel. She has a master's degree in fine arts from the University of South Africa and received her doctorate in literature from Bar-Ilan University, Israel, in 2005. Her research focuses on developmental cognitive psychology, pedagogy, language learning, and creativity. She is the head of the Academic Forum for Literature in Israel, and is publicity chair of the Israel Forum for Academic Writing. Currently she is focusing on enhancing creativity, meta-cognitive thinking, tolerance, and self-reflection among her students.

JULIEN J. SIMON is assistant professor of Spanish and French at Indiana University in Richmond. His main research interests are early modern Spanish literature and cognitive literary studies. He has published articles on early modern literature, Hispanic culture, and literature and cognition. In 2005 he co-founded with Isabel Jaén the Literary Theory, Cognition, and the Brain working group at the Yale University Whitney Humanities Center. Since 2008 he has been a steering committee member of the Center for Cognitive Literary Studies at Purdue University. He is also an executive committee member of the Cognitive Approaches to Literature discussion group of the Modern Language Association.

MICHAEL SINDING is a Marie Curie fellow at the Vrije Universiteit Amsterdam. He studies cognitive approaches to literary and cultural forms, including genre, narrative, and metaphor. He has held postdoctoral fellowships from the Social Sciences and Humanities Research Council of Canada and the Alexander von Humboldt Foundation. He has published articles and reviews in the *Wallace Stevens Journal*, *New Literary History*, *Genre*, *Semiotica*, *Style*, *SubStance*, *Poetics Today*, *Cognitive Linguistics*, *Postmodern Culture*, the *Journal of Literary Theory*, and *Northrop Frye: New Directions from Old*. He has contributed recently to the edited collections *Blending and Narrative* and *Beyond Cognitive Metaphor Theory*.

BRAD SULLIVAN is professor of English at Western New England University. His primary interest has always been learning and knowing—how we do it, how we can facilitate it, how literary encounters may accomplish it. His work has explored early Romantic models of knowing and learning, discussed connections of literature and science in a team-taught environmental literature course, and argued for the value of liberal arts education. He is the author of *Wordsworth and the Composition of Knowledge: Refiguring Relationships among Minds, Worlds, and Words* (2000) and is currently at work on a book-length project tentatively titled *Artful Knowing: British Romanticism, Cognitive Science, and the Practice of Learning*.

memory, ix, 6, 16, 36, 37, 38, 40, 58, 61, 63, 80, 89, 90, 97, 101, 118n6, 128, 186, 207, 217; and anomalous suspense, 38, 39, 41, 50; autobiographical, 107, 185; emotional, 91, 93–94; episodic, 91; long-term, 183, 184; long-term semantic, 96; and narrative experiences, 36; reception and, 23; semantic, 96; short-term, 183; short-term perceptual, 96; working, 91, 96, 183

mentalizing, 66. See also developmental psychology; theory of mind

Merleau-Ponty, Maurice, x, 128, 132, 140n9

metafiction(s), 6, 73–86. See also Don Quixote

metaphor(s), 14, 22, 36, 132, 133, 139n5, 188, 216, 240; conduit, 41; and the construction of meaning, 127; grammatical, 129; as a product of the embodied mind, 22. See also blending; schemas

Metaphors We Live By (Lakoff & Johnson), 14, 216

metrical music, 7; and metrical verse, 179–180

metrical verse, 7, 125. See also counting

Miall, David, xv, 16, 20, 25n4, 128, 183

Middlemarch (Eliot), 22, 139n1

Mimesis (Auerbach), 235, 236

mimetic culture (Donald), 116

mind(s): and anomalous states of consciousness, 71; body problem, 118n6; and brain, 117–118n2; computational model(s) of the, 2, 165; as emerging from physiological processes, 204; and engagement with fiction, 236; feeling (Langer), 131; fictional and real, 20; habits of, 8, 205, 208, 210; and impact of fiction, 1–2; processes in relation to language and literature, 7, 11, 13–15, 125; in relation to learning and social development, 68; as situated within the body, vii. See also embodied mind; fiction

mirror neurons, 18, 25n6, 81, 82, 186

mirth, 79, 98, 99, 103, 155

Mishara, Aaron, 6, 7, 17, 71, 105–123, 252

motion processing, 195; cognitive effects of, 194

motion verbs, 8, 125, 194, 195, 196; and cognitive engagement, 187; somatic effects of, 190

mourning, 71, 89, 90, 102

Murphy, Joseph A., 6, 33, 53–70, 71, 253

narrative: adaptive function of, 6, 20, 21, 66, 68n1, 86; as doubling-self, 115–117; and healing, 116; and internal structure, 64; as perception of object in a trajectory, 64; worldmaking, 16

narrative comprehension, ix, 16, 53–68; elements of, 62; mechanisms underlying, 68; model of, 33, 67; processes in, 63; and sentence-level comprehension, 241; and theory of mind, 66

narrative processing, 41; empirical approach to, 50

narrative psychology, 15

narratives: function of, 22; in face-to-face interaction, 16; and learning and social development, 68; readers' responses to, 36; self-, 68; representation of consciousness in, 16

narrative understanding: role of intentionality in, 16

narratology: cognitive, 15, 16, 24n3; post-classical phase, 15; traditional, 15, 16

neo-phenomenology, 118n6

neurobiology, 55

neuroimaging research: and reading stories, 17; on story comprehension and production, 25n5; and viewing films, 17

neurolinguistics, 61

neuropsychiatry, 17, 253

neuroscience, ix, 3, 7, 17, 18, 35, 55, 57, 61, 67, 86, 105, 107, 117, 118n6

Nordlund, Marcus, 3, 19

novel: cognitive model of, 151; as a developing genre, 145; as a secondary utterance, 146. See also genre

Oatley, Keith, xv, 8, 14, 17, 21, 22, 68, 97, 98, 199, 235–249, 253

social cognition, 21, 22, 111, 119n8
social sciences, vii, viii, 19, 138
somatic marker, 184, 186, 187, 189, 192, 196
Spolsky, Ellen, ix, xin1, 23, 229
Steen, Gerard, ix, 14, 146, 158nn1,2
Sterne, Laurence, 7, 74, 148–159
Stockwell, Peter, xv, 14, 195
story comprehension, 35, 63. *See also* narrative comprehension
structuralism, 15
suicide, 101, 120n15
Sullivan, Brad, 8, 23, 199, 201–218, 254
suspense, 36; anomalous, 36–41, 50, 78–79; narrative strategies of, 131; the paradox of, 6, 37, 41
Swales, John, 148, 158nn1,2,3
Swirski, 19

Talmy, Leonard, 14, 140n11
Taylor, Marjorie, xv, 220, 227
text world theory, 14
theory of mind (ToM), 6, 17, 18, 20, 21, 65–67, 116; and child development, 66–67, 240–243; fMRI research on, 17; Hartley's 8, 199, 201, 204; interaction theory, 25n6; simulation theory, 25n6; theory theory, 25n6
thought: intermental and intramental, 22
Tobin, Vera, 15

Todorov, Tzvetan, 15, 61, 62, 158n2
Tribble, Evelyn, 23
Tristram Shandy (Sterne), 7, 74, 148–159
Tsur, Reuven, xin1, 3, 14, 128, 139n4
Turner, Mark, ix, xin1, 14, 15, 127, 130, 139n4, 146, 156, 158, 217, 239. *See also* blending; conceptual integration network theory; Fauconnier, Gilles

uncanny, the, 77, 85

Van Peer, Willie, 16, 17, 128, 238
Vermeule, Blakey, viii, 19, 21
virtual reality, 16
Vygotsky, Lev, 224–225

Waiting (Ha Jin), 241
Walton, Kendall, 37, 58
Williams, Raymond, 23
willing suspension of disbelief (Coleridge), 73, 78, 238
Wordsworth, William, 8, 131, 199, 201–217
writer's block, 17, 75

Young, Kay, 17, 80

Zunshine, Lisa, ix, xin1, xv, 18, 21, 23, 24, 240
Zyngier, Sonia, 16, 17

CPSIA information can be obtained
at www.ICGtesting.com
Printed in the USA
FFOW02n2324231114
8942FF